N

F

I

F

The Autobiography of Upton Sinclair

The Autobiography
of
UPTON SINCLAIR

New York

HARCOURT, BRACE & WORLD, INC.

© 1962 by Upton Sinclair

Library of Congress Catalog Card Number: 62-19592

Printed in the United States of America

Preface

All through my seventy-one years of writing life—I started at thirteen—I have had from my readers suggestions that I should tell my own story. When I was halfway through those writing years I accepted the suggestion and wrote a book called *American Outpost.* The major part of that book, revised and brought up to date, is incorporated in this volume.

I put myself in the position of a veteran of many campaigns who gathers the youngsters about his knee. He knows these youngsters cannot really share the anguish and turmoil of his early years, for they belong to a new generation which is looking to be entertained and amused. So the old campaigner takes a casual and lighthearted tone.

If any old-timer is offended by this—well, there are any number of serious books, plays, and pamphlets of mine that he can read, plus an anthology and a selection of letters written to me by the really great writers of our time. If that is not enough he can travel to the University of Indiana and there, in the Lilly Library, he can read the 250,000 letters that have been written to me over the years—and the carbon copies of my replies. After he has read all this, I shall have written more.

Contents

List of Illustrations

The Autobiography of Upton Sinclair

1
Childhood

My first recollection of life is one that my mother insisted I could not possibly have, because I was only eighteen months old at the time. Yet there it is in my mind: a room where I have been left in the care of a relative while my parents are taking a trip. I see a little old lady, black-clad, in a curtained room; I know where the bed is located, and the oilstove on which the cooking is done, and the thrills of exploring a new place. Be sure that children know far more than we give them credit for; I hear fond parents praising their precious darlings, and I wince, noting how the darlings are drinking in every word. Always in my childhood I would think: "How silly these grownups are! And how easy to outwit!"

I was a toddler when one day my mother told me not to throw a piece of rag into a drain. "Paper dissolves, but rag doesn't." I treasured up this wisdom and, visiting my Aunt Florence, remarked with great impressiveness, "It is all right to throw paper into the drain, because it dissolves, but you mustn't throw rags in, because they don't dissolve." Wonder, mingled with amusement, appeared on the face of my sweet and gentle relative. My first taste of glory.

Baltimore, Maryland, was the place, and I remember boardinghouse and lodginghouse rooms. We never had but one room at a time, and I slept on a sofa or crossways at the foot of my parents' bed; a custom that caused me no discomfort that I can recall. One adventure recurred; the gaslight would be turned on in the middle of the night, and I would start up, rubbing my eyes, and join in the exciting chase for bedbugs. They came out in the dark and scurried into hiding when they saw the light; so they must be mashed quickly. For thrills like this, wealthy grown-up children travel to the heart of Africa on costly safaris. The more bugs we killed, the fewer there were to bite us the rest of the night, which I suppose is the argument of the lion hunters also. Next morning, the landlady would come, and corpses in the washbasin or impaled on pins would be exhibited to her; the bed would be taken to pieces and "corrosive sublimate" rubbed into the cracks with a chicken feather.

My position in life was a singular one, and only in later years did I understand it. When I went to call on my father's mother, a black-clad, frail little lady, there might be only cold bread and dried herring for Sunday-night supper, but it would be served with exquisite courtesy and overseen by a great oil painting of my grandfather in naval uniform—with that same predatory beak that I have carried through life and have handed on to my son. Grandfather Sinclair had been a captain in the United States Navy and so had his father before him, and ancestors far back had commanded in the British Navy. The family had lived in Virginia, and there had been slaves and estates. But the slaves had been set free, and the homestead burned, and the head of the family drowned at sea in the last year of the Civil War. His descendants, four sons and two daughters, lived in embarrassing poverty, but with the consciousness, at every moment of their lives, that they were persons of great consequence and dignity.

II

Being interested in the future rather than the past, I always considered ancestors a bore. All I knew about mine were a few anecdotes my mother told me. Then my friend Albert Mordell, who was writing a paper for a historical magazine, came upon my great-grandfather. He wrote me: "The life of your ancestors is a history of the American navy." It amused him to discover that a notorious "red" had such respectable forefathers, and he

had a manuscript called *The Fighting Sinclairs,* which may someday be published. Meanwhile, since every biography is required
to have ancestors, I quote a summary that Mr. Mordell kindly
supplied. Those not interested in ancestors are permitted to skip.

Commodore Arthur Sinclair, the great-grandfather of Upton, fought
in the first American naval battle after the Revolution, he being a
midshipman on the *Constellation,* when it fought the *Insurgente,* in
1798. He was also in the latter part of the war with Tripoli. He was
on the *Argus* in the first cruise of the War of 1812, and captured many
prizes. He fought in the leading battle of Lake Ontario under Commander Chauncey. The battle was between the *Pike,* on which he
was captain, and the *Wolf.* He also a little later had command of the
entire squadron on the upper lakes. He commanded the *Congress* in
its cruise to South America in 1818, carrying the commissioners to investigate conditions, and on its cruise was born the Monroe Doctrine,
for the commissioner's report led to the promulgation of the Doctrine.
He also founded a naval school at Norfolk. When he died in 1831,
the flags of all the ships were ordered at half-mast, and mourning
was ordered worn by the officers for thirty days. He was an intimate
friend of practically all the naval heroes in the War of 1812.

He had three sons, Arthur, George T., and Dr. William B., all of
whom became officers in the old navy and resigned in 1861 to join
the Confederacy. Arthur, who is Upton's grandfather, was with Perry
in Japan in the early fifties. He also commanded a ship in the late
fifties—the *Vandalia*—and was compelled to destroy a village of can-
nibals on an island in the Pacific.

His brother, George T., was in the famous voyage of the *Potomac*
around the world in the early thirties, which went to attack a town in
the Malay Islands for some ravages upon an American ship. He also
was with Commander Elliott, the Lake Erie hero, on the *Constitution*
in the Mediterranean. He was in the famous Wilkes exploring expedition around 1840, when they discovered the Antarctic continent; and,
like the rest of the officers, he had trouble with Wilkes, whom they
had court-martialed. He also served in the African Squadron hunting
slavers in the early fifties, and later in the home squadron in the
Wabash under Commander Paulding. It was on this ship that the
famous filibuster, William Walker, who made himself dictator of
Nicaragua, surrendered to Paulding.

The third brother, Dr. William B. Sinclair, was in the Mediterranean Squadron with Commander Isaac Hull about 1840. He was
also in the African Squadron. All these three brothers were in the

Mexican waters during the war, but saw no active service there. At the opening of the Civil War, they became officers in the Confederate Navy and saw various services.

Arthur was compelled to burn his ship the *Mississippi* at the battle of New Orleans to prevent its falling into the hands of his friend (now his enemy) Farragut. He was drowned on a blockade runner when leaving Liverpool toward the end of the war. George built a ship in England for the Confederacy, but it was never taken over by them because the English took hold of it. Dr. Sinclair served as physician in the Confederate Navy.

These three men also had four sons who became officers in the Confederate Navy. Arthur had two sons in this navy—Arthur, Jr., and Terry. Arthur, Jr., an uncle of Upton, was in the battle between the *Monitor* and the *Merrimac,* and wrote an account of it. He served two years on the *Alabama,* and was in the famous fight with the *Kearsarge,* and left a book about his experiences: *Two Years on the Alabama.*

His brother, Terry, also an uncle of Upton, was on the Confederate Cruiser *Florida,* the most important ship next to the *Alabama,* for two years. This was captured unlawfully, and Terry was made a prisoner of war, but was soon released. He left a magazine article about his experience. George T.'s son, William H., commanded a prize ship taken by the *Alabama.* Dr. William B.'s son, William B., Jr., was drowned at the age of eighteen from the *Florida* because he gave his oar to a shipmate who could not swim.

III

My father was the youngest son of Captain Arthur Sinclair and was raised in Norfolk. In the days before the war, and after it, all Southern gentlemen "drank." My father became a whole-sale whisky salesman, which made it easy and even necessary for him to follow the fashion. Later on he became a "drummer" for straw-hat manufacturers, and then for manufacturers of men's clothing; but he could never get away from drink, for the beginning of every deal was a "treat," and the close of it was another. Whisky in its multiple forms—mint juleps, toddies, hot Scotches, egg-nogs, punch—was the most conspicuous single fact in my boyhood. I saw it and smelled it and heard it everywhere I turned, but I never tasted it.

The reason was my mother, whose whole married life was

poisoned by alcohol, and who taught me a daily lesson in horror. It took my good and gentle-souled father thirty or forty years to kill himself, and I watched the process week by week and sometimes hour by hour. It made an indelible impression upon my childish soul, and is the reason why I am a prohibitionist, to the dismay of my "libertarian" friends.

It was not that my father could not earn money, but that he could not keep it. He would come home with some bank notes, and the salvation of his wife and little son would depend upon the capture of this treasure. My mother acquired the habit of going through his pockets at night; and since he never knew how much he had brought home, there would be arguments in the morning, an unending duel of wits. Father would hide the money when he came in late, and then in the morning he would forget where he had hidden it, and there would be searching under mattresses and carpets and inside the lining of clothing—all sorts of unlikely places. If my mother found it first, you may be sure that my father was allowed to go on looking.

When he was not under the influence of the Demon Rum, the little "drummer" dearly loved his family; so the thirty years during which I watched him were one long moral agony. He would make all sorts of pledges, with tears in his eyes; he would invent all sorts of devices to cheat his cruel master. He would not "touch a drop" until six o'clock in the evening; he would drink lemonade or ginger ale when he was treating the customers. But alas, he would change to beer, in order not to "excite comment"; and then after a week or a month of beer, we would smell whisky on his breath again, and the tears and wranglings and naggings would be resumed.

This same thing was going on in most of the homes in Maryland and Virginia of which I had knowledge. My father's older brother died an inebriate in a soldiers' home. My earliest memory of the home of my maternal grandfather is of being awakened by a disturbance downstairs, and looking over the banisters in alarm while my grandfather—a Methodist deacon—was struggling with his grown son to keep him from going out when he was drunk. Dear old Uncle Harry, burly and full of laughter, a sportsman and favorite of all the world—at the age of forty or so he put a bullet through his head in Central Park, New York.

IV

Human beings are what life makes them, and there is no more fascinating subject of study than the origin of mental and moral qualities. My father's drinking accounted for other eccentricities of mine besides my belief in prohibition. It caused me to follow my mother in everything, and so to have a great respect for women; thus it came about that I walked in the first suffrage parade in New York, behind the snow-white charger of Inez Milholland. My mother did not drink coffee, nor even tea; and so, when I visited in England, I made all my hostesses unhappy. No lady had ever been known to smoke in Baltimore—only old Negro women with pipes; therefore I did not smoke—except once. When I was eight years old, a big boy on the street gave me a cigarette, and I started it; but another boy told me a policeman would arrest me, so I threw the cigarette away, and ran and hid in an alley, and have never yet recovered from this fear. It has saved me a great deal of money, and some health also, I am sure.

The sordid surroundings in which I was forced to live as a child made me a dreamer. I took to literature, because that was the easiest refuge. I knew practically nothing about music; my mother, with the upbringing of a young lady, could play a few pieces on the piano, but we seldom had a piano, and the music I heard was church hymns, and the plantation melodies that my plump little father hummed while shaving himself with a big razor. My mother had at one time painted pictures; I recall a snow scene in oils, with a kind of tinsel to make sparkles in the snow. But I never learned this wonderful art.

My mother would read books to me, and everything I heard I remembered. I taught myself to read at the age of five, before anyone realized what was happening. I would ask what this letter was, and that, and go away and learn it, and make the sounds, and very soon I was able to take care of myself. I asked my numerous uncles and aunts and cousins to send me only books for Christmas; and now, three quarters of a century later, traces of their gifts are still in my head. Let someone with a taste for research dig into the Christmas books of the early eighties, and find a generous broad volume, with many illustrations, merry rhymes, and a title containing the phrase "a peculiar family." From this book I learned to read, and I would ask my mother if she knew any such "peculiar" persons; for example, the "little boy who was so dreadfully polite, he would not even sneeze unless he asked you if he might." He sneezed by accident, and "scared all the company into the middle of next week."

While arguments between my father and my mother were going on, I was with Gulliver in Lilliput, or on the way to the Celestial City with Christian, or in the shop with the little tailor who killed "seven at one blow." I had Grimm and Andersen and *The Story of the Bible*, and Henty and Alger and Captain Mayne Reid. I would be missing at a party and be discovered behind the sofa with a book. At the home of my Uncle Bland there was an encyclopedia, and my kind uncle was greatly impressed to find me absorbed in the article on gunpowder. Of course, I was pleased to have my zeal for learning admired—but also I really did want to know about gunpowder.

Readers of my novels know that I have one favorite theme, the contrast between the social classes; there are characters from both worlds, the rich and the poor, and the plots are contrived to carry you from one to the other. The explanation is that as far back as I can remember, my life was a series of Cinderella transformations; one night I would be sleeping on a vermin-ridden sofa in a lodginghouse, and the next night under silken coverlets in a fashionable home. It all depended on whether my father had the money for that week's board. If he didn't, my mother paid a visit to her father, the railroad official in Baltimore. No Cophetua or Aladdin in fairy lore ever stepped back and forth between the hovel and the palace as frequently as I.

V

When *The Metropolis* was published in 1908, the New York critics said it was a poor novel because the author didn't know the thing called "society." As a matter of fact, the reason was exactly the opposite; the author knew "society" too well to overcome his distaste for it. Attempting to prove this will of course lay me open to the charge of snobbery; it is not good form to establish your own social position. But, on the other hand, neither is it good form to tell about your drunken father, or the bedbugs in your childhood couch; so perhaps one admission will offset the other. What I am doing is explaining a temperament and a literary product, and this can be done only by making real to you both sides of my double life—the bedbugs and liquor on the one hand, the snobbery on the other.

My maternal grandfather was John S. Harden, secretary-treasurer of the Western Maryland Railroad. I remember going to his office and seeing rows of canvas bags full of gold and silver coin that were to go into pay envelopes. I remember also that the president of the road lived just up the street from us and that I broke one of his basement windows with a ball. I was sent to confess my crime and carry the money to pay for it.

Grandfather Harden was a pillar of the Methodist Church, which was not fashionable; but even so, the leaders of Baltimore's affairs came to his terrapin suppers, and I vividly recall these creatures—I mean the terrapin—crawling around in the backyard, and how a Negro man speared them through the heads with a stout fork, and cut off their heads with a butcher knife. Apparently it was not forbidden for a Methodist to serve sherry wine in terrapin stew—or brandy, provided it had been soaked up by fruitcake or plum pudding.

I recall the long reddish beard of this good and kindly old man and the large bald spot on the top of his head. It did not occur to me as strange that his hair should grow the wrong way; but I recall that I was fascinated by a mole placed exactly on the top, like a button, and once I yielded to a dreadful temptation and gave it a slap. Then I fled in terror to the top story of the house. I was brought down by my shocked mother and aunts, and ordered to apologize. I recollect this grandfather carving unending quantities of chickens, ducks, turkeys, and hams; but I cannot to save me recall a single word that he spoke. I suppose the reason the carving stands out in my mind is that I was the youngest of the family of a dozen or so and therefore the last to get my plate at mealtimes.

I recall even better my maternal grandmother, a stout, jolly old lady, who made delightful ginger cookies and played on the piano and sang little tunes to which I danced as a child:

> Here we go, two by two,
> Dressed in yellow, pink and blue.

Mary Ayers was her maiden name, and someone who looked up her family tree discovered that she could lay claim to several castles in Ireland. The family got in touch with the Irish connections, and letters were exchanged, with the result that one of the younger sons came emigrating—a country "squire," six feet or more, rosy-cheeked, and with a broad brogue. He told us about his search for a job and of the unloving reception he met when he went into a business place. " 'Git oot,' said the man, and so I thought I'd better git oot." Not finding anything in Baltimore, our Irish squire wound up on the New York police force—a most dreadful humiliation to the family. My mother, of a mischievous disposition, would wait until her fashionable niece and nephew were entertaining company, and then inquire innocently: "By the way, whatever became of that cousin of ours who's a policeman up in New York?"

My mother's older sister married John Randolph Bland, named for John Randolph, the Virginia statesman. This Uncle Bland, as I called him, became one of the richest men in Baltimore. Sometime before his death, I saw him scolded in a country club of his home city because of his dictatorial ways. The paper referred to him as "the great Bland"—which I suppose establishes his position. He knew all the businessmen of the city, and they trusted him. So he was able to sell them shares in a bonding concern he organized. I remember walking downtown with him one day when I was a child. We stopped at a big grocery store while he persuaded the owner to take shares in the company he was founding. Its name was the United States Fidelity and Guaranty Company, and of course he became its president. You have probably heard of it because it has branches all over America and in many of the world's capitals.

After I had taken up my residence in Pasadena, he made a tour of the country to become acquainted with the agents of his company; he gave a banquet to those in southern California.

There must have been two hundred of them, for they filled the biggest private dining room of our biggest hotel. His muckraker-nephew was invited to partake of this feast and listen to the oratory—but not to be heard, you may be sure! We all sang "Annie Laurie" and "Nellie Gray" and other songs calculated to work up a battle spirit and send us out to take away the other fellow's business.

In my childhood, I lived for months at a time at Uncle Bland's. He and his family lived in one of those brick houses—four stories high, with three or four white marble steps—which are so characteristic of Baltimore and were apparently planned and built by the block. Uncle Bland's daughter married an heir of many millions, and through the years of her young ladyhood I witnessed dances and parties, terrapin suppers, punch, dresses, gossip—everything that is called "society." Prior to that came the debut and wedding of my mother's younger sister, all of which I remember, even to the time when she woke my mother in the middle of the night, exclaiming, "Tell me, Priscie, shall I marry him?" For the benefit of the romantically minded, let me say that she did and that they lived happily until his death.

Let me picture for you the training of a novelist of social contrasts! My relatives were intimate with the society editor of Baltimore's leading newspaper; a person of "good family," no common newspaperman, be it understood. His name was Doctor Taylor, so apparently he was a physician as well as a writer. I see him, dapper, blond, and dainty, with a boutonniere made of one white flower in a ring of purple flowers; he was one of those strange, half-feminine men who are accepted as sexless and admitted to the boudoirs of ladies in deshabille to help drape their dresses and design their hats. All the while he kept up a rapid-fire chatter about everybody who was anybody in the city. I sat in a corner and heard the talk—whose grandfather was a grocer and whose cousin eloped with a fiddler. I breathed that atmosphere of pride and scorn, of values based upon material possessions preserved for two generations or more, and the longer the better. I do not know why I came to hate it, but I know that I did hate it from my earliest days. And everything in my later life confirmed my resolve never to "sell out" to that class.

VI

Nor were the members of my father's family content to remain upon a diet of cold bread and dried herring. My father's older sister had lovely daughters, and one of them married a landed estate in Maryland. In 1906, in the days of *The Jungle*, when I went to Washington to see Theodore Roosevelt, I visited this cousin, who was now a charming widow and was being unsuccessfully wooed by Senator Albert J. Beveridge of Indiana. Later she became the wife of General George Barnett, who commanded the United States Marine Corps in France. This marriage gave rise much later to a comic sequence, which required no change to be fitted into one of my novels. I will tell it here—even though it requires skipping thirty years ahead of my story.

It was at the height of the White Terror, after World War I, and one of the cities of which the American Legion had assumed control was Santa Barbara, California. I was so unwise as to accept an invitation to address some kind of public-ownership convention in that city, and my wife and I motored up with several friends, and learned upon our arrival that the Legion chiefs had decreed that I was not to be heard in Santa Barbara.

In the effort to protect ourselves as far as possible, we registered at the most fashionable hotel, the Arlington—shortly afterward destroyed by an earthquake. Upon entering the lobby, the first spectacle that met our anxious eyes was a military gentleman in full regalia: shiny leather boots, Sam Browne belt, shoulder straps and decorations—I don't know the technical names for these things, but there was everything to impress and terrify. "He is watching you!" whispered my wife, and so he was; there could be no doubt of it, the stern military eye was riveted upon my shrinking figure. There has always been a dispute in the family as to whether I did actually try to hide behind one of the big pillars of the hotel lobby. My wife said it was so, and I was never permitted to spoil her marital stories.

The military gentleman disappeared, and a few minutes later came a bellboy. "Are you Mr. Sinclair?" I pleaded guilty, and was told: "There is a lady who wishes to speak to you in the reception room." "Is it an ambush?" I thought. I had been warned

not to go anywhere alone; there were rumors that the Ku Klux
Klan was after me, as well as the Legion. (This proved not to be
true; I was shortly afterward invited to join the Klan!)

In the reception room sat a lady, none other than my cousin
Lelia, somewhat plump, but as lovely as any lady can be with
the help of both nature and art. How glad we were to see each
other! And how much gossip we had to exchange after sixteen
years! "You must meet my hubby," she said, and led me into the
lobby—and who should "hubby" be but the stern-eyed general!
Whatever displeasure he may have felt at having a revolutionary
cousin-in-law he politely concealed, and we discussed the
weather of southern California in the most correct booster spirit.

Presently the general reminded his wife that the military machine of the United States Government was awaiting his arrival
in San Francisco; they had some three hundred and fifty miles
to drive that night. But the Southern beauty shook her proud
head (you see I know the language of chivalry) and said, "I
haven't seen my cousin for sixteen years." So the general paced
the lobby in fierce impatience for two hours, while Lelia chatted
with my wife and my socialist bodyguard—a millionaire woman
friend of my wife, about whom I shall have much to tell later on.
Did I remember the time when I was romping with Kate, and
put a pillow on Kate's head and sat on it, and when they pulled
me off she was black in the face? Yes, I remembered it. Kate was
married to a civil engineer, Walter was ill—and so on.

At last I saw my childhood playmate off in a high-powered
military car, with a chauffeur in khaki and a guard to ride at his
side, both with holsters at their belts; most imposing. It was fine
local color for a novelist—and incidentally it was a knockout for
the American Legion chiefs of Santa Barbara. Since I was cousin-
in-law to the commander in chief of this military district, it was
impossible to prevent my speaking in favor of the public ownership of water power in California!

VII

To return to childhood days: my summers were spent at the
country home of the Bland family or with my mother at summer
resorts in Virginia. My father would be "on the road," and I re-

member his letters, from which I learned the names of all the towns in Texas and the merits of the leading hotels. If my father was "drinking," we stayed in some low-priced boardinghouse— in the city in winter and in the country in summer. On the other hand, if my father was keeping his pledges, we stayed at one of the springs hotels. My earliest memory of these hotels is of a fancy-dress ball, for which my mother fixed me up as a baker, with a white coat and long trousers and a round cap. That was all right, except that I was supposed to carry a wooden tray with rolls on it, which interfered with my play. Another story was told to me by one of the victims, whom I happened to meet. I had whooping cough, and the other children were forbidden to play with me; this seemed to me injustice, so I chased them and coughed into their faces, after which I had companions in misery. I should add that this early venture in "direct action" is not in accordance with my present philosophy.

I remember one of the Virginia boardinghouses. I would ask for a second helping of fried chicken, and the little Negro who waited table would come back and report, " 'Tisn' any mo'." No amount of hungry protest could extract any words except, " 'Tisn' any mo', Mista Upton, 'tisn' any mo'." At another place the formula ran, "Will you have ham or an egg?" I went fishing and had good luck, and brought home the fish, thinking I would surely get enough to eat that day; but my fish was cooked and served to the whole boardinghouse. I recall a terrible place known as Jett's, to which we rode all day in a bumpy stagecoach. The members of that household were pale ghosts, and we discovered that they were users of drugs. There was an idiot boy who worked in the yard, and gobbled his food out of a tin plate, like a dog.

My Aunt Lucy was with us that summer, and the young squires of the country came calling on Sunday afternoons, vainly hoping that this Baltimore charmer with the long golden hair might consent to remain in rural Virginia. They hitched their prancing steeds to a rail in the yard, and I, an adventurer of eight or ten years, would unhitch them one by one and try them out. I rode a mare to the creek, her colt following, and let them both drink; then I rode back, and can see at this hour the expedition that met me—the owner of the mare, my mother and my aunt, many visitors and guests, and farmhands armed with pitchforks and ropes. There must have been a dozen persons, all looking for a tragedy—the mare being reputed to be extremely dangerous. But I had no fear, and neither had the mare. From this and other experiences I believe that it is safer to go through life without fear. You may get killed suddenly, but meantime it is easier on your nerves.

VIII

When I was eight or nine, my father was employed by a New York firm, so we moved north for the winter, and I joined the tribe of city nomads, a product of the new age, whose formula runs: "Cheaper to move than to pay rent." I remember a dingy lodginghouse on Irving Place, a derelict hotel on East Twelfth Street, housekeeping lodgings over on Second Avenue, a small "flat" on West 65th Street, one on West 92nd Street, one on West 126th Street. Each place in turn was home, each neighborhood full of wonder and excitement. Second Avenue was especially thrilling, because the "gangs" came out from Avenue A and Avenue B like Sioux or Pawnees in war paint, and well-dressed little boys had to fly for their lives.

Our longest stay—several winters, broken by moves to Baltimore—was at a "family hotel" called the Weisiger House, on West 19th Street. The hotel had been made by connecting four brownstone dwellings. The parlor of one was the office. The name sounds like Jerusalem; but it was really Virginia, pronounced Wizziger. Colonel Weisiger was a Civil War veteran and had half the broken-down aristocracy of the Old South as his guests; he must have had a sore time collecting his weekly dues.

I learned much about human nature at the Weisiger House, observing comedies and tragedies, jealousies and greeds and spites. There was the lean Colonel Paul of South Carolina, and the short Colonel Cardoza of Virginia, and the stout Major Waterman of Kentucky. Generals I do not remember, but we had Count Mickiewicz from Poland, a large, expansive gentleman with red beard and booming voice. What has become of little Ralph Mickiewicz, whom I chased up and down the four flights of stairs of each of those four buildings—sixteen flights in all, quite a hunting ground! We killed flies on the bald heads of the colonels and majors, we wheedled teacakes in the kitchen, we pulled the pigtails of the little girls playing dolls in the parlor. One of these little girls, with whom I quarreled most of the time, was destined to grow up and become my first wife; and our married life resembled our childhood.

Colonel Weisiger was large and ample, with a red nose, like Santa Claus; he was the judge and ultimate authority in all disputes. His son was six feet two, quiet and reserved. Mrs. Weisiger was placid and kindly, and had a sister, Miss Tee, who made the teacakes—this pun is of God's making, not of mine. Completing the family was Taylor Tibbs, a large black man, who went to the saloon around the corner twice every day to fetch the Colonel's pail of beer. In New York parlance this was known as "rushing the growler," and you will find Taylor Tibbs and his activities all duly recorded in my novel *The Wet Parade.* Later in life I would go over to Metro-Goldwyn-Mayer to see him in the "talkie" they were making of the novel.

IX

In those days at the Weisiger House I was one of Nature's miracles, such as she produces by the millions in tenement streets—romping, shouting, and triumphant, entirely unaware that their lot is a miserable one. I was a perpetual explosion of energy, and I cannot see how anybody in the place tolerated me; yet they all liked me, all but one or two who were "mean." I have a photograph of myself, dressed in kilts; and my mother tells me a story. Some young man, teasing me, said: "You wear dresses; you are a girl." Said I: "No, I am a boy." "But how do you know you are a boy?" "Because my mother says so."

My young mother would go to the theater, leaving me snugly tucked in bed, in care of some old ladies. I would lie still until I heard a whistle, and then forth I would bound. Clad in a pair of snow-white canton-flannel nighties, I would slide down the banisters into the arms of the young men of the house. What romps I would have, racing on bare feet, or borne aloft on sturdy shoulders! We never got tired of pranks; they would set me up in the office and tell me jokes and conundrums, teach me songs—it was the year of McGinty, hero of hilarity:

Down went McGinty to the bottom of the sea;
He must be very wet,
For they haven't found him yet,
Dressed in his best suit of clothes.

These young men would take me to see the circus parade, which went up Broadway on the evening prior to the opening of Barnum and Bailey's. Young Mr. Lee would hold me on his shoulder a whole evening for the sake of hearing my whoops of delight at the elephants and the gorgeous ladies in spangles and tights. I remember a trick they played on one of these parade evenings. Just after dinner they offered me a quarter if I would keep still for five minutes by the watch, and they sat me on the big table in the office for all the world to witness the test. A couple of minutes passed, and I was still as any mouse; until one of the young men came running in at the front door, crying, "The parade is passing!" I leaped up with a wail of despair.

As a foil to this, let me narrate the most humiliating experience of my entire life. Grown-up people do not realize how intensely children feel, and what enduring impressions are made upon their tender minds. The story I am about to tell is as real to me as if it had happened last night.

My parents had a guest at dinner, and I was moved to another table, being placed with old Major Waterman and two young ladies. The venerable warrior started telling of an incident that had taken place that day. "I was walking along the street and I met Jones. 'Come in and have a drink,' said he, and I replied, 'No, thank you'—"

What was to be the end of that story I shall never know in this world. "Oh, Major Waterman!" I burst out, and there followed an appalled silence. Terror gripped my soul as the old gentleman turned his bleary eyes upon me. "What do you mean, sir? Tell me what you mean."

Now, if this had been a world in which men and women spoke the truth to one another, I could have told exactly what I meant. I would have said, "I mean that your cheeks are inflamed and your nose has purple veins in it, and it is difficult to believe that you ever declined anyone's invitation to drink." But it was not a world in which one could say such words; all I could do was to sit like a hypnotized rabbit, while the old gentleman bored me through. "I wish to have an answer, sir! What did you mean by that remark?" I still have, as one of my weaknesses, the tendency to speak first and think afterwards; but the memory of Major Waterman has helped me on the way to reform.

<h1 style="text-align:center">X</h1>

The pageant of America gradually revealed itself to my awakening mind. I saw political processions—I remember the year when Harrison defeated Cleveland, and our torchlight paraders, who had been hoping to celebrate a Democratic triumph, had to change their marching slogan at the last minute. "Four, four, four years more!" they had expected to shout; but they had to make it four months instead. The year was 1888, and my age was ten.

Another date that can be fixed: I remember the excitement when Corbett defeated the people's idol, John L. Sullivan. Corbett was known as Gentleman Jim, and I told my mother about the new hero. "Of course," said the haughty Southern lady, "it means that he is a gentleman for a prize-fighter." But I assured her, "No, no, he is a real gentleman. The papers all say so." This was in 1892, and I was fourteen, and still believed the papers.

There was a Spanish dancer called Carmencita and a music hall, Koster and Bial's; I never went to such places, but I heard the talk. There was a book by the name of *Trilby*, which the ladies blushed to hear spoken of. I did not read it until later, but I knew it had something to do with feet, because thereafter my father always called them "trilbies." There were clergymen denouncing vice in New York, and editors denouncing the clergymen. I heard Tammany ardently defended by my father, whose politics were summed up in a formula: "I'd rather vote for a nigger than for a Republican."

I recall another of his sayings—I must have heard it a hundred times—that Inspector Byrnes was the greatest detective chief in the world. I now know that Inspector Byrnes ran the detective bureau of New York upon this plan: local pickpockets and burglars and confidence men were permitted to operate upon two conditions—that they would keep out of the Wall Street and

Fifth Avenue districts, and would report to Byrnes all outside crooks who attempted to invade the city. Another of my father's opinions—this one based upon knowledge—was that you should never argue with a New York policeman, because of the danger of getting your skull cracked.

What was the size and flavor of Blue Point oysters as compared with Lynnhaven Bay's? Why was it impossible to obtain properly cooked food north of Baltimore? What was the wearing quality of patent-leather shoes as compared with calfskin? Wherein lay the superiority of Robert E. Lee over all other generals of history? Was there any fusel oil in whisky that was aged in the wood? Were the straw hats of next season to have a higher or a lower brim? Where had the Vanderbilts obtained the fifty-thousand-dollar slab of stone that formed the pavement in front of their Fifth Avenue palace? Questions such as these occupied the mind of my little, fat, kindhearted father and his friends. He was a fastidious dresser, as well as eater, and especially proud of his small hands and feet—they were aristocratic; he would gaze down rapturously at his tight little shoes, over his well-padded vest. He had many words to describe the right kind of shoes and vests and hats and gloves; they were "nobby," they were "natty," they were "neat"—such were the phrases by which he sold them to buyers.

I heard much of these last-named essential persons, but cannot recall ever seeing one. They were Jews, or countrymen, and the social lines were tightly drawn; never would my father, even in the midst of drink and degradation, have dreamed of using his aristocratic Southern wife to impress his customers. Nor would he use his little son, who was expected to grow up to be a naval officer like his ancestors. "The social position of a naval officer is the highest in the world," pronounced my father. "He can go anywhere, absolutely anywhere; he can meet crowned heads as their equals." And meantime the little son was reaching out into a strange world of books; reading things of which the father had never heard. "What are you reading?" he would ask, and the son would reply, none too generously, "A book." The father got used to this answer. "Reading a book!" he would say, with pathetic futility. The chasm between the two was widening, never to be closed in this world.

XI

I was ten years old before I went to school. The reason was that some doctor told my mother that my mind was outgrowing my body, and I should not be taught anything. When finally I was taken to a public school, I presented the teachers with a peculiar problem; I knew everything but arithmetic. This branch of learning, so essential to a commercial civilization, had shared the fate of alcohol and tobacco, tea and coffee; my mother did not use it, so neither did I.

The teachers put me in the first primary grade, to learn long division; promising that as soon as I caught up in the subject, I would be moved on. I was humiliated at being in a class with children younger than myself, so I fell to work and got into the grammar school in less than a month, and performed the unusual feat of going through the eight grammar grades in less than two years. Thus at the age of twelve I was ready for the City College —it was called a college, but I hasten to explain that it was in reality only a high school.

Unfortunately the college was not ready for me. No one was admitted younger than fourteen; so there was nothing for me to do but to take the last year of grammar school all over again. I did this at old Number 40, on East 23rd Street; my classmates were the little "toughs" of the East Side tenements. An alarming experience for a fastidious young Southerner, destined for the highest social circles—but I count it a blessing hardly to be exaggerated. That year among the "toughs" helped to save me from the ridiculous snobbery that would otherwise have been my destiny in life. Since then I have been able to meet all kinds of humans and never see much difference; also, I have been able to keep my own ideals and convictions, and "stand the gaff," according to the New York phrase.

To these little East Side "toughs" I was, of course, fully as strange a phenomenon as they were to me. I spoke a language that they associated with Fifth Avenue "dudes" wearing silk hats and kid gloves. The Virginia element in my brogue was entirely beyond their comprehension; the first time I spoke of a "street-cyar," the whole class broke into laughter. They named me

Chappie, and initiated me into the secrets of a dreadful game called "hop, skip, and a lepp," which you ended, not on your feet, but on your buttocks; throwing your legs up in the air and coming down with a terrific bang on the hard pavement. The surgeons must now be performing operations for floating kidney upon many who played that game in boyhood.

The teacher of the class was a jolly old Irishman, Mr. Furey; he later became principal of a school, and I would have voted for his promotion without any reservation. He was a disciplinarian with a homemade method; if he observed a boy whispering or idling during class, he would let fly a piece of chalk at the offender's head. The class would roar with laughter; the offender would grin, pick up the chalk, and bring it to the teacher, and get his knuckles smartly cracked as he delivered it, and then go back to his seat and pay attention. From this procedure I learned that pomposity is no part of either brains or achievement, and I have never in my life tried to impress anyone by being anything but what I am.

One feature of our school was the assembly room, into which we marched by classes to the music of a piano, thumped by a large dark lady with a budding mustache. We sang patriotic songs and listened to recitations in the East Side dialect, a fearful and wonderful thing. This dialect tried to break into the White House in the year 1928, and the rest of America heard it for the first time. Graduates of New York public schools who had made millions out of paving and contracting jobs put up the money to pay for radio "hookups," and the voice of Fulton Fish Market came speaking to the farmers of the corn belt and the fundamentalists of the bible belt. "Ladies and genn'lmun, the foist thing I wanna say is that the findin's of this here kimittee proves that we have the woist of kinditions in our kimmunity." I sat in my California study and listened to Al Smith speaking in St. Louis and Denver, and it took me straight back to old Number 40, and the little desperados throwing their buttocks into the air and coming down with a thump on the hard pavement.

As I read the proofs of this book I have returned from a visit to New York after thirty years. The old "El" roads are gone, and many of the slum tenements have been replaced by sixty-story buildings. The "micks" and the "dagos" have been replaced by Negroes and Puerto Ricans, who have taken possession of Harlem.

XII

Behold me now, a duly enrolled "subfreshman" of the College of the City of New York; a part of the city's free educational system, not very good, but convenient for the son of a straw-hat salesman addicted to periodical "sprees." It was a combination of high school and college, awarding a bachelor's degree after a five-year course. I passed my entrance examinations in the spring of 1892, and I was only thirteen, but my public-school teacher and principal entered me as fourteen. The college work did not begin until September 15, and five days later I would be of the required age, so really it was but a wee little lie.

The college was situated in an old brick building on the corner of Lexington Avenue and 23rd Street. It was a firetrap, but I did not know it, and fortunately never had to learn it. There were about a thousand students in its four or five stories, and we trooped from one classroom to another and learned by rote what our bored instructors laid out for us. I began Latin, algebra, and solid geometry, physics, drawing, and a course called English, which was the most dreadful ordeal I ever had to endure. We had a list of sentences containing errors, which we were supposed to correct. The course was necessary for most of the class because they were immigrants or the sons of immigrants. For me it was unnecessary, but the wretched teacher was affronted in his dignity, and would set traps for me by calling on me when my mind had wandered.

The professor of chemistry and physics was R. Ogden Doremus, a name well known to the public because he testified as an expert in murder trials. He had snowy white mustaches, one arm, and a peppery temper. His assistant was his son, whom he persisted in referring to as Charlie, which amused us, because Charlie was a big man with a flourishing black beard. I managed early in the course to get on the elderly scientist's nerves by my tendency to take the physical phenomena of the universe without due reverence. The old gentleman would explain to us that scientific caution required us to accept nothing on his authority, but to insist upon proving everything for ourselves. Soon afterward he produced a little vial of white powder, remarking, "Now, gentlemen, this vial contains arsenic, and a little pinch of it would be sufficient to kill all the members of this class." Said I, "*You* try that, Professor!"

Really, he might have joined in the laugh. But what he did was to call me an "insolent young puppy," and to predict that I was going to "flunk" his course, in which event he would see to it that I did not get promoted to the next class. This roused my sporting spirit, and I decided to "flunk" his course and get such high marks in all the other courses that I could not be held back. This I did.

The top floor of our building was a big auditorium, where we met every morning for chapel. Our "prexy" read a passage from the Bible, and three of us produced efforts in English composition, directed and staged by a teacher of elocution, who had marked our manuscripts in the margin with three mystic symbols: *rg*, *lg*, and *gbh*. The first meant a gesture with the right hand, the second a gesture with the left hand, and the third a gesture with both hands—imploring the audience, or in extreme emergencies lifted into the air, imploring the deity. In a row, upstage, facing the assembled students, sat our honorable faculty, elderly gentlemen with whiskers, doing their best not to show signs of boredom. Our "prexy" was a white-bearded Civil War veteran, General Webb; and when it was my turn to prepare a composition, I made my debut as a revolutionary agitator with an encomium of my father's favorite hero, Robert E. Lee. My bombshell proved a dud, because General Webb, who had commanded a brigade at Gettysburg, remarked mildly that it was a good paper, and Lee had been a great man. Soldiers, I learned, take a professional attitude to their jobs, and confine their fighting to the field of battle.

XIII

The year I started at this college, we lived in a three- or four-room flat on West 65th Street. Mother did the cooking, and father would put an apron over his little round paunch and wash the dishes; there was much family laughter when father kissed the cook. When the weather was fair, I rode to college on a bicycle; when the weather was stormy, I rode on the Sixth Avenue Elevated and walked across town. I took my lunch in a little tin box with a strap: a couple of sandwiches, a piece of cake, and an apple or banana. The honorific circumstances of college life were missing. In fact, so little did I know about these higher matters that when I was sounded out for a "frat," I actually didn't know what it was, and could make nothing of the high-sounding attempts at explanation. If the haughty upperclassman with the correct clothes and the Anglo-Saxon features had said to me in plain words, "We want to keep ourselves apart from the kikes and wops who make up the greater part of our student body," I would have told him that some of the kikes and wops interested me, whereas he did not.

About two thirds of the members of my class were Jews. I had never known any Jews before, but here were so many that one took them as a matter of course. I am not sure if I realized they were Jews; I seldom realize it now about the people I meet. The Jews have lived in Central Europe for so long, and have been so mixed with the population, that the border line is hard to draw. Since I became a socialist writer, half my friends and half my readers have been Jews. I sum up my impression of them in the verse about the little girl who had a little curl right in the middle of her forehead, and when she was good she was very, very good, and when she was bad she was horrid.

About this time, I threw away another chance for advancement. My uncle, Terry Sinclair, who was an "old beau" in New York and therefore met the rich and had some influence, brought to his bright young nephew the offer of an appointment to the Annapolis Naval Academy. This was regarded as my birthright, but I declined it. I had made up my mind that I wanted to be a lawyer, having come to the naïve conclusion that the law offered a way to combine an honorable living with devotion to books. This idea I carried through college and until I went up to Columbia University, where I had an opportunity to observe the law-school students.

XIV

My Saturdays and holidays I spent racing about the streets and in my playground, Central Park. In the course of these years I came to know this park so well that afterward, when I walked in it, every slope and turn of the winding paths had a story for me. I learned to play tennis on its grass courts; I roller-skated on its walks and ice-skated on its lakes—when the flag with the red ball went up on top of the "castle," thrilling the souls of young folks for miles around. I played hare and hounds, marking up the asphalt walks with chalk; we thought nothing of running all the way around the park, a distance of seven miles.

The Upper West Side was mostly empty lots, with shanties of "squatters" and goats browsing on tin cans—if one could believe the comic papers. Blasting and building were going on, and the Italian laborers who did this hard and dangerous work were the natural prey of us young aborigines. We snowballed them from the roofs of the apartment houses, and when there was no snow, we used clothespins. When they cursed us we yelled with glee. I can still remember the phrases—or at any rate what we imagined the phrases to be. "Aberragotz!" and "Chingasol!"—do those sounds mean anything to an Italian? If they do, it may be something shocking, perhaps not fit to print. When these "dagos" chased us, we fled in terror most delightful.

Sometimes we would raid grocery stores on the avenue and grab a couple of potatoes, and roast them in bonfires on the vacant lots. I was a little shocked at this idea, but the other boys explained to me that it was not stealing, it was only "swiping," and the grocers took it for granted. So it has been easy for me to understand how young criminals are made in our great cities. We manufacture crime wholesale, just as certainly and as definitely as we manufacture alcohol in a mash of grain. And just as we can stop getting alcohol by not mixing a mash, so we can stop crime by not permitting exploitation and economic inequality.

But that is propaganda, and I have sworn to leave it out of this book. So instead, let me tell a story that illustrates the police attitude toward these budding criminals. In my mature days when I was collecting material about New York, I was strolling on the East Side with an elderly police captain. It was during a reform administration, and the movement for uplift had taken the form of a public playground, with swings and parallel bars. The young men of the tenements were developing their muscles after a day's work loading trucks, and I said to the captain, what a fine thing they should have this recreation. The elderly cynic snorted wrathfully: "Porch climbers! Second-story work!"

The Nietzscheans advise us to live dangerously, and this advice I took without having heard it. The motorcar had not yet come in, but there were electric cars and big two-horse trucks, and my memory is full of dreadful moments. Riding down Broadway to college, the wheel of my bicycle slipped into the wet trolley slot, and I was thrown directly in front of an oncoming car. Quick as a cat, I rolled out of the way, but the car ran over my hat, and a woman bystander fainted. Again, skating on an asphalt street, I fell in the space between the front and rear wheels of a fast-moving express wagon, and had to whisk my legs out before the rear wheels caught them. When I was seventeen, I came to the conclusion that Providence must have some special purpose in keeping me in the world, for I was able to reckon up fourteen times that I had missed death by a hairbreadth. I had fallen off a pier during a storm; I had been swept out to sea by a rip tide; I had been carried down from the third story of the Weisiger House by a fireman with a scaling ladder.

I do not know so much about the purposes of Providence now as I did at the age of seventeen, and the best I can make of the matter is this: that several hundred thousand little brats are bred in the great metropolis every year and turned out into the streets to develop their bodies and their wits, and in a rough, general way, those who get caught by streetcars and motorcars and trucks are those who are not quite so quick in their reactions. But when it comes to genius, to beauty, dignity, and true power of mind, I cannot see that there is any chance for them to survive in the insane hurly-burly of metropolitan life. If I wanted qualities such as these in human beings, I would surely transfer them to a different environment. And maybe that is what Providence was planning for me to understand and to do in the world. At any rate, it is what I am trying to do, and is my final reaction to the great metropolis of Mammon.

2

Youth

I

CHILDHOOD lasted long, and youth came late in my life. I was taught to avoid the subject of sex in every possible way; the teaching being done, for the most part, in Victorian fashion, by deft avoidance and anxious evasion. Apparently my mother taught me even too well; for once when I was being bathed, I persisted in holding a towel in front of myself. Said my mother: "If you don't keep that towel out of the way, I'll give you a spank." Said I: "Mamma, would you rather have me disobedient, or immodest?"

The first time I ever heard of the subject of sex, I was four or five years old, playing on the street with a little white boy and a Negro girl, the child of a janitor. They were whispering about something mysterious and exciting; there were two people living across the street who had just been married, and something they did was a subject of snickers. I, who wanted to know about everything, tried to find out about this; but I am not sure my companions knew what they were whispering about; at any rate, they did not tell me. But I got the powerful impression of something strange.

It was several years later that I found out the essential facts. I spent a summer in the country with a boy cousin a year or two younger than I, and we watched the animals and questioned the farmhands. But never did I get one word of information or advice from either father or mother on this subject; only the motion of shrinking away from something dreadful. I recollect how the signs of puberty began to show themselves in me, to my great bewilderment; my mother and grandmother stood helplessly by, like the hens that hatch ducklings and see them go into the water.

Incredible as it may seem, I had been at least two years in college before I understood about prostitution. So different from my friend Sam De Witt, socialist poet, who told me that he was raised in a tenement containing a house of prostitution, and that at the age of five he and other little boys and girls played brothel as other children play dolls, and quarrelled as to whose turn it was to be the "madam"! I can remember speculating at the age of sixteen whether it could be true that women did actually sell their bodies. I decided in the negative and held to that idea until I summoned the courage to question one of my classmates in college.

The truth, finally made clear, shocked me deeply, and played a great part in the making of my political revolt. Between the ages of sixteen and twenty I explored the situation in New York City, and made discoveries that for me were epoch-making. The saloonkeeper, who had been the villain of my childhood melodrama, was merely a tool and victim of the big liquor interests and politicians and police. The twin bases of the political power of Tammany Hall were saloon graft and the sale of women. So it was that, in my young soul, love for my father and love for my mother were transmuted into political rage, and I sallied forth at the age of twenty, a young reformer armed for battle. It would be a longer battle than I realized, alas!

II

Another factor in my life that requires mentioning is the Protestant Episcopal Church of America. The Sinclairs had always belonged to that church; my father was named after an Episcopal clergyman, the Reverend Upton Beall. My mother's father was a Methodist and took the *Christian Herald*, and as a little fellow I read all the stories and studied all the pictures of the conflicts with the evil one; but my mother and aunts had apparently decided that the Episcopal Church was more suited to their social standing, and therefore my spiritual life had always been one of

elegance. Not long ago, seeking local color, I attended a service in Trinity Church; it was my first service in more than thirty
years, yet I could recite every prayer and sing every hymn and
could even have preached the sermon.

In New York, no matter how poor and wretched the rooms in
which we lived, we never failed to go to the most fashionable
church; it was our way of clinging to social status. When we lived
at the Weisiger House, we walked to St. Thomas' on Fifth
Avenue. When we lived on Second Avenue, we went to St.
George's. When we moved uptown, we went to St. Agnes'. Now
and then we would make a special trip to the Church of St.
Mary the Virgin, which was "high" and had masses and many
candles and jeweled robes and processions and genuflections and
gyrations. Always I wore tight new shoes and tight gloves and a
neatly brushed little derby hat—supreme discomfort to the glory
of God. I became devout, and my mother, determined upon making something special of me, decided that I was to become
a bishop. I myself talked of driving a hook-and-ladder truck.

We moved back to the Weisiger House, and I was confirmed at
the Church of the Holy Communion, just around the corner; the
rector, Doctor Mottet, lived to a great age. His assistant was the
Reverend William Wilmerding Moir, son of a wealthy old Scotch
merchant; the young clergyman had, I think, more influence upon
me than any other man. My irreverent memory brings up the first
time I was invited to his home and met his mother, who looked
and dressed exactly like Queen Victoria, and his testy old father,
who had a large purple nose, filled, I fear, with Scotch whisky.
The son took me aside. "Upton," he said, "we are going to have
chicken for dinner, and Father carves, and when he asks you if
you prefer white meat or dark, please express a preference, because if you say that it doesn't matter, he will answer that you
can wait till you make up your mind."

Will Moir was a young man of fashion, but he had gone into
the church because of genuine devoutness and love of his fellowmen. Spirituality is out of fashion at the moment and open to
dangerous suspicion, so I hasten to say that he was a thoroughly
wholesome person; not brilliant intellectually, but warmhearted,
loyal, and devoted. He became a foster father to me, and despite
all my teasing of the Episcopal Church in *The Profits of Religion*

and elsewhere, I have never forgotten this loving soul and what he meant at the critical time of my life. My quarrel with the churches is a lover's quarrel; I do not want to destroy them, but to put them on a rational basis, and especially to drive out the money changers from the front pews.

Moir specialized in training young boys in the Episcopal virtues, with special emphasis upon chastity. He had fifty or so under his wing all the time. We met at his home once a month and discussed moral problems; we were pledged to write him a letter once a month and tell him all our troubles. If we were poor, he helped us to find a job; if we were tempted sexually, we would go to see him and talk it over. The advice we got was always straightforward and sound. The procedure is out of harmony with this modern age, and my sophisticated friends smile when they hear about it. The problem of self-discipline versus self-development is a complicated one, and I can see virtues in both courses and perils in either extreme. I am glad that I did not waste my time and vision "chasing chippies," as the sport was called; but I am sorry that I did not get advice and aid in the task of finding a girl with whom I might have lived wisely and joyfully.

III

I became a devout little Episcopalian, and at the age of fourteen went to church every day during Lent. I taught a Sunday-school class for a year. But I lost interest because I could not discover how these little ragamuffins from the tenements were being made better by learning about Jonah and the whale and Joshua blowing down the walls of Jericho. I was beginning to use my brains on the Episcopalian map of the universe, and a chill was creeping over my fervor. Could it possibly be that the things I had been taught were merely the Hebrew mythology instead of the Greek or the German? Could it be that I would be damned for asking such a question? And would I have the courage to go ahead and believe the truth, even though I were damned for it?

I took these agonies to my friend Mr. Moir, who was not too much troubled; it appeared that clergymen were used to such crises in the young. He told me that the fairy tales did not really matter, he was not sure that he believed them himself; the only thing of importance was the resurrection of Jesus Christ and the redemption by his blood. So I was all right for a time—until I began to find myself doubting the resurrection of Jesus Christ. After all, what did we know about it? Were there not a score of other martyred redeemers in the mythologies? And how could Jesus have been both man and God at the same time? As a psychological proposition, it meant knowing everything and not knowing everything, and was not that plain nonsense?

I took this also to Mr. Moir, and he loaded me up with tomes of Episcopalian apologetics. I remember the Bampton Lectures, an annual volume of foundation lectures delivered at Oxford. I read several volumes, and it was the worst thing that ever happened to me; these devout lectures, stating the position of the opposition, suggested so many new doubts that I was completely bowled over. Literally, I was turned into an agnostic by reading the official defenses of Christianity. I remind myself of this when I have a tendency to worry over the barrage of attacks on socialism in the capitalist press. Truth is as mighty now as it was then.

I told my friend Mr. Moir what had happened, but still he refused to worry; it was a common experience, and I would come back. I felt certain that I never would, but I was willing for him to keep himself happy. I no longer taught Sunday school, but I remained under my friend's sheltering wing, and told him my troubles—up to the time when I was married. Marriage was apparently regarded as a kind of graduation from the school of chastity. My friend did not live to see me as a socialist agitator; he succumbed to an attack of appendicitis—due, no doubt, to his habit of talking Christianity all through dinner and, just before the butler came to remove his plate, bolting his food in a minute or two.

For a time my interest was transferred to the Unitarian Church. I met Minot J. Savage of the Church of the Messiah, now the Community Church; his arguments seemed to me to possess that reasonableness that I had missed in the Bampton Lectures. I never joined his church, and have never again felt the need of formal worship; from the age of sixteen it has been true with me that "to labor is to pray." I have prayed hard in this fashion and have found it the great secret of happiness.

An interesting detail about Dr. Savage: he was the first in-

tellectual man I ever met who claimed to have seen a ghost. Not
merely had he seen one, he had sat up and chatted with it.
I found this an interesting idea, and find it so still. I am the despair of my orthodox materialistic friends because I insist upon
believing in the possibility of so many strange things. My materialistic friends know that these things are *a priori* impossible;
whereas I assert that nothing is *a priori* impossible. It is a question of evidence, and I am willing to hear the evidence about anything whatever.

The story as I recall it is this. Savage had a friend who set out
for Ireland in the days before the cable; at midnight Savage
awakened and saw his friend standing by his bedside. The friend
stated that he was dead, but Savage was not to think that he had
known the pangs of drowning; the steamer had been wrecked on
the coast of Ireland, and the friend had been killed when a beam
struck him on the left side of his head as he was trying to get off
the ship. Savage wrote this out and had it signed by witnesses,
and two or three weeks later came the news that the ship had
been wrecked and the friend's body found with the left side of his
head crushed.

If such a case stood alone, it would of course be nothing. But in
Edmund Gurney's two volumes, *Phantasms of the Living,* are a
thousand or so cases, carefully documented. There is another set
of cases, collected by Dr. Walker Franklin Prince, of the Boston
Society for Psychical Research in Bulletin XIV of that society. I
no longer find these phenomena so difficult of belief, because my
second wife and I demonstrated long-range telepathy in our
personal lives. Later on, I shall be telling about our book, *Mental Radio.*

IV

In my class in college there was a Jewish boy by the name of
Simon Stern, whom I came to know well because we lived in the
same neighborhood and often went home together. Simon wrote
a short story, and one day came to class in triumph, announcing
that this story had been accepted by a monthly magazine published by a Hebrew orphans' home. Straightway I was stirred to
emulation. If Simon could write a story, why could not I? Such

was the little acorn that grew into an oak, with so many branches that it threatens to become top-heavy.

I wrote a story about a pet bird. For years it had been my custom every summer to take young birds from the nest and raise them. They would know me as their only parent, and were charming pets. Now I put one of these birds into an adventure, making it serve to prove the innocence of a colored boy accused of arson. I mailed the story to the *Argosy*, one of the two Munsey publications in those early days, and the story was accepted, price twenty-five dollars. You can imagine that I was an insufferable youngster on the day that letter arrived; especially to my friend Simon Stern, who had not been paid for his story.

Our family fortunes happened to be at a low ebb just then, so I fell to digging in this new gold mine. I found several papers that bought children's stories at low prices; also, before long, I discovered another gold mine—writing jokes for the comic papers. At seventeen, jokes were my entire means of support. My mother and I spent that winter on West 23rd Street, near the river. My weekly budget was this: for a top-story hallroom in a lodging-house, one dollar twenty-five; for two meals a day at an eating house, three dollars; and for a clean collar and other luxuries, twenty-five cents. It seems a slender allowance, but you must remember that I had infinite riches in the little room of the college library.

The quantity production of jokes is an odd industry, and for the aid of young aspirants I will tell how it is done. Jokes are made up hind end forward, so to speak; you don't think of the joke, but of what it is to be about. There are tramp jokes, mother-in-law jokes, plumber jokes, Irishman jokes, and so on. You decide to write tramp jokes this morning; well, there are many things about tramps that are jokable; they do not like to work, they do not like to bathe, they do not like bulldogs, and so on. You decide to write about tramps not liking to bathe; very well, you think of all the words and phrases having to do with water, soaps, tubs, streams, rain, etc., and of puns or quirks by which these words can be applied to tramps.

I have a scrapbook in which my mother treasured many of the jokes for which I was paid one dollar apiece, and from this book, my biographer, Floyd Dell, selected one, in which a tramp calls attention to a sign, "Cleaning and Dyeing," and says he always knew those two things went together. Out of this grew a joke more amusing than the one for which I was paid. My enterprising German publishers prepared a pamphlet about my books, to be sent to critics and reviewers in Germany, and they quoted this joke as a sample of my early humor. The Germans didn't think it was very good. And no wonder. The phrase in translation appeared as "*Waescherei und Faeberei*," which, alas, entirely destroys the double meaning of "Dyeing." It makes me think of the Irishman on a railroad handcar who said that he had just been taking the superintendent for a ride, and had heard a fine conundrum. "What is the difference between a railroad spike and a thief in the baggage room? One grips the steel and the other steals the satchels."

My jokes became an obsession. While other youths were thinking about "dates," I was pondering jokes about Scotchmen, Irishmen, Negroes, Jews. I would take my mother to church, and make up jokes on the phrases in the prayer book and hymnbook. I kept my little notebook before me at meals, while walking, while dressing, and in classes if the professor was a bore. I wrote out my jokes on slips of paper, with a number in the corner, and sent them in batches of ten to the different editors; when the pack came back with one missing, I had earned a dollar. I had a bookkeeping system, showing where each batch had been sent; jokes number 321 to 330 had been sent to *Life, Judge,* and *Puck,* and were now at the *Evening Journal.*

I began taking jokes to artists who did illustrating. They would pay for ideas—if you could catch them right after they had collected the money. It was a New York bohemia entirely unknown to fame. Dissolute and harum-scarum but good-natured young fellows, they were, inhabiting crudely furnished "studios" in the neighborhood of East 14th Street. I will give one glimpse of this artist utopia: I entered a room with a platform in the center and saw a tall lanky Irishman standing on it, bare-armed and bare-legged, a sheet wrapped around him, and an umbrella in his hand, the ferule held to his mouth. "What is this?" I asked, and the young artist replied, "I am doing a set of illustrations of the Bible. This is Joshua with the trumpet blowing down the walls of Jericho."

V

The editor of *Argosy* who accepted my first story was Matthew White, Jr., a genial little gentleman, who had been the great Munsey's associate from the earliest days, when that future master of magazine merchandising and chain grocery stores had sat in a one-room office in his shirt sleeves and kept his own accounts. White invited me to call on him, and I went, and we had a delightful chat; at any rate, I found it so. Finally the editor asked me if I would not like to see the "plant," whereupon he led me through two or three rooms full of bookkeepers and office girls stamping envelopes, and then paused casually at the elevator and rang the bell. So I learned that an author is not so great a novelty to an editor as an editor is to an author. The device of "showing the plant" is one which I have employed many times with callers who fail to realize that I am more of a novelty to them than they are to me.

I wrote other stories for the *Argosy*, and also odds and ends for *Munsey's*. They had a department called "Fads," and I racked my imagination for new ones that could be humorously written up; each one would be a meal ticket for a week. In the summer—1895, I think it was—my mother and I went to a hotel up in a village called Pawlet, Vermont, and Matthew White, a bachelor, came to join us for his vacation. My experience at that hotel requires considerable courage to tell.

My father was drinking, and we were stranded. Rather than be dependent upon our relatives, I had answered an advertisement for a hotel clerk, and there I was, the newly arrived employee of this moderately decent country establishment. I was supposed to do part-time work to earn the board of my mother and myself, and the very first night of my arrival, I discovered that one of the duties of the so-called clerk was to carry up pitchers of ice water to the guests. I refused the duty, and the outcome of the clash of wills was that the proprietor did it instead. I can see in my mind's eye this stoop-shouldered, elderly man, with a long brown beard turning gray; he was kindhearted, and doubtless saw the kind of decayed gentlefolk he had got on his hands. He was sorry for my mother, and did not turn us away.

I performed such duties as were consistent with my notion of my own dignity, but they were not many. Among them was copying out the dinner menus every day; that brought me into clash with the cooks of the establishment—they were husband and wife, and had a notion of their importance fully equal to my own. I would sometimes fail to copy all the fancy French phrases whereby they sought to glorify their performances. Ever since then, I lose my appetite when I hear of "prime ribs of beef au jus."

I remember that among the guests was the painter, J. G. Brown, famous for depicting newsboys and village types. I took long walks with him and learned his notion of art, which was that one must paint only beautiful and cheerful things, never anything ugly or depressing. His children were not so democratic as their father and refused to overlook my status as an employee. His oldest daughter was named Mabel, and all the young people called her that. I, quite innocently, did the same—until she turned upon me in a fury and informed me that she was "Miss Brown."

Yet my status as a college student apparently kept me in the amateur class, for I was on the tennis team that played matches with other hotels in the neighborhood. I remember a trip we made, in which I received a lesson in table manners as practiced in this remote land of the Yankees. It was the custom to serve vegetables in little bird bathtubs, which were ranged in a semi-circle about each plate, five or six of them. The guests finished eating, and I also finished; all the other plates were cleared away, but mine remained untouched, and I did not know why. The waitress was standing behind me, and I remarked gently, "I am through"—the very precise language that my mother had taught me to use; never "I am done," but always, "I am through." But this waitress taught me something new. Said she, in a voice of icy scorn: "*Stack your dishes!*"

VI

The venerable faculty of the College of the City of New York, who had charge of my intellectual life for five years, were nearly all of them Tammany appointees, and therefore Catholics. It was the first time I had ever met Catholics, and I found them kindly,

but set in dogma, and as much given to propaganda as I myself
was destined to become.

For example, there was "Herby." Several hours a week for
several years I had "Herby," the eminent Professor Charles
George Herbermann, editor of the *Catholic Encyclopedia* and
leading light of the Jesuits. He was a stout, irascible old gentleman with a bushy reddish beard. "Mr. Sinclair," he would roar,
"it is so because I *say* it is so!" But that did not go with me at all;
I would say, "But, Professor, how *can* it be so?" We would have a
wrangle, pleasing to other members of the class, who had not
prepared their lessons and were afraid of being called upon. (We
learned quickly to know each professor's hobbies, and whenever we were not prepared to recite, we would start a discussion.)

"Herby" taught me Latin, "Tizzy" taught me Greek, and Professor George Hardy taught me English. He was a little round
man of the Catholic faith, and his way of promoting the faith
was to set a class that was sixty per cent Jewish to learning Catholic sentimentality disguised as poetry. I remember we had to
recite Dobson's "The Missal," and avenged ourselves by learning
it to the tune of a popular music-hall ditty of the hour, "Ta-ra-ra-
boom-de-ay." Hardy was a good teacher, except when the Pope
came in. He told us that Milton was a dangerous disturber of the
peace of Europe, and that it was a libel to say that Chaucer was a
Wycliffite. What a Wycliffite was nobody ever mentioned.

Our professor of history had no dogma, so I was permitted to
learn English and European history according to the facts. I was
interested, but could not see why it was necessary for me to learn
the names of so many kings and dukes and generals, and the
dates when they had slaughtered so many human beings. In the
effort to keep them in my mind until examination day, I evolved
a memory system, and once it tripped me in a comical way. "Who
was Lord Cobden?" inquired the professor; and my memory system replied: "He passed the corncob laws."

But the prize laugh of my history class had to do with a lively
witted youngster by the name of Fred Schwed, who afterward
became a curb broker. Fred never prepared anything and never
paid attention, but trusted to his gift of the gab. He was suddenly called upon to explain the origin of the title, Prince of
Wales. Said the grave Professor Johnston: "Mr. Schwed, how did

it happen that an English prince, the son of an English king, was born on Welsh soil?" Fred, called suddenly out of a daydream or perhaps a game of crap shooting, gazed with a wild look and stammered: "Why—er—why, you see, Professor—his mother was there."

VII

Also, I remember vividly Professor Hunt, who taught us freehand drawing, mechanical drawing, and perspective. A lean gentleman with a black mustache and a fierce tongue, he suffered agonies from bores. You may believe that in our class we had many; and foreigners struggling with English were also a trial to him. I recall a dumb Russian by the name of Vilkomirsson; he would gaze long and yearningly, and at last blurt out some question that would cause the class to titter. In perspective it is customary to indicate certain points by their initials; the only one I recall now is "V.P.," which means "vanishing point." The poor foreigner could never get these abbreviations straight, and he would take a seat right in front of the professor in the hope of being able to ask help without disturbing the rest of the class. "Professor, I don't understand what you mean when you say that the V.P. is six inches away." "Mr. Vilkomirsson," demanded the exasperated teacher, "if I were to tell you that the D.F. is six feet away, what would you understand me to mean?"

Our freehand drawing was done in a large studio with plaster casts all around the room. We took a drawing board and fastened a sheet of paper to it, and with a piece of charcoal proceeded to make the best possible representation of one of the casts; Professor Hunt in the meantime roamed about the room like a tiger at large, taking a swipe with his sharp claws at this or that helpless victim. That our efforts at "free" art were not uniformly successful you may judge from verses that I contributed to our college paper portraying the agony of mind of a subfreshman who, forgetting what he was drawing, took his partly completed work from the rack and wandered up and down in front of a row of plaster casts, exclaiming: "Good gracious, is it Juno, or King Henry of Navarre?"

I contributed a number of verses and jokes to this college paper

and to a class annual that we got up. I have some of them still in
my head, and will set down the sad story of "an imaginative poet"
who

> Came to C.C.N.Y.
> Dreaming of nature's beauty
>   And the glories of the sky.
> He learned that stars are hydrogen,
>   The comets made of gas;
> That Jupiter and Venus
>   In elliptic orbits pass.
> He learned that the painted rainbow,
>   God's promise, as poets feign,
> Is transverse oscillations
>   Turning somersaults in rain.

And so on to the sorrowful climax:

> His poetry now is ruined,
>   His metaphors, of course;
> He's trying to square the circle
>   And to find the five-toed horse.

I will relate one other incident of these early days, in which
you may see how the child is father to the man. The crowding in
our ramshackle old school building had become a scandal, and
an effort was under way to persuade the legislature to vote funds
for new buildings uptown. No easy matter to persuade politicians to take an interest in anything so remote as higher education! We students were asked to circulate petitions, to be signed
by voters; and I, in an access of loyalty to my alma mater, gave
my afternoons and Saturdays to the task for a month or two, and
went the rounds of department stores and business houses. Not
many of the persons invited to sign had ever heard of the matter, but it cost them nothing, and they were willing to take the
word of a nice jolly lad that a free college was a good thing. I
brought in some six or eight hundred signatures, and got my
name in the college paper for my zeal. You see here the future
socialist, distributing leaflets and making soapbox speeches—to
the same ill-informed and indifferent crowd.

VIII

Simon Stern and I went into partnership and wrote a novel of many adventures about which I don't remember a thing. Together we visited the office of Street and Smith, publishers of "thrillers" for boys, and met one of the editors, who was amused to hear two boys in short trousers announce themselves as joint authors of a novel. He read it, and did not accept it, but held out hopes and suggested that we write another novel, according to his needs. We agreed to do so and went away, and to the consternation of the editor came back in a week with the novel complete. I have since learned that you must never do that. Make the editor think you are taking a lot of time because that is one of his tests of excellence—despite the examples of Dumas and Balzac and Dickens and Dostoevski and other masters.

I am not sure what became of that story. All I remember is that during the ensuing summer I was working at a full-length novel of adventure, which I am ashamed to realize bore a striking resemblance to *Treasure Island*. The difference was that it happened on land, having to do with an effort to find buried gold hidden by some returning forty-niners before they were killed by Indians. *The Prairie Pirates* was the title, and I don't know if the manuscript survives; but I recall having read it at some later date and being impressed by my idea of "sex appeal" at the age of seventeen. The hero had accompanied the beautiful heroine all the way from California and rescued her many times from Indian marauders and treacherous half-breeds. At the end he told her blushingly that he loved her, and then, having obtained permission, "he placed upon her forehead a holy kiss."

I was working on that novel in some country boardinghouse in New Jersey, and I mounted my bicycle with a bundle of manuscript strapped upon it, and rode to New York and up the Hudson into the Adirondack mountains, to a farmhouse on Brant Lake. At this retreat I enjoyed the companionship of a girl who was later to be my wife; her mother and my mother had become intimate friends, and we summered together several times for that reason. She was a year and a half younger than I, and we gazed at each other across a chasm of misunderstanding. She was a quiet, undeveloped, and unhappy girl, while I was a self-confident and aggressive youth, completely wrapped up in my own affairs. To neither of us did fate give the slightest hint of the trick it meant to play upon us four years later.

That fall I was invited to visit my clergyman friend, William Moir, in his brother's camp at Saranac Lake. I got on my bicycle at four o'clock one morning and set out upon a mighty feat—something that was the goal in life of all cycling enthusiasts in those far off eighteen-nineties. "Have you done a century?" we would ask one another, and it was like flying across the Atlantic later on. All day I pedaled, through sand and dust and heat. I remember ten miles or so up the Schroon River—no doubt it is a paved boulevard now, but in 1896 it was a ribbon of deep sand, and I had to plod for two or three hours. I remember coming down through a pass into Keene Valley—on a "corduroy road" made of logs, over which I bumped madly. In those days you used your foot on the front tire for a brake, and the sole of my shoe became so hot that I had to dip it into the mountain stream. I remember the climb out of Keene Valley, eight miles or so, pushing the wheel uphill; there was Cascade Lake at sunset, a beautiful spot, and I heard Tennyson's bugles blowing—

> The long light shakes across the lakes
> And the wild cataract leaps in glory.

I came into the home of my friend at half past ten at night, and was disappointed of my hopes because the total had been only ninety-six miles. I had not yet "done a century." I took the same ride back a couple of weeks later, and was so bent upon achievement that it was all my mother could do to dissuade me from taking an extra night ride from the farmhouse to the village and back so as to complete the hundred miles. From this you may see that I was soundly built at that age and looking for something to cut my teeth upon. If it should ever happen that a "researcher" wants something to practice on, he may consult the files of the New York *Evening Post* for the autumn of 1896 and find a column article describing the ride. I am not sure it was signed, but I remember that Mr. Moir, job-maker extraordinary, had given me a letter to the city editor of the *Evening Post*, and I had become a reporter for a week. I gave it up because the staff was too crowded, and all there was for this bright kid just out of knicker-bockers was a few obituary notices, an inch or two each.

It was the *Post* I read in the afternoon, and the *Sun* in the morning, and in my social ideas I was the haughtiest little snob that ever looked down upon mankind from the lofty tur-rets of an imitation-Gothic college. I can recollect as if it were yesterday my poor father—he was showing some signs of evolv-ing into a radical, having been reading editorials by Brisbane in the *Evening Journal,* a sort of steam calliope with which Willie Hearst had just broken loose on Park Row. Oh, the lofty scorn with which I spurned my father! I would literally put my fingers into my ears in order that my soul might not be sullied by the offensive sounds of the Hearst calliope. I do not think my father ever succeeded in making me hear a word of Brisbane's assaults upon the great and noble-minded McKinley, then engaged in having the presidency purchased for him by Mark Hanna.

IX

My poor father was no longer in position to qualify as an edu-cator of youth. Every year he was gripped more tightly in the claws of his demon. He would disappear for days, and it would be my task to go and seek him in the barrooms that he frequented. I would find him, and there would be a moral battle. I would argue and plead and threaten; he would weep, or try to assert his authority—though I cannot recall that he ever even pre-tended to be angry with me. I would lead him up the street, and every corner saloon would be a new contest. "I must have just one more drink, son. I can't go home without one more. If you only knew what I am suffering!" I would get him to bed and hide his trousers so that he could not escape, and mother would make cups of strong black coffee, or perhaps a drink of warm water and mustard.

Later on, things grew worse yet. My father was no longer to be found in his old haunts; he was ashamed to have his friends see him and would wander away. Then I had to seek him in the dives on the Bowery—the Highway of Lost Men, as I called it in *Love's Pilgrimage.* I would walk for hours, peering into scores of places, and at last I would find him, sunk into a chair or sleeping with his arms on a beer-soaked table. Once I found him literally in the gutter—no uncommon sight in those days.

I would get a cab and take him—no longer home, for we could not handle him; he would be delirious, and there would be need of strong-armed attendants and leather straps and iron bars. I would take him to St. Vincent's Hospital, and there, with crucified saviors looking down on us, I would pay twenty-five dollars to a silent, black-clad nun, and my father would be entered in the books and led away, quaking with terror, by a young Irish husky in white ducks. A week or two later he would emerge, weak and unsteady, pasty of complexion but full of moral fervor. He would join the church, sign pledges, vote for Sunday closing, weep on my shoulder and tell me how he loved me. For a week or a month or possibly several months he would struggle to build up his lost business and pay his debts.

X

My liberal friends who read *The Wet Parade* found it sentimental and out of the spirit of the time. To them I made answer that the experiences of my childhood were "reality," quite as much so as the blood and guts of the Chicago stockyards or the birth scene in *Love's Pilgrimage*. It is a fact that I have been all my life gathering material on the subject of the liquor problem. I know it with greater intimacy than any other theme I have ever handled. The list of drunkards I have wrestled with is longer than the list of coal miners, oil magnates, politicians, or any other group I have known and portrayed in my books.

My experiences with my father lasted thirty years; during this period several uncles and cousins, and numerous friends of the family, Southern gentlemen, Northern businessmen, and even one or two of their wives were stumbling down the same road of misery. Later on, I ran into the same problem in the literary and socialist worlds: George Sterling, Jack London, Ambrose Bierce, W. M. Reedy, O. Henry, Eugene Debs—a long list. I have a photograph of Jack and George and the latter's wife, Carrie, taken on Jack's sailboat on San Francisco Bay; three beautiful people, young, happy, brilliant—and all three took poison to escape the claws of John Barleycorn. And then came a new generation,

many of whom I knew well: Sinclair Lewis, Edna Millay, Eugene
O'Neill, Dylan Thomas, Scott Fitzgerald, Ernest Hemingway,
Theodore Dreiser, William Faulkner.

The experience with my father of course made me prematurely
serious. I began questioning the world, trying to make out how
such evils came to be. I soon traced the saloon to Tammany and
blamed my troubles on the high chieftains of this organization. I
remember writing of Richard Croker that "I would be willing
with my own hands to spear him on a pitchfork and thrust him
into the fires of hell." A sound evangelical sentiment! I had not
yet found out "big business"—and of course I would not, until I
had outgrown E. L. Godkin of the *Evening Post* and Charles A.
Dana of the *Sun*.

It was my idea at this time that the human race was to be saved
by poetry. Men and women were going to be taught noble
thoughts, and then they would abandon their base ways of living. I had made the acquaintance of Shelley and conceived a pas-
sionate friendship for him. Then I became intimate with Hamlet,
Prince of Denmark; he came to the library of my Uncle Bland,
in Baltimore, where I spent the Christmas holidays, and we had
much precious converse. I too was a prince, in conflict with a
sordid and malignant world; at least, so I saw myself, and lived
entirely in that fantasy, very snobbish, scornful, and superior.
Any psychiatrist would have diagnosed me as an advanced case
of delusion of grandeur, messianic complex, paranoia, narcissism,
and so to the end of his list.

XI

Along with extreme idealism, and perhaps complementary to
it, went a tormenting struggle with sexual desire. I never had
relations with any woman until my marriage at the age of twenty-
two; but I came close to it, and the effort to refrain was more
than I would have been equal to without the help of my clergyman friend. For a period of five years or more I was subject
to storms of craving; I would become restless and miserable and
wandering out on the street, look at every woman and girl I
passed and dream an adventure that might be a little less than
sordid. Many of the daughters of the poor, and more than once a

daughter of the rich, indicated a "coming-on disposition"; there would begin a flirtation, with caresses and approaches to intimacy. But then would come another storm—of shame and fear; the memory of the pledge I had given; the dream of a noble and beautiful love, which I cherished; also, of course, the idea of venereal disease, of which my friend Moir kept me informed. I would shrink back and turn cold; two or three times, with my reformer's impulse, I told the girl about it, and the petting party turned into a moral discourse. I have pictured such a scene in *Love's Pilgrimage,* and it affords amusement to my "emancipated" radical friends.

What do I think about these experiences after sixty-five years of reflection? The first fact—an interesting one—is that I am still embarrassed to talk about them. My ego craves to be dignified and impressive and is humiliated to see itself behaving like a young puppy. I have to take the grown-up puppy by the back of the neck and make him face the facts—there being so many young ones in the world who have the same troubles. Frankness about sex must not be left to the cynical and morally irresponsible.

There are dangers in puritanism, and there are compensations. My chastity was preserved at the cost of much emotional effort, plus the limitation of my interests in certain fields. For example, I could not prosecute the study of art. In the splendid library of Columbia University were treasures of beauty, costly volumes of engravings; and in my usual greedy fashion I went at these, intending to learn all there was to know about Renaissance art in a week or two. But I found myself overwhelmed by this mass of nakedness; my senses reeled, and I had to quit. I might have gone back when I was mature; but alas, I was by then too busy trying to save the world from poverty and war. This confession resembles Darwin's—that his concentration upon the details of natural science had the effect of atrophying his interest in music and other arts.

What did I get in return for this? I got intensity and power of concentration; these elements in my make-up were the product of my efforts to resist the tempter. I learned to work fourteen hours a day at study and creative effort because it was only by being thus occupied that the craving for woman could be kept out of my soul. I told myself the legend of Hercules and recited the wisdom attributed to Solomon: "He that ruleth his spirit is greater than he that taketh a city."

For years now we have heard a great deal about mental troubles caused by sex repression; we have heard little about the complexes that may be caused by sex indulgence. But my observation has been that those who permit themselves to follow every sexual impulse are quite as miserable as those who repress them. I remember saying to a classmate in college, "Did it ever occur to you to stop and look at your own mind? Everything that comes to you is turned into sex." He looked surprised, and I saw that it was a new idea to him; he thought it over and said, "I guess you are right."

This problem of the happy mean in sex matters would require a volume for a proper discussion. As it happens, I have written such a volume, *The Book of Life,* and it is available to those who are interested. So I pass on.

XII

I was becoming less and less satisfied with college. It had become an agony for me to sit and listen to the slow recitation of matters that I either knew already or did not care to know. I was enraged by professors whose idea of teaching was to catch me being inattentive to their dullness. At the same time, I had to have my degree because I was still planning to study law. I fretted and finally evolved a scheme; I made application to the faculty for two months' leave of absence, on the ground that I had to earn some money—which was true. They gave me the leave, and I earned the money writing stories, and spent the rest of my time in a hall bedroom reading Shelley, Carlyle, and Emerson. I forced myself to read until one or two in the morning, and many a time I would wake at daybreak and find that I had sunk back on my pillow and slept with my book still open and the gaslight burning—not a very hygienic procedure.

It was the lodginghouse on West 23rd Street, kept by a Mrs. Carmichael, whose son also was a would-be genius—only he was a religious mystic and found his thrills in church music. We used to compare notes, each patronizing the other, of course—two

young stags in the forest, trying out their horns. I remember that
Bert went up to display his musical skill to a great composer,
Edward MacDowell, of whom I thus heard for the first time. The
youth came back in excitement to report that the composer had
praised him highly and offered him free instruction. But after the
first lesson, Bert was less elated, for his idol had spoken as follows: "Mr. Carmichael, before you come again, please have your
hair cut and wash your neck. The day of long-haired and greasy
musicians is past."

I went back to college, made up my missing studies in a week
or two, and was graduated without distinction, exactly in the
middle of my class. I remember the name of the man who carried off all the honors, and I look for that name in *Who's Who*,
but do not find it. I won some sort of prize in differential calcu-
lus, but that was all; nothing in literature, nothing in oratory,
philosophy, history. Such talents as I had were not valued by my
alma mater, nor would they have been by any other alma mater
then existing in America so far as I could learn. I was so little interested in the college regime that I did not wait for commence-
ment, but went off to the country and received my diploma by
mail.

I had sold some jokes and stories, and I now spent a summer
writing more, while drifting about in a skiff among the Thousand Islands in the upper St. Lawrence River. I caught many
black bass and ate them; read the poems of Walter Scott and the
novels of Thackeray and George Eliot, made available in the
Seaside Library, which I purchased wholesale for eight cents a
copy. The life I got from those classics is one reason why I believe in cheap books and have spent tens of thousands of dollars
trying to keep my own books available to students.

XIII

I still meant to be a lawyer, but first I wanted a year of literature and philosophy at Columbia University. "If you do that,
you'll never be a lawyer," said some shrewd person to me—and
he was right. But to Columbia I would go, and how was I to live
meantime? I went back to New York to solve this problem and
called upon the Street and Smith editor who had once suggested

a serial story to Simon Stern and myself. Now I reaped the reward of persistence, obtaining a meal ticket for the next three years of my life.

The name of this editor was Henry Harrison Lewis, and he later became editor of one of the fighting organs of the open-shop movement. I remember expounding to him my views of life and my destiny therein, and how he protested that it was not normal for a youth to be so apocalyptic and messianic. My evil career was assuredly not Mr. Lewis' fault.

He showed me proofs of the *Army and Navy Weekly*, a five-cent publication with bright red and blue and green and yellow covers, which the firm was just starting. The editor himself was to write every other week a story of life at the Annapolis Naval Academy and wanted someone to write in alternate weeks, a companion story of life at the West Point Military Academy. Would I like to try that job? My heart leaped with excitement.

My first experience in the gathering of local color! I got from Mr. Moir a letter of introduction to an army officer at West Point, and went up and stayed at a cheap hotel in the village. I roamed about the grounds and watched the cadets, and made copious notes as to every detail of their regimen. I recollect being introduced to a stern and noble-looking upperclassman. I revealed to him what I was there for, and said that I needed a hero. "Well, why not use me?" inquired this cadet. "I am president of the senior class, I am captain of the football team, and I have made the highest records in this and that," and so on. I looked into the man's face for any trace of a smile, but there was none. He stays in my memory as a type of the military mind. Doubtless he is a great general by now.

I went back to New York, and under the pen name of Lieutenant Frederick Garrison, USA, produced a manuscript of some twenty-five or thirty thousand words, a rollicking tale of a group of "candidates" who made their appearance at the academy to start their military career. The Mark Mallory stories they were called, and they were successful, so I was definitely launched upon a literary career. I was paid, I believe, forty dollars per story; it was a fortune, enough to take care of both my mother and myself. The local color was found satisfactory. Lewis told me that Smith, head of the firm, asked if that new writer had been through West Point. "Yes," replied Lewis, "he went through in three days."

XIV

This episode of my hack writing I find always interests people, so I may as well finish it here, even though it involves running ahead of my story. After I had been doing the work for a while, the firm needed Mr. Lewis' services for more editing, and he asked me if I could do his stint as well as my own. I always thought I could do everything, so I paid a visit to Annapolis, haunted by the ghosts of my grandfathers. I went through this place also in three days. Thereafter I was Ensign Clarke Fitch, USN, as well as Lieutenant Frederick Garrison, USA. I now wrote a novelette of close to thirty thousand words every week, and received forty dollars a week.

Shortly after that, Willie Hearst with his New York *Evening Journal* succeeded in carrying the United States into a war with Spain. ("You make the pictures, and I'll make the war," cabled Willie to Frederick Remington in Cuba.) So my editor sent for me and explained that the newsboys and messenger boys who followed the adventures of Mark Mallory and Clif Faraday would take it ill if these cadets idled away their time in West Point and Annapolis while their country was bleeding; I must hurry up and graduate them, and send them to the battlefield.

No sooner said than done. I read a book of Cuban local color and looked up several expletives for Spanish villains to exclaim. I remember one of them, "Carramba!" I have never learned what it means, but hope it is not too serious, for I taught it to all the newsboys and messenger boys of the eastern United States. When I hear people lamenting the foolishness of the movies, I remember the stuff I ground out every week, which was printed in large editions.

From that time on my occupation was killing Spaniards. "What are you going to do today?" my mother would ask, and the answer would be, "I have to kill Spaniards." I thought nothing of sinking a whole fleet of Spanish torpedo boats to make a denouement, and the vessels I sank during that small war would

have replaced all the navies of the world. I remember that I had
my hero explode a bomb on a Spanish vessel and go to the bottom with her; in the next story I blandly explained how he had
opened a porthole and swum up again. Once or twice I killed a
Spanish villain, and then forgot and brought him to life again.
When that occurred, I behaved like President Coolidge and Governor Fuller and President Lowell, and the other great ones of
Massachusetts—I treated my critics with silent contempt.

I was never told how my product was selling; that was the
affair of my masters. But they must have been satisfied, for presently came another proposition. There was a boom in war literature, and they were going to start another publication—I think
the title was the *Columbia Library*—to be issued monthly and
contain fifty-six thousand words. Could I add this to my other
tasks? I was a young shark, ready to devour everything in sight.
So for some months I performed the feat of turning out eight
thousand words every day, Sunday included. I tell this to literary
men, and they say it could not be done; but I actually did it, at
least until the end of the Spanish-American War. I kept two ste-
nographers working all the time, taking dictation one day and
transcribing the next. In the afternoon I would dictate for about
three hours, as fast as I could talk; in the evening I would revise
the copy that had been brought in from the previous day, and
then take a long walk and think up the incidents of my next day's
stunt. That left me mornings to attend lectures at Columbia University and to practice the violin. I figured out that by the time I
finished this potboiling I had published an output equal in volume to the works of Walter Scott.

What was the effect of all this upon me as a writer? It both
helped and hurt. It taught me to shape a story and to hold in
mind what I had thought up; so it fostered facility. On the other
hand, it taught me to use exaggerated phrases and clichés, and
this is something I have fought against, not always successfully.
Strange as it may seem, I actually enjoyed the work while I was
doing it. Not merely was I earning a living and putting away a
little money; I had a sense of fun, and these adventures were a
romp. It is significant that the stories pleased their public only
so long as they pleased their author. When, at the age of twenty-

one, I became obsessed with the desire to write a serious novel,
I came to loathe this hackwork, and from that time on I was
never able to do it with success, even though, driven by desperate need, I several times made the effort. It was the end of my
youth.

3

Genius

WAS it really genius? That I cannot say. I only know it seemed
like it, and I took it at its face value. I tell the story here as objectively as possible, and if the hero seems a young egotist, do not
blame me, because that youth is long since dead.

The thing I believed was genius came to me first during one of
those Christmas holidays I spent in Baltimore, at the home of
my Uncle Bland. I had always enjoyed these holidays, having a
normal boy's fondness for turkey and plum pudding and other
Christmas delights. I used to say that anybody might wake me at
three o'clock in the morning to eat ice cream; my Aunt Lelia Montague, mother of the general's wife, declared that the way to my
heart was through a bag of gingersnaps.

But on this particular Christmas my uncle's home meant to
me a shelf of books. I read Shakespeare straight through during
that holiday and, though it sounds preposterous, I read all
of Milton's poetry in those same two weeks. Literature had become a frenzy. I read while I was eating, lying down, sitting,
standing, and walking; I read everywhere I went—and I went
nowhere except to the park to read on sunshiny days. I averaged
fourteen hours a day, and it was a routine matter to read all of
Shakespeare's comedies in two or three days, and all his tragedies in the next two or three, and the historical plays over the
weekend. In my uncle's library reposed beautiful volumes, untouched except by the hand of the parlormaid; now I drew them

forth, with love and rapture, and gave them a reason for being. Some poet said to a rich man, "You own the land and I own the landscape." To my kind uncle I said, "You own the books and I own the literature."

My mind on fire with high poetry, I went out for a walk one night. A winter night, with hard crunching snow on the ground and great bright lights in the sky; the tree branches black and naked, crackling now and then in the breeze, but between times silence, quite magical silence—and I walking in Druid Hill Park, mile on mile, lost to the world, drinking in beauty, marveling at the mystery of life. Suddenly this thing came to me, startling and wonderful beyond any power of words to tell; the opening of gates in the soul, the pouring in of music, of light, of joy that was unlike anything else and therefore not to be conveyed in metaphors. I stood riveted to one spot, and a trembling seized me, a dizziness, a happiness so intense that the distinction between pleasure and pain was lost.

If I had been a religious person at this time, no doubt I would have had visions of saints and holy martyrs, and perhaps developed stigmata on hands and feet. But I had no sort of superstition, so the vision took a literary form. There was a campfire by a mountain road, to which came travelers who hailed one another and made high revelry there without alcohol. Yes, even Falstaff and Prince Hal were purified and refined, according to my teetotal sentiments! There came the melancholy Prince of Denmark, and Don Quixote—I must have been reading him at this time. Also Shelley—real persons mixed with imaginary ones, but all equal in this realm of fantasy. They held conversation, each in his own character, yet glorified, more so than in the books. I was laughing, singing with the delight of their company; in short, a perfect picture of a madman, talking to myself, making incoherent exclamations. Yet I knew what I was doing, I knew what was happening, I knew that this was literature, and that if I could remember the tenth part of it and set it down on paper, it would be read.

The strangest part about this ecstasy is the multifarious forms it assumes, the manifold states of consciousness it involves, all at one time. It is possible to be bowed with grief and transported with delight; it is possible to love and to hate, to be naïve and calculating, to be hot and cold, timid and daring—all contradictions reconciled. But the most striking thing is the conviction that you are in the hands of a force outside yourself. Without trace of a preconception, and regarding the thing as objectively as you know how, the feeling is that something is taking hold of you, pushing you along, sweeping you away. To walk in a windstorm and feel it beating upon you is a sensation of the body no more definite and unmistakable than this windstorm of the spirit, which has come to me perhaps a hundred times in my life. I search for a metaphor and picture a child running, with an older and swifter person by his side taking his hand and lifting him off the ground, so that his little leaps become great leaps, almost like flying.

You may call this force your own subconscious mind, or God, or cosmic consciousness—I care not what fancy name you give; the point is that it is there, and always there. If you ask whether it is intelligent, I can only say that you appear to be the intelligence, and "it" appears to be the cause of intelligence in you. How anything unintelligent can be the cause of intelligence is a riddle I pass by. Life is built upon such antinomies.

II

This experience occurred in unexpected places and at unpredictable times. It was associated with music and poetry, but still more frequently with natural beauty. I remember winter nights in Central Park, New York, and tree branches white with snow, magical in the moonlight; I remember springtime mornings in several places; a summer night in the Adirondacks, with moonlight strewn upon a lake; a summer twilight in the far wilds of Ontario, when I came over a ridge and into a valley full of clover, incredibly sweet of scent—one has to go into the North in summer to appreciate how deep and thick a field of red clover can grow and what overpowering perfume it throws upon the air at twilight.

This experience, repeated, made me more of a solitary than ever. I wanted to be free to behave like a lunatic, and yet not have anybody think me one. I remember a highly embarrassing moment when I was walking down a lane bordered with wild roses in June, and two little girls seated on a fence, unnoticed by me, suddenly broke into giggles at the strange sight of a man laughing and talking to himself. I became a haunter of mountain-tops and of deep forests, the only safe places. I had something that other people did not have and could not understand—other-wise, how could they behave as they were doing? Imagine any-one wanting a lot of money, or houses and servants, or fine rai-ment and jewels, if he knew how to be happy as I did! Imagine anyone becoming drunk on whisky when he might become drunk on poetry and music, sunsets, and valleys full of clover!

For a time it seemed to me that music was the only medium in which my emotions could be expressed. I longed to play some instrument, and began very humbly with a mandolin. But that was not enough, and presently I took the plunge and paid sev-enty-five of my hard-earned dollars for a violin. In my class at college had been Martin Birnbaum, a Bohemian lad, pupil of a really great teacher, Leopold Lichtenberg. Martin played the violin with an ease and grace that were then, and have remained ever since, my life's great envy. Each of us wants to do what he cannot.

With all my potboiling and my work at Columbia University, I could find only limited time for practice in the winter. But in the summer I was free—except for three or four days in each fortnight, when I wrote my stories and earned my living. I took myself away to a summer hotel, near Keeseville, New York, on the east edge of the Adirondacks, and I must have seemed one of the oddest freaks ever seen outside of an asylum. Every morning I got up at five o'clock and went out upon a hillside to see the sunrise; then I came back for breakfast, and immediately there-after got my violin and a book of music and a stand and went out into the forest and set up my stand and fiddled until noon-time; I came back to dinner, and then sallied out again and prac-ticed another four hours; then I came in and had supper, and went out on the hillside to sit and watch the sunset; finally I went upstairs and shut myself in a little room and practiced the violin by the light of an oil lamp; or, if it was too hot in the room, I went down to the lake to watch the moon rise behind the mountains.

The wild things of the forest got used to this odd invasion. The squirrels would sit on the pine-tree branches and cock their heads and chatter furiously when I made a false note. The partridges would feed on huckleberries all about me, apparently understanding clearly the difference between a fiddlebow and a gun. Foxes took an interest, and raccoons and porcupines—and even humans.

The guests from the cities arrived on an early morning train and were driven to the hotel in a big four-horse stage. One morning, one of these guests arrived, and at breakfast narrated a curious experience. The stage had been toiling up a long hill, the horses walking, and alongside was an old Italian woman with a couple of pails, on her way to a day of berry picking. She was whistling cheerily, and the tune was the *Tannhäuser* march. The new arrival, impressed by this evidence of culture in the vicinity, inquired through the open window, "Where did you learn that music?" The reply was, "Dey ees a crazy feller in de woods, he play it all day long for t'ree weeks!"

III

I have got ahead of my story and must go back to the fall of 1897, when I registered at Columbia University as a special student. This meant that I was free to take any courses I preferred. As at the City College, I speedily found that some of the teachers were tiresome, and that the rules allowed me to drop their courses and begin others without extra charge. Upon my declaring my intention to take a master's degree, all the tuition fees I paid were lumped together until they totaled a hundred and fifty dollars, after which I had to pay no more. Until I had completed one major and two minors, I was at liberty to go on taking courses and dropping them with no extra expense.

The completing of a course consisted of taking an examination, and as that was the last thing in the world I ever wanted to do, I never did it; instead, I would flee to the country, and come back the next fall and start a new set of courses. Then I would get the professors' points of view and the list of books to be read —and that was all there was to the course. Four years in succession I did this, and figured that I had sampled more than forty courses; but no one ever objected to my singular procedure. The great university was run on the assumption that the countless thousands of young men and women came there to get degrees. That anyone might come merely to get knowledge had apparently not occurred to the governing authorities.

In the first year I remember Professor George Rice Carpenter setting out to teach me to write English. It was the customary process of writing "themes" upon trivial subjects; and the dominating fact in my life has been that I have to be emotionally interested before I can write at all. When I went to the professor to tell him that I didn't think I was getting anything out of the course, his feelings were hurt, and he said, "I can assure you that you don't know anything about writing English." I answered that this was no doubt true, but the question was, could I learn by his method. Four or five years later, as a reader for Macmillan, Professor Carpenter got hold of some of my manuscripts; I paid several visits to his home, and he was so gracious as to ask how I thought the writing of English might be taught in colleges. My formula was simple—find something the student is interested in. But Carpenter said that was no solution—it would limit the themes to football and fraternities.

Professor W. P. Trent, a famous scholar, undertook to teach me about poetry, and this effort ended in an odd way. Something came up in the class about grammatical errors in literature, and the professor referred to Byron's famous line, "There let him lay." Said the professor: "I have the impression that there is a similar error in Shelley, and some day I am going to run through his poetry and find it." To my fastidious young soul that seemed *lèse-majesté;* I pictured a man reading Shelley in such a mood, and I dropped the course.

IV

Since we are dealing with the phenomena of genius, I will tell about the one authentic man of genius I met at Columbia. Edward MacDowell was the head of the department of music, and he was struggling valiantly to create a vital music center in America; he was against heavy odds of philistinism, embodied in the banker trustees of the great university. MacDowell gave two courses in general musical culture. These I took in successive years, and they were not among the courses I dropped. The composer was a man of wide culture and full of a salty humor, a delightful teacher. There were fewer than a dozen students taking the course—such was the amount of interest in genius at Columbia.

Early in the course I noted that MacDowell suffered in his efforts to say in words something that could only be said in music, and I suggested to him that instead of trying to describe musical ideas, he should play them for us. This suggestion he at once accepted, and thereafter the course consisted in a piano rendition of the great music of the world, with incidental running comments. MacDowell was a first-rate concert pianist, and truly noble were the sounds that rumbled from that large piano in the small classroom.

Since I was going in for the genius business myself, I was interested in every smallest detail of this great man's behavior and appearance. Here was one who shared my secret of ecstasy; and this set him apart from all the other teachers, the dull plodding ones who dealt with the bones and dust of inspirations. Almost thirty years afterward I wrote about him in an article published in the *American Mercury* (January 1928), and so vivid were my recollections I was able to quote what I felt certain were the exact words of MacDowell's comments on this and that item of music and literature. Shortly afterward I met the composer's widow, who told me that she recognized many of the phrases, and that all of them sounded authentic to her.

Here was a man who had the true fire and glory, yet at the same time was perfectly controlled; it was only now and then, when some bit of philistinism roused his anger, that I saw the sparks fly. He found it possible to display a gracious courtesy; in fact, he might have been that little boy in my nursery poem, "who would not even sneeze unless he asked you if he might." I remember that he apologized to the young ladies of the class for telling a story that involved the mention of a monkey; this surprised me, for I thought my very proper mother had warned me against all possible social improprieties. Some of his pupils had sent the composer flowers on his birthday and put in a card with the inscription from *Das Rheingold:* "*O, singe fort, so suess und fein*"; a very charming thing to say to a musician. Mac-

Dowell's story was that on opening the box he had started to read the inscription as French instead of as German, and had found himself hailed: "O, powerful monkey!"

V

Shortly after I left Columbia, MacDowell left on account of disagreements with Nicholas Murray Butler, the newly elected president of the great university. I had taken a course in Kantian philosophy with Butler and had come to know him well; an aggressive and capable mind, a cold and self-centered heart. In his class I had expressed my surprise that Kant, after demonstrating the impossibility of metaphysical knowledge, should have turned around and swallowed the system of Prussian church orthodoxy at one gulp. I asked the professor whether this might be accounted for by the fact that the founder of modern critical philosophy had had a job at a Prussian state university. I do not remember Butler's reply to this, but you may be sure I thought of it when Butler declared himself a member of the Episcopal Church—this being a required preliminary to becoming president of Columbia. I am prepared to testify before the Throne of Grace—if the fact has not already been noted by the recording angel—that Butler in his course on Kant made perfectly plain that he believed no shred of Christian dogma.

I divided my Columbia courses into two kinds, those that were worth while and I completed, and those that were not worth while and I dropped. In the years that followed I made note of a singular phenomenon—all of the teachers of the second group of courses prospered at Columbia, while all teachers of the first group were forced out, or resigned in disgust. It seemed as if I had been used as a litmus paper, and everybody who had committed the offense of interesting me was *ipso facto* condemned. This fate befell MacDowell and George Edward Woodberry, who gave me two never-to-be-forgotten courses in comparative literature; and Harry Thurston Peck, who gave a vivid course on Roman civilization—poor devil, I shall have a story to tell about him; and James Harvey Robinson—I took a course with him on the culture of the Renaissance and Reformation that was a revelation of what history teaching might be. Also poor James Hyslop, kindly but eccentric, who taught me applied ethics; later on he took to spooks and learned that no form of eccentricity would be tolerated at the "University of Morgan."

On the other hand, Butler himself throve, and Brander Matthews throve—he had made me acquainted with a new type, the academic "man of the world" I did not want to be. W. P. Trent throve—perhaps to find that grammatical error in Shelley's poetry. George Rice Carpenter throve while he lived, and so did the professors of German and Italian and the instructor of French. I have forgotten their names, but I later met the French gentleman, and he remembered me, and we had a laugh over our failure to get together. The reason was plain enough—I wanted to learn to read French in six weeks, while the Columbia machine was geared to lower speeds.

VI

My experience with the college teaching of foreign languages became the subject of two magazine articles in the *Independent*, which attracted some attention. Professor William Lyon Phelps once recalled them in his department in *Scribner's Magazine*, acknowledging this as one service I had performed for him. I can perhaps repeat the service here for a new generation.

For five years at the City College I had patiently studied Latin, Greek, and German the way my teachers taught me. I looked up the words in the dictionary and made a translation of some passage. The next day I made a translation of another passage, looking up the words for that; and if some of the words were the same ones I had looked up the day before, that made no difference, I looked them up again—and never in the entire five years did anyone point out to me that by learning the meaning of the word once and for all, I might save the trouble of looking it up hundreds of times in the course of my college career.

Of course it did happen that, involuntarily, my mind retained the meanings of many words. At the end of five years I could read very simple Latin prose at sight; but I could not read the simplest Greek or German prose without a dictionary, and it was the literal truth that I had spent thousands of hours looking up words in the dictionary. Thousands of words were as familiar to

sight and sound as English words—and yet I did not know what
they meant!

At Columbia I really wanted to read German, for the sake of
the literature it opened up; so I hit upon the revolutionary idea
of learning the meaning of a word the first time I looked it up.
Instead of writing it into a translation, I wrote it into a notebook; and each day I made it my task to fix that day's list of
words in my mind. I carried my notebook about with me and
studied it while I was eating, while I was dressing and shaving,
while I was on my way to college. I took long walks, during
which I reviewed my lists, making sure I knew the meanings of
all the words I had looked up in the course of recent readings. By
this means I eliminated the drudgery of dictionary hunting, and
in two or three weeks was beginning to read German with pleasure.

In my usual one-track fashion, I concentrated on German literature and for a year or so read nothing else. I went through
Goethe as I had once gone through Shakespeare, in a glow of delight. I read everything of Schiller and Heine, Lessing and
Herder, Wagner's operas and prose writings. I read the Golden
Treasury collection of German poetry so many times that I knew
it nearly by heart—as I do the English one to this day. I read the
novelists down to Freitag and even tried my teeth on Kant, reading the *Critique of Pure Reason* more than once in the original.

VII

Next I wanted French and Italian. I am not sure which I
took first, but I remember a little round Italian professor and a
grammar called *Grandgent's*, and I remember reading Gerolamo
Rovetta's novel, *Mater Dolorosa*, and getting the author's permission to translate it into English, but I could not interest a publisher in the project. I read *I Promessi Sposi*, a long novel, and
also, oddly enough, an Italian translation of Sienkiewicz's *Quo
Vadis*. But a few years later I ruined my Italian by studying Es-
peranto; the two are so much alike that thereafter I never knew
which one I was trying to speak, and when I stepped off a
steamer in Naples, in the year 1912, and tried to communicate

my wants to the natives, they gazed at me as if I were the man from Mars.

With French I began an elementary course, along with a class of Columbia freshmen or sophomores, and stayed with it just long enough to get the pronunciation and the elements of grammar; after which I went my own way, with a text of the novel *L'Abbé Constantin* and a little notebook to be filled with all the words in that pretty, sentimental story. In six weeks I was reading French with reasonable fluency; and then, according to my custom, I moved to Paris in spirit. I read all the classics that are known to Americans by reputation; all of Corneille, Racine, and Molière; some of Rousseau and Voltaire; a sampling of Bossuet and Chateaubriand; the whole of Musset and Daudet, Hugo and Flaubert; about half of Balzac and Zola; and enough of Maupassant and Gautier to be thankful that I had not come upon this kind of literature until I was to some extent mature, with a good hard shell of puritanism to protect me against the black magic of the modern Babylon.

Since then, such depraved literature has been poured in a flood over America, and our bright young intellectuals are thoroughly initiated; they have no shells of puritanism, but try fancy liquors and drugs, and play with the esoteric forms of heterosexuality and homosexuality, and commit suicide in the most elegant continental style. Those who prefer to remain alive are set down as old fogies. I must be one of the oldest.

VIII

My Uncle Bland was in the habit of coming to New York every now and then, and I always went to the old Holland House or the Waldorf-Astoria to have lunch or dinner with him and my aunt. One of these visits is fixed in my mind, because I was proud of my achievement in learning to read French in six weeks and told my uncle about it. It was then that he made me a business offer; he was going soon to have a Paris branch of his company, and if I would come to Baltimore and learn the business, he would put me in charge of his Paris branch, starting at six thousand a year. I thanked my good uncle, but I never considered the offer, for I felt sure of one thing, that I would never engage in any form of business. Little did I dream that fate had in store for me the job of buying book paper by the carload, and making and selling several million books; to say nothing of a magazine, and a socialist colony, and a moving picture by Eisenstein!

At this time, or a little later, my uncle was occupied in establishing the New York office of his bonding company; this played an important part in my education. To his favorite nephew the president of the great concern talked freely, and he gave me my first real knowledge of the relationship between government and big business in America. This Baltimore company, desiring to break into the lucrative New York field, proceeded as follows: one of the leaders of Tammany Hall, a man by the name of O'Sullivan, became manager of the New York office; Richard Croker, the "big chief," received a considerable block of stock, and other prominent Tammany men also received stock. My uncle explained that, as a result of this procedure, word would go forth that his company was to receive the bonding business of the city and all its employees.

It was the system that came to be known as "honest graft." You can see that it was no crime for a Tammany leader to become manager of a bonding company; and yet his profits would be many times as great as if he were to steal money from the city treasury. Some time afterward my uncle told me that he planned to open an office in Albany, and was going to get the business of the state machine also; he had just named the man who was to be elected state treasurer on the Democratic ticket—and when I asked him what this meant, he smiled over the luncheon table and said, "We businessmen have our little ways of getting what we want."

So there I was on the inside of America, watching our invisible government at work. The pattern that my uncle revealed to me in youth served for the arranging of all the facts I later amassed. I have never found anything different, in any part of America; it is thus that big business deals with government at every point where the two come into contact. Every government official in America knows it, likewise every big businessman knows it; talking in private, they joke about it; in public they deny it with great indignation.

The fact that the man from whom I learned this secret was one of the kindest and most generous persons I have ever known ought to have made me merciful in my judgments. With the wisdom of later years, I know that the businessmen who finance political parties and pull the strings of government cannot help what they do; they either have to run their business that way or give place to somebody who will run it no differently. The blame lies with the system, in which government for public service is competing day by day with business for private profit. But in those early days I did not understand any of this; I thought that graft was due to grafters, and I hated them with all my puritanical fervor.

Also, I thought that the tired businessman ought to be an idealist like myself, reading Shakespeare and Goethe all day. When my uncle, thinking to do me a kindness, would buy expensive theater tickets and take my mother and myself to a musical comedy, I would listen to the silly thumping and strumming and the vulgar jests of the comedians, and my heart would almost burst with rage. This was where the world's money was going—while I had to live in a hall bedroom and slave at potboilers to earn my bread!

It happened that at this time I was taking a course in "Practical Ethics" under Professor James Hyslop at Columbia. The second half of this course consisted of an elaborate system that the professor had worked out, a set of laws and constitutional changes that would enable the voters to outwit the politicians and the big businessmen. From the very first hour it was apparent to me that the good professor's elaborate system was a joke. Before any law or constitutional change could be made, it would have to be explained to the public, which included the politicians and their paymasters. These men were quite as shrewd as any college professor and would have their plans worked out to circumvent the new laws a long time before those laws came into operation.

IX

At this time the graft of Tammany Hall was only in process of becoming "honest"; the main sources of revenue of Richard

Croker and his henchmen were still the saloonkeeper and the "madam." There came forth a knight-at-arms to wage war upon this infamy, a lawyer by the name of William Travers Jerome. He made speeches, telling what he had seen and learned about prostitution in New York; and I went to some of these meetings and listened with horrified soul. No longer could I doubt that women did actually sell their bodies; I heard Jerome tell about the brass check that you purchased at the counter downstairs and paid to the victim of your lust. I heard about a roomful of naked women exhibited for sale.

Like many others in the audience, I took fire, and turned out to help elect Jerome. I went about among everybody I knew and raised a sum of money and took it to the candidate at the dinner hour at his club. He thanked me cordially and took the money; but my feelings were a trifle hurt because he did not stay to chat with me while his dinner got cold. Having since run for office myself, and had admirers swarm about to shake my hand, I can appreciate the desire of a public man to have his dinner hour free.

At this election I was one of a group of Columbia students who volunteered as watchers in the interests of the reform ticket. I was assigned to a polling place over on the East Side, a strong Tammany district; all day I watched to prevent the stuffing of the ballot box, and after the closing hour I saw to an honest count of the votes that had been cast. I had against me a whole set of Tammany officials, one or two Tammany policemen, and several volunteers who joined in as the quarrel grew hot. I remember especially a red-faced old police magistrate, apparently summoned for the purpose of overawing this presumptuous kid who was delaying the count. But the great man failed of his effort, because I knew the law and he didn't; my headquarters had provided me with a little book of instructions, and I would read out the text of the law and insist upon my right to forbid the counting of improperly marked ballots.

I was probably never in greater danger in my life, for it was a common enough thing for an election watcher to be knocked over the head and dumped into the gutter. What saved me was the fact that the returns coming in from the rest of the city convinced the Tammany heelers that they had lost the fight anyhow, so a few extra votes did not matter. The ballots to which I objected were held for the decision of an election board, as the law required, and everybody went home. The Tammany police magistrate, to my great surprise, shook hands with me and offered me a cigar, telling me I would be all right when I had learned about practical politics.

I learned very quickly, for my hero-knight, Jerome, was elected triumphantly and did absolutely nothing, and all forms of graft in New York City went on just as they always had. They still went on when the speakeasy was substituted for the saloon, and the night club for the brothel. The naked women are now on the stage instead of in private rooms; and the drinking is out in the open.

There is one story connected with this campaign that I ought to tell, as it came home to me in a peculiar way. It was known during the campaign as "Jerome's lemon story." Said the candidate on the stump to his cheering audience: "Now, just to show you what chances there are for graft in a city like New York, let us suppose that there is a shortage of lemons in the city, and two ships loaded with lemons come into port. Whichever ship can get its cargo first to the market can make a fortune. Under the law, the city fruit inspectors are required to examine every box of lemons. But suppose that one of them accepts a bribe, and lets one cargo be landed ahead of the other—you can see what graft there would be for somebody." Such was the example, made up out of his head, so Jerome declared; the story appeared in the morning papers, and during the day Jerome chanced to meet a city inspector of fruit whom he knew intimately. "Say, Bill," demanded this official, "how the hell did you find out about those lemons?"

The story impressed me especially for the reason that I happened to know this particular inspector of fruit; he was the brother of an intimate friend of my mother's. We knew all the family gossip about "Jonesy," as we called him; we heard not merely the lemon story but many others, and knew that Jonesy was keeping a wife in one expensive apartment and a mistress in another—all on a salary of two thousand dollars a year. Bear this gentleman in mind, for when we come to the days of *The Jungle*, I shall tell a still funnier story. In a serious emergency I had to get Jonesy on the telephone late at night, before the morning pa-

pers went to press; the only way this could be managed was to
call up his wife and ask her for the telephone number of his mistress. Let no one say that romance is dead in the modern world!

X

It was at this time that I was writing the half-dime novels, or
killing Spaniards. I spent the summer in the home of an old sea
captain, in the little town of Gananoque, Ontario, on the St.
Lawrence River. The old captain was ill of tuberculosis, and his
wife fed me doughnuts for breakfast and ice cream left over from
the night before, and whenever I caught a big pike, we had cold
baked fish for three days.

I did my writing late at night, when everything was quiet;
and one night I was writing a vivid description of a fire, in which
the hero was to rescue the heroine. I went into detail about the
starting of the fire, portraying a mouse chewing on a box of
matches. Just why a mouse should chew matches I do not know;
I had heard of it somehow, and no guarantee went with my
stories in those days. I described the tongues of flame starting in
the box and spreading to some papers, and then licking their way
up a stairway. I described the flames bursting from a window;
then I laid down my pencil—and suddenly the silence of the
night outside was broken by a yell of "Fire!"

For a moment I wasn't sure whether I was still in my story or
outside it. I looked out of the window and sure enough, there
was a cottage in flames. I helped to rouse the people in it, and
watched, with the amused superiority of a New Yorker, the efforts of village firemen to put out the blaze. I remember how they
squirted the hose in at one window, and the jet came out at the
opposite window. I will leave it for specialists in the occult to
explain whether the fire was caused by the excessive vividness of
my writing, or whether it was a case of clairvoyance, or possibly
telepathy from the mind of a mouse. (Perhaps I ought to explain
that the above is meant as humor, lest someone cite it as one
more example of my credulity.)

Early that spring I had taken a fishing trip to the far north of
Ontario, traveling on several railroads and then on a bicycle, and
staying in a pioneer cabin near a tiny jewel of a lake. I did not

get many fish, for the reason that I absent-mindedly left my tackle behind in a railroad station along the way, and it did not arrive until the day I departed; but I saw wild geese and a bear, which was a grand thrill; also I saw mosquitoes in clouds that darkened the sky and made me run through the swamps for my very life. On my way back to the railroad I came upon that field of deep clover in the twilight, and experienced the ecstasy I have described.

It was a good thing for a youth to see how our pioneer ancestors lived on this continent. The family with which I stayed lived on flour and bacon; they didn't even have a cow. Once or twice a year, when they traveled to a store, they traded skins for salt and cartridges. Later that summer, on a canoe trip, I stayed with some old people who had a cow, and lived on skimmed milk and potatoes, trading butter at the store for tea and sugar. On another trip I met a French-Canadian settler, with a swarm of half-nourished babies, who did not even have a rifle to keep the bears out of his pigsty.

XI

Having arranged to meet my mother and some friends at Charleston Lake, which lies at the head of the little Gananoque River, I bought a canoe, bundled my stuff into the bow, and set off—so eager for the adventure that I couldn't wait until morning. I paddled most of the night up the misty river, with bullfrogs and muskrats for company, and now and then a deer—all delightfully mysterious and thrilling to a city youth. I got lost in the marshes—but the mosquitoes found me, rest assured. After midnight I came to a dam, roused the miller, and went to sleep in his garret—until the miller's bedbugs found me! Then I got out, watched the sunrise up the river gorge, and stood on the dam and threw flies for black bass that jumped half a dozen at a time.

I paddled all that day, and stayed a while at a lonely farmhouse, and asked a hundred questions about how pioneer farmers lived. I remember coming out onto Charleston Lake, very tired from paddling and from carrying my canoe over the dams; the wind was blowing up the lake, so after getting the canoe started, I lay down and fell asleep. When I woke, my frail craft was grating on the rocks at the far end of the long lake. I paddled to the hotel; there was a dock, and summer guests watching the new arrival. I had made the whole journey without mishap; but now I put out my hand to touch the dock, a sudden gust of wind carried me out of reach—and over I went into the water with everything I owned!

This lake was a famous fishing resort, and there were rich men from the cities amusing themselves with deep-water trolling for large lake trout. They had expensive tackle, and reclined at ease while guides at four dollars a day rowed them about. I paddled my own canoe, so I did not catch so many trout, but I got the muscular development, which was more important. Doubtless it was my Christian duty to love all the rich persons I watched at this and other pleasure resorts; but here is one incident that speaks for itself. The son of a wealthy merchant from Syracuse, New York, borrowed a shotgun from me, stuck the muzzle into the sand, and then fired the gun and blew off the end of the barrel. I had rented this gun in the village and now had to pay for the damage out of my slender earnings; the wealthy father refused to reimburse me, saying that his son had had no authority to borrow the gun.

You may notice that here again I was meeting rich and poor; going back and forth between French-Canadian settlers and city sportsmen.

XII

By the beginning of the year 1900, the burden of my spirit had become greater than I could carry. The vision of life that had come to me must be made known to the rest of the world, in order that men and women might be won from their stupid and wasteful ways of life. It is easy to smile over the "messianic delusion"; but in spite of all smiles, I still have it. Long ago my friend Mike Gold wrote me a letter, scolding me severely for what he called my "Jesus complex"; I answered, as humbly as I could, that the world needs a Jesus more than it needs anything else, and volunteers should be called for daily.

I was no longer any good at potboiling and could not endure the work. I had a couple of hundred dollars saved, and it was my purpose to write the much talked-of "great American novel." I counted the days until spring would be far enough advanced so that I could go to the country. I had in mind Lake Massawippi in Quebec, just over the New York border; I was so impatient that I set out in the middle of April, and when I emerged upon the platform of the sleeping car and looked at the lake, I found it covered with ice and snow; the train was creeping along at three or four miles an hour, over tracks a foot under water.

My one desire was to be alone; far away, somewhere in a forest, where the winds of ecstasy might sweep through my spirit. I made inquiries of real-estate agents, who had no poetry in their souls and showed me ordinary cottages. At last I set out in a snowstorm, and walked many miles down the lake shore, and discovered a little slab-sided cabin—a dream cottage all alone in a place called Fairy Glen. It belonged to a woman in Baltimore and could be rented for May, June, and July for twenty-five dollars. With the snow still falling, I moved in my belongings. The place had one large room, a tiny bedroom, and a kitchen, everything a would-be poet could desire.

I built a fire in the open fireplace, and warmed my face while my back stayed cold; that first night I fiddled vigorously to keep my courage up, while creatures unknown made noises in the forest outside and smelled at my bacon hanging on the back porch. Next day I walked to town to do some purchasing. Snow was still falling. I met a farmer driving a load of straw or something to town, and he pulled up his horses and stared at the unexpected stranger. "Hello! Be you a summer boarder?" "Yes," I confessed. "Well"—and the old fellow looked about at the snowflakes in the air—"which summer?"

I had fires of the heart to warm me, and I began to write my wonderful novel—the story of a woman's soul redeemed by high and noble love. *Springtime and Harvest* I called it, and it was made out of the life story of a woman I had known, a girl of great beauty who had married a crippled man for his money, and had come to understand his really fine mind. At least that is what I imagined had happened; I didn't really know either the woman or the man—I didn't know anything in those days except music and books and my own emotions.

I would, I fear, be embarrassed to read *Springtime and Har-*

vest now; not even loyalty to this present task has caused me to open its pages. But at that time I was sure it was the most wonderful novel ever written. I always do think that about every book I write; the blurb the publisher puts on the jacket—"This is Upton Sinclair's best work"—is perfectly sincere so far as the author is concerned. I write in a fine glow, expecting to convert my last hostile critic; and when I fail, the shock of disappointment is always as severe as ever.

XIII

Springtime came at last, and the Fairy Glen was carpeted with flowers. The little brook in front of the door sang songs to me, and I to it:

> I ask you where in your journey
>   You see so fair a sight,
> That you have joy and singing
>   All through the winter night.

The sunrise over the lake was a daily miracle, and the great winds that lashed the forest trees were brothers to my soul. Again and again that ecstasy came to me—no one to interfere with it now—and I labored days and nights on end to catch it and imprison it in words.

There were comical incidents in my hermithood, of course. Wild things came to steal the butter that I kept in the spring; I set a trap, and behold, it was nothing more romantic than a skunk. The little devil ruined a pair of trousers for me—I not knowing his ways. I left the trousers to soak in the stream for a week, but all in vain. Worse yet, my drinking place was ruined for the entire summer.

Also, I must mention the French-Canadian family that lived up on the mountain side and sent me fresh milk and eggs and butter by a little ragged boy. I tried out my homemade French on them, and the *mère* of the household paid me a high compliment. "Oh, you speak *French* French!" Now and then she would write me notes, in homemade spelling, and one of these deserves a wider audience. She explained that she would not be able to send milk on the morrow because she was going to the town—"*il*

me faut faire arracher dedans." The vision of the poor woman
having herself "pulled out inside" disturbed me greatly, until I
realized that she meant *some teeth* (*des dents*).

Summer came, and the city boarders. Halfway to town was a
golf links—a new game, then coming in. I saw able-bodied men
driving a little white ball about a field all day, and it seemed to
me more than ever necessary that they should have a new ideal.
I was impatient of every form of human vanity and stupidity,
and if I have become less so with the passage of the years, it has
been merely to spare my digestion.

The summer brought my mother and some friends, including
the girl with whom I was to fall in love. But that is a story I'll
save for the next chapter; here, I am dealing with the book. I
labored over it, sometimes five or six hours without moving from
my seat, and for days at a time without seeing a soul or thinking
about anything else. The human organism is not made to stand
such strain, and I began to notice stomach trouble. It grew worse
and plagued me for years—until I humbled my stubborn pride
and learned mother nature's lesson—to limit the number of hours
of brainwork, and get some exercise and recreation every day.
Many years later I came upon a saying of old John Burroughs,
which came home to me as truth immortal and ultimate. "This
writing is an unnatural business; it makes your head hot and
your feet cold, and it stops the digestion of your food."

On the first of August the owner of my fairy cabin took it for
her own use, and I moved up to a lonely farmhouse on the mountainside, where I became the sole and solitary boarder. I would
go out into the woods—sugar-maple trees they were, and for
breakfast I had their juice in a thick dark syrup, freshly melted.
I always have to have a place to walk up and down while I am
working out my stories, and in that sugar-maple forest I wore a
path six inches deep—back and forth, back and forth, for hours
on end every day.

There were mosquitoes, almost as annoying to me as human
beings, and when they found me, I would go out and sit in the
middle of a field of clover hay and do my writing. The crickets
hopped over my manuscript, and the fieldmice nibbled at my
shoes; and then came the mowers to destroy my hiding place.
I remember one little French-Canadian whom I engaged in con-

versation, and how he rolled up his sleeves and boasted of the power of his stringy muscles. "You want to mow avec me, il you faut très strong bras!" I remember also walking miles down the road in the morning to meet the mail carrier; I had sent the first part of my great novel to a publisher and was hoping for a reply, but none came. It was the beginning of an agony that lasted many weary years. My curses upon those publishers who let manuscripts pile up on their desks unread!

September came, and an invitation from my clergyman friend, Mr. Moir, who now had a camp at Lake Placid. He asked me to visit him for a couple of weeks. I was so near the end of my story, I ventured out of hiding; but I found it was a mistake, because I could do no work at all when I had to fit myself to the meal hours and other habits of the world. I tried in vain for a week or two; I remember that I read the letters of Robert Louis Stevenson in this interval—and very thin and poor they seemed in comparison with what filled my soul.

At last, in desperation, because cold weather was coming fast, I went out on one of the islands of Lake Placid and found a little "cook house"—a tiny cabin with no windows and no furniture but a stove. I rented it for the sum of five dollars, and spread a couple of blankets; and with the brown leaves falling in showers about me, and the cries of blue jays and the drumming of partridges in the air, I wrote the closing scenes of my tragedy. I later used that little cook house in *The Journal of Arthur Stirling*. Also I used the siege of the publishers that was still to come. But of that I had no vision as I bundled up my belongings and returned to New York, a conquering hero in my own fantasy. I was carrying in my suitcase the great American novel for which all the critics of those days were waiting on tiptoe!

4
Marriage

I

I BELIEVE that marriage can be studied as a science, and practiced as an art; that like every other natural phenomenon, it has its laws, psychological, moral, and economic. At present it would seem that many others hold this belief. We have seen the rise of marriage counselors, and I have heard that marriage is even the subject of courses in college. But when I was young, it was generally taken for granted that marriages had to be ill-assorted and that married couples had to quarrel and deceive each other. Here is a case record, an example of what happens when marriage is entered into in utter ignorance of all its practical problems.

The story was told in *Love's Pilgrimage,* with the variation of a few details. In ancient Greek pastorals, Corydon and Thyrsis were two shepherds; but the lines in Milton's "L'Allegro" caught my fancy:

> Where Corydon and Thyrsis met
> Are at their savory supper set,
> Of herbs and other country messes.

And so I said, "For purposes of this tale let Corydon be a girl."

In writing the book, I told the story as the girl wanted it told. If it seemed to her that the manuscript failed to give a sufficiently vivid account of the hardheadedness and unreasonableness of Thyrsis, I would say, "You write it the way it ought to be." So Corydon would write a paragraph, or maybe a page or a scene,

75

and in it would go. I was so sorry for the fate of women that I found it hard to contend with them.

The marriage of Corydon and Thyrsis was dominated by the most pitiful ignorance. Both parties had been taught very little, and most of that was wrong. Corydon had lived the solitary life of a child of the city nomads; her father had been a newspaper reporter, then deputy clerk of a court, and she had been moved about from boardinghouses to apartments; and in the course of twenty years of life she had picked up one intimate girl friend, a poor stenographer dying of tuberculosis, and no men friends whatever. As for Thyrsis, he had, besides Corydon, one girl friend.

Let not Laura Stedman fail of her due place in this story: little Laura, golden-haired and pretty, prim and precise. She was the granddaughter of Edmund Clarence Stedman, the poet, and happened to live in the apartment house next to me for two or three years. We had our childish "scrap," and I vaguely remember pulling her pigtail, or something brutal like that. Later, at the age of fifteen or so, I would go to call upon her, and experience tumultuous thrills; I recall one occasion when I purchased a new hat, of a seductive pearl gray, and went walking with Laura in this regalia, so excited that my knees would hardly hold me up.

We discoursed learnedly about the books we were reading, among these *Romola,* a "classic." First there is a Greek seducer named Tito Melema, and I remarked sapiently that I considered him "magnificent." Laura flushed and exclaimed, "I think he is a perfect beast!" I had to explain that I was speaking from the technical point of view; the character was well drawn. So then the little lady from New England consented to forgive me.

II

Between Corydon and Thyrsis the determining factor, as in nine tenths of marriages, was propinquity. Corydon came to the place where Thyrsis was writing his great novel; she visited the romantic cabin in the Fairy Glen; and since someone had to read the manuscript, she carried it off, and came back flushed with the discovery that this hateful, egotistical, self-centered youth whom she had known and disliked for ten years or more

was a hothearted dreamer, engaged in pouring out a highly romantic love story destined soon to be recognized as the great
American novel. "Oh, it is wonderful!" she exclaimed; and the
rest of the scene tells itself. Literary feelings turned quickly into
personal ones, and the solitary poet had a companion and supporter.

But, oh, the grief of the parents on both sides of this ill-assorted
match! Quite literally, if a bomb had exploded in the midst of
their summer vacation, it could not have discommoded them
more. A clamor of horrified protests broke out. "But you are
crazy! You are nothing but children! And you have no money!
How can people get married without a cent in the world!" The
two mothers fell to disagreeing as to which of their offspring was
the more to blame, and so an old-time friendship passed into
temporary eclipse. Corydon was hastily spirited away to another
summer resort; but not until she had taken a solemn vow—to
learn the German language more rapidly than Thyrsis had
learned it!

At the end of October the poet returned to New York with an
invisible crown on his brow and inaudible trumpets pealing in
his ears. He and Corydon proceeded to spend all day and half
the night reading Goethe's *Iphigenia in Tauris* and practicing
Mozart's sonatas for violin and piano. But there developed grave
obstacles to this program. Corydon's family was inconvenienced
if Thyrsis arrived at the apartment before breakfast; also, the
mother of Thyrsis adhered stubbornly to the idea that Corydon
ought not to play the piano later than eleven in the evening, and
should be taken home before her family went to bed. There was
only one way in the world to escape such fetters—by means of a
marriage license.

Thyrsis had only ten or fifteen dollars, but was wealthy in the
certain future of his masterpiece. So the young couple went to the
study of the Reverend Minot J. Savage at the Church of the Messiah and were pronounced man and wife. By this step, as Thyrsis
quickly discovered, he had deprived himself of the last chance of
getting help in his literary career. With one accord, all relatives
and friends now agreed that he must "go to work." And by this
phrase they did not mean eight hours a day of Goethe plus six of
Mozart; they did not mean even the writing of great American

novels; they meant getting a job with a newspaper, or perhaps with a bonding company.

III

Something happened that the author of *Springtime and Harvest* had not dreamed of in his most pessimistic moment; a publisher rejected the novel. Several publishers rejected it, one after another! The Macmillans were first, and Scribner's second; Brander Matthews kindly read the manuscript and passed it on to W. C. Brownell, literary adviser of Scribner's, and I went to see this soft-spoken, gray-bearded critic, who explained his opinion that the book was not one that would sell. What that had to do with the matter was not clear to me. Again and again those in authority had to explain that they were representing businessmen who had capital invested in the publishing of books and who desired to receive dividends on that capital. I could understand such a business fact; what I couldn't understand was how men employed for such a purpose could consider themselves critics, and be solemnly discussed as critics by other critics like themselves.

Professor Matthews saw me at his home—very fashionable, on West End Avenue, the walls of the study lined with rare editions and autographed pictures and such literary trophies. He was sorry, he said, but he had no further suggestions to offer. When I asked about the possibility of publishing the book myself, he advised strongly against it; there would be no way to market the book. When I suggested that I might market it to everybody I knew, a chill settled over the conversational atmosphere. "Of course, if you are willing to do anything like *that*—" When I persisted in talking about it, I completely lost caste with my "man of the world" professor, and never regained it.

I wrote a potboiler, and earned a couple of hundred dollars, and borrowed another two hundred from my uncle, and went downtown and shopped among printers until I found one who would make a thousand copies of a cheap and unattractive-looking little red volume, such as my ascetic notions required. The book contained a preface, telling how it had been written and what a wonderful book it was. This preface was made into a pamphlet and sent to everybody I knew—not so very many, but by dint of including my father's friends and my mother's, there were several hundred names. The price of the book was one dollar; about two hundred copies were sold, just enough to pay back the debt to my uncle.

The pitiful little book with its pitiful little preface was sent to all the New York newspapers; two of them, the *Times* and the *American*, sent a reporter to see the author. Hopes mounted high, but next morning they dropped with a thud. All the picturesque details about the young poet and his wife were there, but not one word of the wonderful message he hoped to deliver to mankind. Incidentally, the author learned the value of personal publicity in the marketing of literature. As a result of a column apiece in the two largest morning papers of New York, he sold two copies of *Springtime and Harvest*. He knew—because they were the only two copies sold to strangers.

Corydon and Thyrsis were now fast in the "trap" of marriage; living in one crowded room, opening on an airshaft, in a flat belonging to the mother and father of Thyrsis. The would-be creative artist was writing potboilers in order to pay the board of his wife and himself; incidentally, he was learning the grim reality behind those mother-in-law jokes he had written so blithely a few years back! The mother of Thyrsis did not like Corydon; she would not have liked a female angel who had come down to earth and taken away her darling son, until recently destined to become an admiral, or else a bishop, or else a Supreme Court judge. Neither did the mother of Corydon like Thyrsis; she would not have liked a male angel who had taken a daughter without having money to take proper care of her.

The idea of a marriage that involved no more than the reading of German and the playing of violin and piano duets had been broken up by an old family doctor, who insisted that it was not in accordance with the laws of physiology. He made Thyrsis acquainted with the practice of birth control; but alas, it turned out that his knowledge had not been adequate; and now suddenly the terrified poet discovered the purpose of the trap into which mother nature had lured him. Corydon was going to have a baby; and so the reading of German and the playing of violin and piano duets gave place to visiting other doctors, who professed to know how to thwart the ways of nature; then rambling about in the park on chilly spring days, debating the problem of "to be or not to be" for that incipient baby.

These experiences were harrowing and made indelible scars upon two young and oversensitive souls. Aspects of life that should have been full of beauty and dignity became freighted with a burden of terror and death. Under the law, what the young couple contemplated was a state-prison offense, and the fact that it is committed by a million American women every year does not make it any the less ghastly. Thyrsis saw himself prisoned in a cage, the bars being made not of steel but of human beings; everybody he knew was a bar, and he hurled himself against one after another, and found them harder than steel.

IV

Springtime and Harvest had been sent to the leading book reviews, and now came a letter from Edward J. Wheeler, editor of the *Literary Digest*. His attention had been caught by the preface; he had read the novel, and, strange to say, agreed with the author's high opinion of it. Would the author come to see him? The outcome was a proposition from Funk and Wagnalls to take over the book, put it into type again, and issue it under a new title, with illustrations and advertisements and blurbs and other appurtenances of the great American novel.

So once more Thyrsis was swept up to the skies, and it became possible for a baby to be born into the world. All the editors and readers and salesmen and officeboys of a great publishing firm were sure that *King Midas* would be a best seller; and anyhow it did not matter, since a new novel, still more brilliant, was gestating in the writer's brain. It was springtime again, and the apron of mother nature was spilling flowers. Corydon and Thyrsis boarded a train for the Thousand Islands, and on one of the loveliest and most remote of these they built a wooden platform, and set up a small tent, and began the back-to-nature life.

This canvas home contained two tables and two sets of shelves built of boards by an amateur carpenter, who could saw straight if he kept his mind upon it, but seldom did. It contained two canvas cots, a bundle of bedding, a little round drum of a stove, a frying pan, a couple of saucepans, and a half a dozen dishes. Outside there swung two hammocks, one close to the tent for the young expectant novelist. The tent stood on an exposed point, for the sake of the scenery and the avoidance of mosquitoes; it commanded an uninterrupted sweep of Lake Erie, and the gales would seize the little structure and shake it as with a giant's hand, a raging and tireless fury that lasted for days at a time.

The regime of this literary household was of primordial simplicity. Drinking water was dipped from the mighty St. Lawrence. Waste was thrown into the stream a little farther down. Soiled dishes were not washed in hot water but taken to the shore and filled with sand and scrubbed round and round. Black bass and yellow perch could be caught from the rocky point, and now and then, when strange cravings of pregnancy manifested themselves, a pine squirrel or a yellowhammer could be shot in the interior of the island. There may have been game laws, but Thyrsis did not ask about them; this Leek Island was on the Canadian side, the nearest town many miles away, and the long arm of Queen Victoria did not reach these campers.

The post office was on Grindstone Island, on the American side, and thither the young author sailed in a leaky little skiff, purchased for fifteen dollars. He bought groceries, and from a nearby farmhouse, milk and butter. The farmer's wife quickly made note of Corydon's condition and was full of sympathy and anecdotes. An odd freak this gypsy camper must have seemed, wearing a big straw hat, such as are made for haymakers, with a bit of mosquito netting wound about it for decoration.

It was a place of sudden and terrific thunderstorms, and the sight of scores of lightning flashes playing about the wide bay and the pine-tree covered islands was inspiring or terrifying according to one's temperament. Thyrsis was standing by the opening of the tent watching the spectacle, his arm upraised, holding onto the tentpole, when there came a sudden flash, an all-enveloping mass of light, and an all-enveloping crash of sound; the upraised hand was shaken as by some huge vibrating machine and fell numb to the side. Lightning had struck one of the pine trees to which the tent was anchored, and the tree crashed to the ground.

After the storm there was found in the tree a nest of the red-eyed vireo, a silent little forest bird that you see bending under twigs and picking tiny green worms from the undersides. Two of the young birds were alive, and the campers took them in and raised them by hand—most charming pets. They would gulp down big horny grasshoppers and then regurgitate the hard shells in solid lumps; on this rather harsh diet they throve, and it was amusing to see them refuse to heed their own proper parents and fly to their fosterparents instead. At sundown they would be taken into the tent, and flying swiftly about, they would clean from the walls every fly, mosquito, spider, and daddy longlegs. They would sit on the boom of the skiff during the crossing of the channel, and on the heads of their fosterparents during the trip to the post office—something that greatly interested the village loungers, also the village cats. Now and then fishing parties would land on the island, and be surprised to have two full-grown birds of the forest fly down and alight on their hats.

V

The product of that summer's activities was the novel *Prince Hagen*, story of a Nibelung, grandson of the dwarf Alberich, who brings his golden treasures up to Wall Street and Fifth Avenue, and proves the identity between our Christian civilization and his own dark realm. The tale was born of the playing of the score of *Das Rheingold* to so many squirrels and partridges in the forests of the Adirondacks and in the Fairy Glen on the Quebec lake. The opening chapter was sent to Bliss Perry, editor of the *Atlantic Monthly*, who wrote that he was delighted with it and wished to consider the completed work as a serial. The hopes of the little family rose again; but alas, when the completed work was read, it was adjudged too bitter and extreme. "We have a very conservative, fastidious, and sophisticated constituency," wrote the great editor, and the disappointed young author remarked sarcastically that one could have that kind of thing in Boston. The truth was that the story was not good enough; the writer was strong on emotions but weak on facts.

King Midas had failed wholly to produce the hoped-for effect; it had sold about two thousand copies and brought its author two or three hundred dollars. So now the publishers were not interested in *Prince Hagen,* and no other publishers were interested; they would take the manuscript and promise to read it, and then manifest annoyance when a hungry young writer came back after two or three weeks to ask for a decision.

Thus occurred the painful incident of Professor Harry Thurston Peck, told with much detail in *The Journal of Arthur Stirling.* Besides being professor of Latin at Columbia, Peck was editor of the *Bookman* and literary adviser to Dodd, Mead and Company. He read *Prince Hagen* for his former pupil and called it a brilliant and original work, which he would recommend to the firm. Then began a long siege—six weeks or more—the culmination of which was the discovery that the firm had never seen the manuscript they were supposed to be reading.

The cries of rage and despair of the young author will not be repeated here. Poor Harry Peck has long been in a suicide's grave; President Butler kicked him out of Columbia after some widow had sued him for breach of promise and given his sweetish love letters to the press. Perhaps the reason he neglected the young author's manuscript was that he was busy with that widow, or with some other one. Harry was a devotee of decadent literature, and he broke the one law that is sacred—he got caught.

VI

That dreadful winter Corydon went back to her parents, while Thyrsis lived in a garret room, and haunted publishers and editors, and wrote potboilers that he could not sell. He did sell a few jokes and a few sketches, book reviews for the *Literary Digest,* and articles for the *Independent.* He wrote a blank-verse narrative called *Caradrion,* portions of which are in *Love's Pilgrimage;* also a novelette, *The Overman,* an attempt to portray ecstasy and speculate as to its source. Many critics have quarreled with Thyrsis because of so much "propaganda" in his books; but here was a work with no trace of this evil, and the critics never heard of it, and it existed only in the Haldeman-Julius five-cent books.

The literary editor of the *Independent,* who had the saying of thumbs up or thumbs down on book reviews, was Paul Elmer More, of whom Thyrsis saw a great deal before the days of More's repute. A man of very definite viewpoint—as oddly different from his young contributor as the fates could have contrived. Thyrsis, always eager to understand the other side, was moved to a deep respect for his cold, calm intelligence, akin to godhead, subsequently revealed to the world in the series of *Shelburne Essays.* More never made propaganda, nor carried on controversy; he spoke once, and it was the voice of authority. The hothearted young novelist would go off and ponder and wish he could be like that; but there were too many interesting things in the world, and too many vested evils.

There are two factors in the process of growth that we call life; the expanding impulse and the consolidating and organizing impulse. In the literary world these impulses have come to be known, somewhat absurdly, as romanticism and classicism. Both impulses are necessary, both must be present in every artist, and either without the other is futile. Paul Elmer More spoke for the classical tradition and carried it to the extreme of condemning everything in his own time that had real vitality. Many times I pointed out to him that his favorite classical authors had all been rebels and romantics in their own day; but that meant nothing to him. He had understood and mastered these writers, so to him they meant order and established tradition; whereas the new things were uncomprehended and therefore disturbing. It was amusing to see More publish essays in appreciation of writers like Thoreau and Whitman, the revolutionists of their time. What would he say about the same sort of writers of our own day? The answer was, he never mentioned them, he never read them, or even heard of them.

The young wife had her baby, and the young husband sat by and held her hand during the fourteen-hour ordeal. Soon afterward he converted the experience into seven thousand words of horrifying prose. He took these to Paul Elmer More, and the cold Olympian intelligence spoke briefly. "It is well done, supposing one wants to do that kind of thing. But it seems to me one shouldn't. Anyhow, it is unpublishable, so there is no use saying any more." Said the young writer: "It will be published, if I have to do it myself." Eight or nine years later this material appeared as the birth scene in *Love's Pilgrimage,* and for some reason the censors did not find out about it. Now, being half a century old, it is presumably a "classic," and safe.

More gave the *congé* to his tempestuous young contributor; after that I saw him only once, an accidental encounter in the subway at the height of the excitement over *The Jungle.* I asked, "May I send you a copy?" The reply was, "Some time ago I made up my mind I was through with the realists." So there was no more to say. Later, the stern critic was forced to return to the realists; in his book, *The Demon of the Absolute,* I found him condemning Sinclair Lewis and Theodore Dreiser. Myself he did not condescend to mention.

The *Independent* published my paper on "Teaching of Languages" (February 27, 1902) and a follow-up article, "Language Study: Some Facts" (June 19, 1902). I sent a questionnaire to a thousand college graduates, and discovered that among those who had been out ten years, practically none could read the languages they had studied in college. Another article was called "A Review of Reviewers" (February 6, 1902), occasioned by the odd contrast between the reviews of *Springtime and Harvest,* a pitiful, unattractive little volume published by the author, and the reviews of the same novel when it was issued under the name of *King Midas,* in conventional costume by an established publishing house. It was, quite unintentionally, a test of book reviewers and their independence of judgment. *Springtime and Harvest* had a preface, which had crudity and inexperience written all over it; accordingly, the thirteen reviewers of the United States who found the little book worth mentioning employed such phrases as: "proofs of immaturity" . . . "this tumult of young blood" . . . "a crude one, showing the youth, the inexperience of the writer" . . . "betrays the fact that he is a novice in literature" . . . "considering his youth," etc.

But then came *King Midas,* a stately volume illustrated by a popular artist and bearing the imprint of Funk and Wagnalls. It carried the endorsement of Edwin Markham, Thomas Wentworth Higginson, Barrett Wendell, and George Santayana; also a rousing publisher's blurb: "Full of power and beauty; an American story of today by a brilliant writer; no novel we have ever published equals this in the wonderful reception accorded to it, in advance of publication, in commendations from the critics and in advance orders from the trade."

In the face of this barrage, what became of the crudity and inexperience? In the first eight weeks after publication, fifty reviews appeared; and setting aside half a dozen that connected the book with *Springtime and Harvest,* only one critic noted crudity and inexperience! The "novice in literature" had come to display "the mind of a master"; the "tumult of young blood" had become "musical and poetic fervor, at times bordering on the inspired"; the "crude work" had become "a novel of tremendous power"; "the youth, the inexperience of the writer" had developed, according to the *Outlook,* into "workmanship that may be called brilliant . . . sincerity as well as knowledge are apparent on every page"—and so on through a long string of encomiums. The article made amusing reading for the public but cannot have been very pleasing to the critics upon whom a young writer's future depended.

VII

Corydon went to spend the summer with her parents in the Catskills, and Thyrsis went back alone to Leek Island, which seemed home to him because it was full of memories of the previous summer. He put up the tent on the same spot, and sailed the same little skiff, older and still leakier, across the stormy channel. He had gone too early, because of a new book that was clamoring to be written, and the icy gales blowing through the tent almost froze him in his chair. He built the fire too hot in the little round drum of a stove, and set fire to his tent, and had to put it out with the contents of his water pail. For several days the channel could not be crossed at all, and the author lived on dried apples and saltine crackers. The fish would not bite, and the author went hunting, but all he could get was a crow, which proved to have a flesh of deep purple, as strong in texture as in flavor.

From the library of Columbia University, the author had taken a strange German book called *Also Sprach Zarathustra.* While waiting for the muse to thaw out, the author lay wrapped in blankets reading this volume. He put an account of it into his new work, *The Journal of Arthur Stirling*, which helped to launch the Nietzsche cult in America. The vision revealed in Zarathustra is close to the central doctrine of all the seers, and in a chapter on Nietzsche in *Mammonart* I pointed out its curious resemblance to the beatitudes. My friend Mencken, reviewing the book, declared that nothing could be more absurd than to compare Jesus and Nietzsche. My friend Emanuel Haldeman-Julius took up the cudgels, declaring that Mencken was an authority on Nietzsche to whom I should bow—overlooking the fact that *Arthur Stirling* was published in 1903, and Mencken's book on Nietzsche in 1908. I could not induce either Mencken or his champion to publish the words from *Zarathustra* that are so curiously close to the beatitudes.

Arthur Stirling was written in six weeks of intense and concentrated labor; that harrowing, fourteen-hour-a-day labor that is destroying to both mind and body. Of course, my stomach went on strike; and I went to consult a country doctor, who explained a new scientific discovery whereby I could have my food digested for me by the contents of the stomach of a pig. This appealed to me as an advanced idea, and for several weeks I took after each meal a spoonful of pink liquid containing pig pepsin. But gradually its magic wore off, and I was back where I was before. So began a long siege, at the end of which I found it necessary to become my own doctor and another kind of "crank."

Arthur Stirling was sent to a publisher, and I went into the Adirondacks, on the Raquette River, and spent several weeks in the company of hunters and lumbermen. I was a reasonably good hunter for the first ten minutes of any hunt; after that, I would forget what I was doing and be a thousand miles away in thought; a deer would spring up in front of me, and I would see a flash of white tail over the top of the bushes. The reader, having been promised laughter, is invited to contemplate the spectacle of a young author lying on the edge of a mountain meadow in November, watching for deer at sunset, wrapped in a heavy blanket against the cutting frost—and reading a book until the deer should arrive! The deer must have come up and smelled the back of my neck; anyhow, there was a crash five or ten feet behind me, and a deer going twenty feet at a leap, and me pulling the trigger of an uncocked gun!

VIII

For months I had been living in fancy with Arthur Stirling, and this poet had become as real to me as myself. Why not let this poet's diary pass as a true story—as in the spiritual sense it was? In New York was a stenographer who had worked for me for several years, and he inserted in the New York papers a notice of the death by suicide of the poet Arthur Stirling. The reporters took it up, and published many biographical details about the unfortunate young man.

So now the firm of D. Appleton and Company was interested in the dairy of this suicide. Their literary adviser was Ripley Hitchcock. He happened to be in the Adirondacks and we had a meeting. I told him the facts, and he made no objection to the hoax. It has always seemed to me a harmless one; but a few solemn persons, such as my old teacher, Brander Matthews, and my old employer, the New York *Evening Post*, held it a high crime against literature. The book appeared in February of 1903 and created a tremendous furor. Practically everybody accepted it as true—which did not surprise me at all, because, as I have said, it was true in the inner sense.

The papers had long articles about the book, and some of them were deeply felt. The best was written by Richard LeGallienne. Having nobody to advise me about the customs of the world, I debated anxiously whether it would be proper for me to write a letter of thanks to a man who had praised my book. I decided that it would seem egotistical, tending to make personal something that was purely a matter of art.

The hoax did not last very long. A shrewd critic pointed out the resemblances in style between *King Midas* and *Arthur Stirling*, and that was the end of it. I wrote a manifesto on the subject of starving poets and their wrongs, and how I was going to make it my life task to save them from ignominy in the future. "I, Upton Sinclair, would-be singer and penniless rat"—so began this war whoop published in the *Independent,* May 14, 1903. I looked this up, intending to quote some of it, but I found that I could not even read it without pain.

My friend and biographer, Floyd Dell, read the manuscript

of *Arthur Stirling* in 1927, and complained that "it fails to do justice to a very interesting person." He explained his feeling: "It is too unsympathetic to its hero—strange as that may seem! It is only in spots that you lend complete imaginative sympathy to the younger Upton Sinclair." Later in his letter, he remarked: "I suspect that I am more interested in Upton Sinclair as a human being than you are." So here I give my friend a chance to discuss this unusual essay and what it meant to him. He says:

Reading your MS., I came upon a few words from one of your youthful manifestoes—"I, Upton Sinclair, would-be singer and penniless rat"—and it made me remember what that article meant to me when I was sixteen. I too was a would-be singer and penniless rat— and your manifesto stirred me like a trumpet call. It sang itself into my heart. I really think it is one of America's great poems. I think that in that prose poem you achieved the greatness as a poet which you missed in your rhymes. I think it is a pity that it is not in all the anthologies. I do not know how many other youths it affected as it did me. Perhaps many of them have forgotten, as I did till I re-read it just now. But that prose poem gave me the courage to face an ugly and evil world; it gave me courage in my loneliness; it made me spiritually equal to the burden of being a dreamer in an alien world. It is no small thing to give strength to youth. Perhaps it is the greatest thing that literature can do.

I think it was in the following year that I found you again, in the *Appeal to Reason*; in the meantime, like you, I had found it impossible to wage war on the world alone, and I had identified my cause with that of the workers of the world. It is true that there are not in America at present many young people who can as readily identify their own hurts and aims with yours as I could; but there are many all through the world, and there will be more. And to all these you will be a person of great importance for that deeply personal reason. If you will not think I am mocking you, I will say that you will be in a true sense their saint. A saint, you know, in the true sense, is one who has suffered as we have suffered, and triumphed as we hope to triumph. One man's saint is often no use to the next man; each of us must have a saint of his own. And the real difficulty with a good deal of your fiction is that your heroes do not suffer enough nor sin at all. That is why your life is more edifying in some respects than your novels.

But you are not yet in the frame of mind to confess your sins—you are still self-defensively persuaded that some of the worst of them were virtues. That is why many people don't like you—who, indeed, could possibly like anybody who was half as good as you have always been persuaded that you were? But in *The Journal of Arthur Stirling* and *Love's Pilgrimage*, you gave yourself away. It is no wooden doll who walks through those pages—it is a living, suffering bundle of conceit, cruelty, selfishness and folly, such as we know ourselves to be. And you make us feel the nobility and generosity that lies behind all that conceit, cruelty, selfishness and folly—you make us feel that we, too, may, with all our faults, achieve something for mankind. I do not value greatly your present wisdom, which suits you better than it would me—I have a wisdom that I shouldn't trade for yours if you threw that of the Seven Wise Men of Greece in with it. I do value your power as an imaginative artist, as you know, greatly. But just as Keats' life has for us a value in addition to his poetry, so has yours.

To put it in the simplest terms, all over the world there are young people who wish sincerely to devote their lives to revolutionary better-ment of the world; and those same young people will probably fall in love with the wrong people, and suffer like hell, and believe this and that mistaken idea about themselves and the other sex and love; and while Upton Sinclair cannot prevent that, nor tell them what to do about it when it happens (or be believed when he tells them), he can do them good by letting them know that he went through some of the same things. Among these "same things" I include asceticism—a com-moner youthful sin than you seem to think. Many grown people are horribly ashamed of their youthful asceticism. It would do them good to have you confess yours, admitting all you lost by it (and knowing really just what you lost), but explaining the apparently frightful terms upon which "freedom" was offered to youth, and the impossi-bility of accepting it upon such terms; and explaining the way in which the ascetic life came to be associated with everything that was good— and again with a full recognition of the deceitfulness of the combina-tion, and the years of pain and struggle ahead before the tangle of falsehood could be unraveled.

IX

The manifesto in the *Independent* had proclaimed my personal independence—"I having consummated a victory," and so on. I really thought it meant something that the literary world had hailed my book with such fervor. But in the course of time the publishers reported less than two thousand copies sold, and called my attention to a tricky clause in the contract whereby they did not have to pay any royalties until the book had earned its expenses—which, of course, it never did. This was before the authors of America had formed a league, and learned how contracts should be drawn.

So there were Corydon and Thyrsis, more fast in the trap than ever. Corydon and her baby were staying with her parents; while Thyrsis lived in a lodginghouse, this time up in Harlem. He was not permitted to see his wife whom he could not support. He had not seen his son for six months, and was naturally, anxious to know what that son looked like. It was arranged between the young parents that the Negro maid who took care of the child should wheel the baby carriage to a certain spot in Central Park at a certain hour of the afternoon, and Thyrsis would be there and watch the little one go by. The father kept the appointed tryst, and there came a Negro nursemaid, wheeling a baby carriage, and the father gazed therein and beheld a horrifying spectacle—a red-headed infant with a flat nose and a pimply skin. The father went away, sick at soul—until he had the inspiration to send a telegram, and received an answer informing him that the nursemaid had been prevented from coming.

The lodginghouse where Thyrsis had a room was kept by an elderly widow who had invested her little property in United States Steel common and had seen it go down to six dollars. As fellow lodgers, there was the father of Thyrsis, who was drinking more and more; and that Uncle Harry who had almost reached the stage where he put a bullet through his brain. Meanwhile, the uncle considered it his duty to give worldly-wise advice to a haggard young author who refused to "go to work." The mother of Thyrsis, distracted, kept repeating the same formula; half a dozen other occupants of the lodginghouse, broker's clerks, and other commercial persons, took an interest in the problem and said their say.

Such was the life of a would-be prophet in a business world! So that winter I wrote the most ferocious of my stories, *A Captain of Industry*, which became a popular item in the list of the State Publishing House of Soviet Russia. The manuscript was submitted to the Macmillans, and the president of that concern was kind enough to let me see the opinion of one of his readers.

"What is the matter with this young author?" was the opening sentence. The answer of course was that the young author was unable to get enough to eat.

Critics of *Arthur Stirling* and of *Love's Pilgrimage* complain of the too-idealistic characters portrayed, the lack of redeeming weaknesses in the hero. Let the deficiency be supplied by one detail—that during that dreadful winter I discovered my vice. Living in these sordid surroundings, desperate, and utterly without companionship, I was now and then invited to play cards with some of my fellow lodgers. I had played cards as a boy, but never for money; now I would "sit in" at a poker game with the young broker's clerks and other commercial persons with whom fate had thrown me.

So I discovered a devastating emotion; I was gripped by a dull, blind frenzy of greed and anxiety, and was powerless to break its hold. The game was what is called penny ante, and the stakes were pitifully small, yet they represented food for that week. I cannot recall that I ever won, but I lost a dollar or two on several occasions. I remember that on Christmas Eve I started playing after dinner, and sat at a table in a half-warmed room gray with tobacco smoke until two or three in the morning; the following afternoon I began playing again and played all night. So it appeared that I was an orthodox Southern gentleman, born to be a gambler! After that Christmas experience I took a vow, and have never played cards for money since that time.

X

Not all the humiliation, rage, and despair could keep new literary plans from forming themselves, colossal and compelling. Now it was to be a trilogy of novels, nothing less. Ecstasy was taking the form of battles, marches, and sieges, titanic efforts of the collective soul of America. *Manassas, Gettysburg,* and *Appomattox* were to be the titles of these mighty works, and by contemplation of the heroism and glory of the past, America was to be redeemed from the sordidness and shame of the present. The problem was to find some one capable of appreciating such a literary service, and willing to make it possible.

I went up to Boston, headquarters of the culture that I meant to glorify. I stayed with my cousin, Howard Bland, then a student at Harvard, and devoted myself to the double task of getting local color and an endowment. I succeeded in the first part only. Thomas Wentworth Higginson had read *Springtime and Harvest*, and he introduced me to what was left of the old guard of the abolitionists; I remember several visits to Frank B. Sanborn and one to Julia Ward Howe. I went to a reunion of a Grand Army post and heard stories from the veterans—though not much of this was needed, as the Civil War has been so completely recorded in books, magazines, and newspapers. I inspected reverently the Old Boston landmarks and shrines; for I had exchanged my Virginia ideals for those of Massachusetts and was intending to portray the Civil War from the Yankee point of view.

I thought Boston ought to be interested and warmhearted. Why was Boston so cold? Perfectly polite, of course, and willing to invite a young novelist to tea and listen to his account of the great work he was planning; but when the question was broached, would anyone advance five hundred dollars to make possible the first volume of such a trilogy, they all with one accord began to make excuses. Among those interviewed I remember Edwin D. Mead, the pacifist, and Edwin Ginn, the schoolbook publisher, a famous philanthropist. Mr. Ginn explained that he had ruined the character of a nephew by giving him money, and had decided that it was the worst thing one could do for the young. In vain I sought to persuade him that there might be differences among the young.

It was in New York that a man was found, able to realize that a writer has to eat while writing. George D. Herron was his name, and he happened to be a socialist, a detail of great significance in the young writer's life. But that belongs to the next chapter; this one has to do with the fate of Corydon and Thyrsis, and what poverty and failure did to their love. Suffice it for the moment to say that the new friend advanced a couple of hundred dollars and promised thirty dollars a month, this being Thyrsis' estimate of what he would need to keep himself and wife and baby in back-to-nature fashion during the year it would take to write *Manassas*. The place selected was Princeton, New Jersey, because that university possessed the second-largest Civil War collection in the country—the largest being in the Library of Congress. So in

May 1903 the migration took place, and for three years and a half
Princeton was home.

XI

On the far side of a ridge three miles north of the town, a patch
of woods was found whose owner was willing to rent it as a literary encampment. The tent had been shipped from Canada, and
a platform was built, and an outfit of wooden shelves and tables.
Also there was a smaller tent, eight feet square, for the secret sessions with Clio, muse of history. Both canvas structures were
provided with screen doors, against the inroads of the far-famed
Jersey mosquito. Water was brought in pails from a farmer's well,
and once a week a horse and buggy were hired for a drive to
town—to purchase supplies, and exchange one load of books
about the Civil War for another load.

Manassas: A Novel of the War—so ran the title; the dedication
said: "That the men of this land may know the heritage that is
come down to them." The young historian found himself a
stamping ground in the woods, a place where he could pace
back and forth for hours undisturbed, and there the scenes of
the dreadful "new birth of freedom" lived themselves over in his
mind. The men of that time came to him and spoke in their own
persons, and with trembling and awe he wrote down their actions and words.

His method of working had evolved itself into this: he would
go through a scene in his imagination, over and over again, until
he knew it by heart, before setting down a word of it on paper.
An episode like the battle scene of *Manassas*, some ten thousand words in length, took three weeks in gestation; the characters and incidents were hardly out of the writer's mind for a
waking moment during that time, nor did the emotional tension
of their presence relax. And in between these bouts of writing
there was reading and research in the literature of sixty years
past: newspapers, magazines, pamphlets, works of biography
and reminiscence. The writing of *Manassas* must have entailed
the reading of five hundred volumes, and the consulting of as
many more.

In the meantime Corydon took care of the baby, a youngster

of a year and a half, who seemed to know exactly what he wanted and would yell himself purple in the face to get it; the inexperienced young parents sometimes wondered whether he would kill himself by such efforts. During his incarceration in the city the child had suffered from rickets, and now a "child specialist" had outlined an extremely elaborate diet, which took hours of the young mother's time to prepare. Under it the infant throve and became yet more aggressive.

Corydon and Thyrsis had wanted nothing but to be together; and now they had what they wanted—almost too much of it. Now and then they met the farmer and his wife, a gentle old couple; when they drove to Princeton, they met the clerks in the stores and in the college library; they met no one else. Possibly some women could have stood this long ordeal, but Corydon was not of that tough fiber. While her husband went apart to wrestle with his angel, she stayed in the tent to wrestle with demons. She suffered from depression and melancholy, and it was impossible to know whether the trouble was of the mind or of the body.

Nowadays, every disciple of Freud in Greenwich Village would know what to tell her. But this was in the days before the invention of the Freudian demonology. Birth control, as explained by a family doctor, had failed, and could not be trusted; since another pregnancy would have meant the death of the young writer's hopes, there was no safety but in returning to the original idea of brother and sister. Since caressing led to sexual impulse, and therefore to discontent, it was necessary that caressing should be omitted from the daily program, and love-making be confined to noble words and the reading aloud of Civil War literature. Thyrsis could do that, being completely absorbed in his vision. Whether Corydon could do it or not was a superfluous question—since Corydon *had* to do it. This was, of course, a cruelty, and prepared the way for a tragedy.

XII

Prince Hagen, after having been declined by seventeen magazines and twenty-two publishing houses, had been brought out by a firm in Boston and, as usual, disappointed its author's hopes.

But there came one or two hundred dollars in royalties, almost enough to pay for the building of a house. An old carpenter and his son drove from the village, and Thyrsis worked with them and learned a trade. In two or three weeks they built a cabin on the edge of the woods, sixteen feet by eighteen, with a living room across the front and a tiny bedroom and kitchen in the back. It was roofed with tar paper, and the total cost was two hundred and fifty-six dollars. Ten per cent of this price was earned by the device of writing an article about the home-made dwelling and selling it to the *World's Work*, for the benefit of other young authors contemplating escape from civilization. The baby, now two years old, watched the mighty men at work, and thereafter the problem of his upbringing was solved; all that was necessary was to put him out of doors with a block of wood, a hammer, and a supply of nails, and he would bang nails into the wood with perfect contentment for hours.

But the problem of the young mother was less easy of solution. Winter came howling from the north and smote the little cabin on the exposed ridge. Snow blocked the roads, and walking became impossible for a woman tired by housework. She could get to town in a sleigh, but there was no place to stay in town with a baby; and what became of the woman's diversion of shopping, when the family had only thirty dollars a month to live on? There occurred the episode of the turkey-red table cover. It was discovered as a bargain in a notion store, price thirty cents, and Corydon craved it as one pitiful trace of decoration in their home of bare lumber. She bought it, but Thyrsis was grim and implacable, insisting that it be folded up and taken back. Thirty cents was a day's food for a family, and if they ran up bills at the stores, how would the soul of America be saved?

Sickness came, of course. Whether you were rich or poor in America in those days, you were subject to colds and sore throats, because you knew nothing about diet, and ate denatured foods out of packages and cans. Corydon had obscure pains, and doctors gave obscure opinions about "womb trouble." She paid a dollar a bottle for Lydia Pinkham's Vegetable Compound, which was supposed to remedy "female complaints," and did so—by the method of dulling the victim's sensations with opium. The time came when Thyrsis awakened one winter night and heard his wife sobbing, and found her sitting up in bed in the moonlight, with a revolver in her hand, something she kept for protection while her husband was working in the college library. She had been trying for hours to get up courage to put a bullet into her head, but did not have that courage.

XIII

The grip of dreadful winter was broken, and it was possible to walk once more. Flowers blossomed in the woods, and also in the two tormented souls. For the great novel had been completed, and this time it was promptly accepted. The great firm of Macmillan called it a distinguished piece of fiction, paid five hundred dollars advance upon it, and agreed to publish it in the autumn. So it was possible for the little family to buy a turkey-red table cover, and also a vase to fill with woodland flowers, and to get the horse and buggy more frequently—one dollar per afternoon—and drive to town and ramble about the campus and listen to the students singing their songs at twilight.

A town full of handsome young college men was a not disagreeable place of residence for the girl-wife of a solitary genius, condemned by grim fate to celibacy. It was not long before Corydon had met a young instructor of science who lived only a mile or two away on the ridge. He came to call; having horse and buggy, he took Corydon driving, and she would come back from these drives refreshed and enlivened. Life became still more promising.

Presently the time came when she told her preoccupied husband a quaint and naïve story of what had happened. The young instructor had admitted, shyly and humbly, that he was falling somewhat in love with her. It was innocent and idyllic, quite touching; and Thyrsis was moved—he could understand easily how anyone might fall in love with Corydon, for he had done so himself. He was glad it was so noble and high-minded; but he suggested, very gently, that it would be the part of wisdom not to go driving with the young man any more. Corydon was surprised and pained by this; but after a few more drives she admitted that it might indeed be wiser.

So again she was lonely for a while; until it happened that in the course of her search for health, she encountered a high-minded and handsome young surgeon, a Scotchman. Strangely enough, the same thing happened again; the surgeon admitted, shyly and humbly, that he was falling somewhat in love with his patient; this time he himself suggested that it would be wiser if he did not see her any more. Corydon told Thyrsis all about it, and it was excellent material for a would-be novelist who lived a retired life and had few experiences of romantic emotions. But in the end, the novelty wore off—it happened too many times.

5

Revolt

Floyd Dell, contemplating his biography of myself, which was published in 1927, asked me to explain the appearance of a social rebel in a conventional Southern family. I thought the problem over and reported my psychology as that of a "poor relation." It had been my fate from earliest childhood to live in the presence of wealth that belonged to others.

Let me say at once that I have no idea of blaming my relatives. They were always kind to me; their homes were open to me, and when I came, I was a member of the family. Nor do I mean that I was troubled by jealousy. I mean merely that all my life I was faced by the contrast between riches and poverty, and thereby impelled to think and to ask questions. "Mamma, why are some children poor and others rich? How can that be fair?" I plagued my mother's mind with the problem, and never got any answer. Since then I have plagued the ruling-class apologists of the world with it, and still have no answer.

The other factor in my revolt—odd as it may seem—was the Protestant Episcopal Church. I really took the words of Jesus seriously, and when I carried the train of Bishop Potter in a confirmation ceremony in the Church of the Holy Communion, I thought I was helping to glorify the rebel carpenter, the friend of the poor and lowly, the symbol of human brotherhood. Later, I read in the papers that the bishop's wife had had fifty thousand dollars' worth of jewels stolen, and had set the police to hunting for the thief. I couldn't understand how a bishop's wife could own fifty thousand dollars' worth of jewels, and the fact stuck in my mind, and had a good deal to do with the fading away of my churchly ardor.

From the age of perhaps seventeen to twenty-two, I faced our civilization of class privilege absolutely alone in my own mind; that is to say, whatever I found wrong with this civilization, I thought that I alone knew it, and the burden of changing it rested upon my spirit. Such was the miracle that capitalist education had been able to perform upon my young mind during the eleven or twelve years that it had charge of me. It could not keep me from realizing that the rule of society by organized greed was an evil thing; but it managed to keep me from knowing that there was anybody else in the world who thought as I did; it managed to make me regard the current movements, Bryanism and Populism, which sought to remedy this evil, as vulgar, noisy, and beneath my cultured contempt.

I knew, of course, that there had been a socialist movement in Europe; I had heard vaguely about Bismarck persecuting these malcontents. Also, I knew there had been dreamers and cranks who had gone off and lived in colonies, and that they "busted up" when they faced the practical problems of life. While emotionally in revolt against Mammon worship, I was intellectually a perfect little snob and tory. I despised modern books without having read them, and I expected social evils to be remedied by cultured and well-mannered gentlemen who had been to college and acquired noble ideals. That is as near as I can come to describing the jumble of notions I had acquired by combining John Ruskin with Godkin of the New York *Evening Post,* and Shelley with Dana of the New York *Sun.*

It happened that I knew about anarchists because of the execution of the Haymarket martyrs when I was ten years old. In the "chamber of horrors" of the Eden Musée, a place of waxworks, I saw a group representing these desperados sitting round a table making bombs. I swallowed these bombs whole, and shuddered at the thought of depraved persons who inhabited the back rooms of saloons, jeered at God, practiced free love, and conspired to blow up the government. In short, I believed in 1889 what ninety-five per cent of America believes in 1962.

II

Upon my return to New York in the autumn of 1902, after the writing of *Arthur Stirling*, I met in the office of the *Literary Digest* a tall, soft-voiced, and gentle-souled youth by the name of Leonard D. Abbott; he was a socialist, so he told me, and he thought I might be interested to know something about that movement. He gave me a couple of pamphlets and a copy of *Wilshire's Magazine.*

It was like the falling down of prison walls about my mind; the amazing discovery, after all those years, that I did not have to carry the whole burden of humanity's future upon my two frail shoulders! There were actually others who understood; who saw what had gradually become clear to me, that the heart and center of the evil lay in leaving the social treasure, which nature had created and which every man has to have in order to live, to become the object of a scramble in the market place, a delirium of speculation. The principal fact the socialists had to teach me was that they themselves existed.

One of the pamphlets I read was by George D. Herron; it moved me to deep admiration, and when I took it to my editor and critic, Paul Elmer More, it moved him to the warmest abhorrence. I wrote to Herron, telling him about myself, and the result was an invitation to dinner and a very curious and amusing experience.

I was in no condition to dine out, for my shoes were down at the heel, and my only pair of detachable cuffs were badly frayed; but I supposed that a socialist dinner would be different, so I went to the address given, a hotel on West Forty-fourth Street. I found myself in an apartment of extreme elegance, with marble statuary and fine paintings; I was received by a black-bearded gentleman in evening dress and Windsor tie—a combination I had never heard of before—and by an elegant lady in a green velvet Empire gown with a train. One other guest appeared, a small man with a black beard and mustache trimmed to sharp points, and twinkling mischievous eyes—for all the world the incarnation of Mephistopheles, but without the tail I had seen him wearing at the Metropolitan Opera House. "Comrade Wilshire," said my host, and I realized that this was the editor of the magazine I had been reading.

We four went down into the dining room of the hotel, and I noted that everybody in the room turned to stare at us, and did not desist even after we were seated. Dinner was ordered, and presently occurred a little domestic comedy that I, the son of an extremely proper mother, was able to comprehend. The waiter served our meat, set the vegetables on the table, and went away to fetch something else. I saw my host look longingly at a platter of peas that lay before him; I saw his hand start to move, and then he glanced at his wife, and the wife frowned; so the hand drew back, and we waited until the waiter came and served us our peas in proper fashion.

Before long I learned the tragic story of my new friend. A Congregational clergyman of Grinnell, Iowa, he had converted a rich woman to socialism, and she had endowed a chair in Grinnell College for him. Being an unhappily married man, he had fallen in love with the rich woman's daughter, and had refused to behave as clergymen were supposed to behave in such a crisis. Instead, he had behaved like a resident of Fifth Avenue and Newport; that is to say, he had proposed to his wife that she divorce him and let him marry the woman he loved. There ensued a frightful scandal, fanned red hot by the gutter press, and Herron had to give up his professorship. Here he was in New York, with his new wife and her mother, preaching to the labor movement instead of to the churches and the colleges.

An abnormally sensitive man, he had been all but killed by the fury of the assault upon him, and before long I persuaded him to go abroad and live and do his writing. He went, but not much writing materialized. During World War I he swallowed the British propaganda as I did, and became a confidential agent of Woodrow Wilson in Switzerland, and made promises to the Germans that Wilson did not keep; so poor Herron died another death. His book, *The Defeat in the Victory*, told the story of his despair for mankind.

He was a strange combination of moral sublimity and human frailty. I won't stop for details here, but will merely pay the personal tribute that is due. I owe to George D. Herron my survival as a writer. At the moment when I was completely exhausted

and blocked in every direction, I appealed to him; I gave him
Arthur Stirling and the manuscript of *Prince Hagen*, and told him
about *Manassas*, which I wanted to write. I had tried the public
and got no response; I had tried the leading colleges and universities, to see if they would give a fellowship to a creative writer; I
had tried eminent philanthropists—all in vain. Now I tried a socialist, and for the first time found a comrade. Herron promised
me money and kept the promise—altogether about eight hundred dollars. How I could have lived and written *Manassas* without that money I am entirely unable to imagine.

III

The other guest at the dinner was likewise a person worth
hearing about. Gaylord Wilshire had made a fortune in billboard advertising in Los Angeles (Wilshire Boulevard is named
after him). Then out of a clear sky he announced his conversion
to socialism, made a speech in one of the city parks, and was
sent to jail for it. He started a weekly; he then brought it to New
York and turned it into a monthly. He was spending his money
fast, offering prizes such as grand pianos and trips around the
world for the greatest number of new subscribers. He had a
standing offer of ten thousand dollars to William Jennings Bryan
to debate socialism with him, but the canny "boy orator" never
took that easy money; he knew nothing about socialism, and the
quick-witted editor would have made a monkey of him.

Wilshire always insisted that his conversion was purely a matter of intellect; he had become convinced that capitalism was
self-eliminating, and that its breakdown was near. But as a matter of fact, a sense of justice and a kind heart had much to do
with his crusade. To hear him talk, you would think him a cynical man of the world, a veritable Mephisto; but his greatest faults
were generosity, which made it impossible for him to keep
money, and a sort of "Colonel Sellers" optimism, which made him
sure he was going to get a lot more at once. The advertising men
in New York had assured him that the problem of a monthly
magazine was solved when it got four hundred thousand subscribers, because at that mark the advertising made any magazine self-sustaining. Hence the prizes; but alas, when the four

hundred thousand mark was reached, it was discovered that the big national advertisers would not patronize a magazine that in its reading columns threatened their privileges. So Wilshire was "stuck," and went into the business of mining gold in order to keep his magazine going in spite of the advertisers. That is a tale I shall tell later.

The editor took me uptown and introduced me to two sisters, of whom the older soon became his wife. The couple came to Princeton on their honeymoon and became our intimate friends. Mary Wilshire was a sort of older sister to me—though as a matter of fact I believe she was younger. "Gay" printed my picture in his magazine, and introduced me to the socialist movement as a coming novelist. I wrote for his columns—I remember "The Toy and the Man," wherein I poked fun at the desire of grown-up Americans to accumulate quantities of unnecessary material things. If you look about you at the America of sixty years later, you will see that my sermon failed entirely of its effect.

It was either that summer or the next that the Wilshires took us with them for a two-week trip to Halifax, the editor having got transportation in exchange for advertising. We drove about and saw the Nova Scotia country, at its loveliest in early summer, and went swimming by moonlight in an inland lake. Incidentally, I discovered some cousins—it seems that a branch of the Sinclairs had left Virginia after the Civil War; so here was a surgeon at this British Army station. Somehow I got the impression that he was not entirely proud of his young genius relative, with an unmodish wife who took care of her own baby. He did not invite us to meet the wealth and fashion of the British Army, and we had time to ramble alone on the beach, where the baby filled his chubby fists with masses of squashy starfish.

IV

Manassas was completed in the spring of 1904 and published in August. Meanwhile I was reading the socialist weekly, *Appeal to Reason*, which was published in Girard, Kansas; it then had a circulation of half a million, and doubled it in the next few years. At that time two Western Miners' officials, Moyer and Haywood, were being tried for a murder that they probably did not commit. The *Appeal* was sure of their innocence. I was too, and in general I was becoming a red-hot "radical." When the twenty thousand workers in the Chicago stockyards had their strike smashed in a most shocking way, I wrote a manifesto addressed to them: "You have lost the strike, and now what are you going to do about it?" This was just the sort of thing the *Appeal* wanted, and they made it into a shouting first-page broadside and distributed hundreds of thousands of copies. I wrote a second broadside, "Farmers of America, Unite!" The *Appeal* paid me for this by sending me twenty or thirty thousand copies, which was like a present of a herd of white elephants! I had to hire a boy and a horse and buggy for a couple of weeks to distribute them over the countryside around Princeton. Two years later I ran for Congress on the socialist ticket in that district, and maybe my propaganda got me half a dozen extra votes.

I learned something about the American small farming community during my three and a half years near Princeton. What their fathers had done, they did; as their fathers had voted, so voted they, and thought it was for Lincoln, or perhaps Tilden. They lived in pitiful ignorance and under the shadow of degeneracy. I often thought of writing a book about them—but you would not have believed me, because the facts fitted so perfectly into my socialist thesis that you would have been sure I was making them to order.

In a neighborhood two miles square, which I knew by personal contact and the gossip of neighbors, the only decent families were half a dozen that lived on farms of a hundred acres or more. The families that lived on ten or twenty-acre farms contained drunkards, degenerates, mental or physical defectives, semi-idiots, victims of tuberculosis or of venereal disease, and now and then a petty criminal. You could descend in the scale, according to the size of the farm, until you came to the Jukes—I don't recall their real name, but students of eugenics will accept that substitute. The Jukes had no farm at all, but squatted in an old barn, and had six half-naked brats, and got drunk on vinegar, and beat each other, and howled and screamed and rioted, and stole poultry and apples from the neighbors.

These small farmers of New Jersey and other eastern states represented what had been left behind from wave after wave of mi-

gration—either to the West or to the cities. The capable and
active ones escaped, while the weak ones stayed behind and constituted our "farm problem." Prohibition did not touch them because they made their own "applejack," with sixty per cent alcohol. Politics touched them only once a year, when they were
paid from two to five dollars for each vote the family could produce. They worked their children sixteen hours a day and sent
them to school three or four months in winter, where they
learned enough to figure a list of groceries, and to read a local
weekly containing reports of church "sociables" and a few canned
items supplied by the power trust; also a Methodist or Baptist
paper, with praises of the "blood of the Lamb" and of patent
medicines containing opium and coal-tar poisons. Such was agri-
cultural New Jersey almost sixty years ago. The farms still go on
voting for Lincoln and McKinley, and hating the labor unions
that force up the prices of the things farmers have to buy.

V

A play called *Candida* by a new British dramatist had been
produced in New York. I had no money to see plays, but I borrowed the book, and it was like meeting Shelley face to face, a
rapturous experience. Then came *Man and Superman*—I remember reading it in the summertime, lying in a hammock by my
woodland cabin and kicking my heels in the air with delight
over the picture of the British aristocracy in heaven—not understanding the music, and being bored to death, but staying because they considered that their social position required it.

I was supporting my wife now, after a fashion, and so was in
better standing with my father-in-law. He had a six-week vacation in the latter half of the summer, and invited me to accompany him on a canoe trip in northern Ontario. My father-in-law
was a city-bred man with a passion for the primitive; he wanted
to get to some place where no man had ever been before, and
then he would explode with delight and exclaim, "Wild as hell!"
We went up to the head of Lake Temeskaming, made a long
portage, and paddled over a chain of lakes some two or three
hundred miles, coming out by the Sturgeon River to Lake Win-
nipeg. We took two canoes, and lugged them heroically on our

shoulders, and learned to use a "tumpline," and ran dangerous
rapids with many thrills, and killed a dozen great pike in a day,
and paddled up to a dozen moose so close that we could have
touched them with our paddles. This country, which is full
of cobalt and copper, is now a great mining region, but at that
time there were not even trails, and the only white man we saw
in several weeks was the keeper of a Hudson's Bay Company
post.

Here were Indians living in their primitive condition, and this
interested me greatly. I asked many questions, and the trader at
the post told me how in wintertime these Indians would kill a
moose, and then move to the moose, and camp there until they
had picked the bones. When I was writing *Oil!* I remembered
this; I told about "Dad," my oilman, who would drill a well, and
move his family to the well; I compared him to the Indians who
moved their families to a moose. Later in the book I remarked,
"Dad had moved to another moose"; and this got me into trouble
with printers and proofreaders, who would insist upon making
"moose" into "house." I changed it back two or three times—until
finally I received a letter from one of the executives of the firm,
calling my attention to the difficulty; surely I could not be
meaning to say that Dad had moved to a *moose!*

Going back home, I found *Manassas* about to appear, and this
was the psychological moment to make a killing with the magazines. Gertrude Atherton had published in the *North American
Review* an article speculating as to why American literature, with
so many opportunities to be robust, should be so bourgeois. I
wrote a reply, interpreting American literature in terms of economics; but the *Review* turned me down. I took the article to
Collier's, then edited by Norman Hapgood, and he published it.
The article was one of the strongest I have ever written, but there
was not a line about it in the capitalist newspapers. I could not
comprehend this; but now, after it has happened to me so many
times, I know what to think.

Collier's published another article of mine, telling the American people what socialists believed and aimed at. But that was
the last. The editors accepted an open letter to Lincoln Steffens
about his series of articles on "The Shame of the Cities," which
was appearing in *McClure's*. I had written a criticism of his arti-

cles, pointing out that the corruption he reported came about
because big business bought the politicians or elected them; and
that there could never be an end to it until the government
owned businesses, especially the public utilities. I sent the article
to Steffens. He wrote me that it was the best criticism of his work
that he had seen; he wanted *McClure's* to publish it, but they
didn't dare to. So I turned it into an open letter and sent it to
Collier's. I have told in *The Brass Check* how I was invited
to Robbie Collier's for dinner, and how old Peter Collier, ex-pack-
peddler, announced to me that he would not permit my articles
to appear in his paper and "scare away" his half-million subscribers. The greater part of the letter to Steffens was published
in my book, *The Industrial Republic*, long since out of print. It
contained a remarkable prophecy of our successive world crises.

Steffens and I became friends at that time. He remained
always one of my closest and dearest friends, and we met whenever we were in the same neighborhood. In 1914, I remember, he
came out to Croton, near New York, where we had rented a little
house, and spent several weekends with us. Once I took him for
a tramp in the snow before he had had his coffee. He appealed
to my wife never to let that happen again, and she promised.

VI

Manassas appeared, and won critical praise, but sold less than
two thousand copies. The "men of this land" did not care about
the heritage that was come down to them; or, at any rate, they
did not care to hear about it from me. The five-hundred-dollar
advance on this book was about all I got for my labors. I had
written in the course of four and one half years a total of six novels or novelettes, published four of them, and the sum of my receipts therefrom was less than one thousand dollars.

Nevertheless, *Manassas* was the means of leading me out of the
woods. The editor of the *Appeal to Reason* read it and wrote
me with enthusiasm; I had portrayed the struggle over chattel
slavery in America, and now, why not do the same thing for wage
slavery? I answered that I would do it, provided he would stake
me. The editor, Fred D. Warren, agreed to advance five hun-

dred dollars for the serial rights of the novel, and I selected the Chicago stockyards as its scene. The recent strike had brought the subject to my thoughts; and my manifesto, "You have lost the strike," had put me in touch with socialists among the stockyard workers.

So, in October 1904 I set out for Chicago, and for seven weeks lived among the wage slaves of the Beef Trust, as we called it in those days. People used to ask me afterward if I had not spent my life in Chicago, and I answered that if I had done so, I could never have written *The Jungle*; I would have taken for granted things that now hit me a sudden violent blow. I went about, white-faced and thin, partly from undernourishment, partly from horror. It seemed to me I was confronting a veritable fortress of oppression. How to breach those walls, or to scale them, was a military problem.

I sat at night in the homes of the workers, foreign-born and native, and they told me their stories, one after one, and I made notes of everything. In the daytime I would wander about the yards, and my friends would risk their jobs to show me what I wanted to see. I was not much better dressed than the workers, and found that by the simple device of carrying a dinner pail I could go anywhere. So long as I kept moving, no one would heed me. When I wanted to make careful observations, I would pass again and again through the same room.

I went about the district, talking with lawyers, doctors, dentists, nurses, policemen, politicians, real-estate agents—every sort of person. I got my meals at the University Settlement, where I could check my data with the men and women who were giving their lives to this neighborhood. When the book appeared, they were a little shocked to find how bad it seemed to the outside world; but Mary MacDowell and her group stood by me pretty bravely—considering that the packers had given them the cots on which the strike breakers had slept during their sojourn inside the packing plants in violation of city laws!

I remember being invited to Hull House to dinner and sitting next to the saintly Jane Addams. I got into an argument with her consecrated band, and upheld my contention that the one useful purpose of settlements was the making of settlement workers into socialists. Afterward Jane Addams remarked to a friend that

I was a young man who had a great deal to learn. Both she and I went on diligently learning, so that when we met again, we did not have so much to argue over.

One stroke of good fortune for me was the presence in Chicago of Adolphe Smith, correspondent of the *Lancet*, the leading medical paper of Great Britain. Smith was one of the founders of the Social-Democratic Federation in England, and at the same time an authority on abattoirs, having studied the packing plants of the world for the *Lancet*. Whenever I was in doubt about the significance of my facts—when I wondered if possibly my horror might be the oversensitiveness of a young idealist—I would fortify myself by Smith's expert, professional horror. "These are not packing plants at all," he declared; "these are packing boxes crammed with wage slaves."

At the end of a month or more, I had my data and knew the story I meant to tell, but I had no characters. Wandering about "back of the yards" one Sunday afternoon I saw a wedding party going into the rear room of a saloon. There were several carriages full of people. I stopped to watch, and as they seemed hospitable, I slipped into the room and stood against the wall. There the opening chapter of *The Jungle* began to take form. There were my characters—the bride, the groom, the old mother and father, the boisterous cousin, the children, the three musicians, everybody. I watched them one after another, fitted them into my story, and began to write the scene in my mind, going over it and over, as was my custom, fixing it fast. I went away to supper, and came back again, and stayed until late at night, sitting in a chair against the wall, not talking to anyone, just watching, imagining, and engraving the details on my mind. It was two months before I got settled at home and first put pen to paper; but the story stayed, and I wrote down whole paragraphs, whole pages, exactly as I had memorized them.

VII

Our life in the little sixteen-by-eighteen cabin had been wretched, and we had set our hearts upon getting a regular farmhouse. We had gone riding about the neighborhood, imagining ourselves in this house and that—I looking for economy, and Corydon looking for beauty, and both of us having the "blues" because the two never came together. Finally Corydon had her way—in imagination at any rate; we chose a farm with a good eight-room house that could be bought for $2,600, one thousand cash and the rest on mortgage. There were sixty acres to the place, with good barns, a wood lot, and three orchards; we imagined a cow, some chickens, a horse and buggy—and persuaded ourselves that all this would pay for itself.

Now, before starting on *The Jungle*, I went to call upon Dr. Savage, who had married us; I poured out my woes upon his devoted head. I told him how Corydon had come close to suicide the previous winter and how I dreaded another siege in our crowded quarters. I so worked upon his feelings that he agreed to lend me a thousand dollars, and take another mortgage on the farm as security. Poor, kind soul, he must have listened to many a painful story in that big church study of his! He assured me he was not a rich man, and I was glad when I was able to repay the money at the end of a year.

We moved into the new, palatial quarters, elegantly furnished with odds and ends picked up at the "vendues" that were held here and there over the countryside whenever some one died or moved away. You stood around in the snow and stamped your feet, and waited for a chance to bid on a lot of three kitchen chairs, with one seat and two rungs missing, or a dozen dishes piled in a cracked washbasin. You paid cash and had twenty-four hours in which to fetch your goods. I purchased a cow at such a sale, also a horse and buggy.

For my previous winter's writing I had built with my own hands a little cabin, eight feet wide and ten feet long, roofed with tar paper, and supplied with one door and one window. In it stood a table, a chair, a homemade shelf for books, and a little round potbellied stove that burned coal—since the urgencies of inspiration were incompatible with keeping up a wood fire. This little cabin was now loaded onto a farmer's wagon and transported to the new place, and set up on an exposed ridge; in those days I valued view more than shelter, but nowadays I am less romantic, and keep out of the wind. To this retreat I repaired on Christmas Day, and started the first chapter of *The Jungle*.

For three months I worked incessantly. I wrote with tears and anguish, pouring into the pages all the pain that life had meant to me. Externally, the story had to do with a family of stockyard workers, but internally it was the story of my own family. Did I wish to know how the poor suffered in wintertime in Chicago? I had only to recall the previous winter in the cabin, when we had had only cotton blankets, and had put rugs on top of us, and cowered shivering in our separate beds. It was the same with hunger, with illness, with fear. Ona was Corydon, speaking Lithuanian but otherwise unchanged. Our little boy was down with pneumonia that winter, and nearly died, and the grief of that went into the book.

VIII

. Three months of incessant work and little exercise put my stomach nearly out of commission. A relative offered me some kind of pass on a steamer to Savannah, and I took this trip, and went on to Florida, and spent a couple of weeks roaming the beaches and fishing in the surf; I came back refreshed, and put in the spring and summer on my task. The story had begun in the *Appeal to Reason*—circulation half a million—and I was getting letters from readers; I realized that this time I had something that would be read. "I am afraid to trust myself to tell you how it affects me," wrote David Graham Phillips.

Of course I had some human life during that year. There were times when the country was beautiful; when the first snow fell, and again when the peach orchard turned pink, the pear orchard white, and the apple orchard pink and white. We had a vegetable garden, and had not yet discovered that it cost us more than buying the vegetables. We bought some goose eggs, hatched a flock of eight or ten, and chased them all over the countryside until one day they disappeared into the stomachs of the foxes or the Jukeses. I worked on the place all my spare time in summer and became a jack-of-all-trades. I drove a hayrake, which was picturesque and romantic—except that the clouds of pollen dust set me to sneezing my head off. I was continually catching cold in those days, and was still at the stage where I went to doc-

tors, and let them give me pills and powders, and pump my nose
full of red and blue and green and yellow-colored liquids, which
never had the slightest effect that I could discover.

Shortly before the completion of the book, I set to work at the
launching of the Intercollegiate Socialist Society. I had reflected
much upon my education in college and university, and made
sure that my ignorance of the modern revolutionary movement
had not been an accident. Since the professors refused to teach
the students about modern life, it was up to the students to teach
themselves; so I sent a circular letter to all the college socialists
I knew of and invited them to organize. On September 12, 1905,
we had a dinner at Peck's Restaurant on Fulton Street in New
York, and chose Jack London as our president. The newspapers
gave three or four inches to the doings of this peculiar set of
cranks. I remember calling up the secretary of some university
club to ask for the membership list, and I could not make him
understand the strange name of our organization. "Intercollegiate
Socialist Society, you say?" The Catholic Anarchist League, the
Royal Communist Club, the Association of Baptist Bolsheviks!

We had no income, of course, and everything was done by
volunteer labor. Many times I sat up until two or three in the
morning, wrapping packages of literature to be mailed to persons who did not always want them and sometimes wrote to say
so. One who attended our first meeting was a young student at
Wesleyan by the name of Harry Laidler, and for several years it
was my dream that some day we might have an income of eighteen dollars per week so that Harry could be our full-time secretary. The organization, now known as the League for Industrial
Democracy, has not merely Harry W. Laidler but Norman
Thomas also, and has raised about fifty thousand dollars a year.
Not so much, compared with the resources of the power trust,
but we have interested and trained two generations of socialists,
progressives, and liberals. The league has been at the same address, 112 East 19th Street, New York, for some fifty-five years—
in itself an achievement; if you want to know about it, send a
postcard.

Soon after our start, we organized a mass meeting at Carnegie
Hall at which the principal speaker was to be Jack London. I
had corresponded with him from the time of his first novel. At

this time he had had his great success with *The Sea Wolf*. He was on the crest of the wave of glory and a hero in the movement of social protest. He was traveling from California to Florida by sea, then by train to New York, and he was due to arrive on the very evening of the meeting. His train was late, and I had been asked to keep the crowd entertained until he arrived. The hall was packed. I was in something of a panic because I didn't think that I was equal to the assignment. But just as I started for the platform, a roar of cheers broke out—our hero and his wife were walking down the aisle.

Jack was not much taller than I, but he was broadly built—the picture of an athlete. That night he gave us the substance of his famous discourse, "Revolution," later published in a little red paper pamphlet. The crowd that listened so raptly was not, I must admit, very collegiate. A few students came, but most of the audience was from the Lower East Side; the ushers were Jewish boys and girls wearing red badges. The socialist fervor of that evening now seems like even more ancient history than it is. A good part of it went into the communist movement, of course, and my friend Scott Nearing used to ask me how I could continue to belong to the Socialist Party, made up of lawyers and retired real-estate speculators!

IX

The first chapters of *The Jungle* had been read by George P. Brett of the Macmillan Company, who was impressed by the book, and gave me an advance of five hundred dollars. The last chapters were not up to standard, because both my health and my money were gone, and a second trip to Chicago, which I had hoped to make, was out of the question. I did the best I could—and those critics who didn't like the ending ought to have seen it as it was in manuscript! I ran wild at the end, attempting to solve all the problems of America; I put in the Moyer-Haywood case, everything I knew and thought my readers ought to know. I submitted these chapters to a test and got a cruel verdict; the editor of the *Appeal* came to visit me, and sat in my little living room one evening to hear the story—and fell sound asleep! The polite author went on reading for an hour or so, hoping that his guest would wake up and be spared the embarrassment of being "caught!" (I cut the material out.)

I was called to New York for an interview with Mr. Brett. He wanted me to cut out some of the "blood and guts" from the book; nothing so horrible had ever been published in America —at least not by a respectable concern. Brett had been a discerning but somewhat reserved critic of my manuscripts so far; if I had taken his advice, I would have had an easier time in life— but I would have had to be a different person. Out of his vast publishing experience he now assured me that he could sell three times as many copies of my book if I would only consent to remove the objectionable passages; if I were unwilling to do this, his firm would be compelled to decline the book. I remember taking the problem to Lincoln Steffens, an older muckraker than I. Said he: "It is useless to tell things that are incredible, even though they may be true." But I could not take his advice; I had to tell the truth, and let people make of it what they could.

I forget who were the other publishers that turned down *The Jungle.* There were five in all; and by that time I was raging and determined to publish it myself. The editor of the *Appeal* generously consented to give space to a statement of my troubles. Jack London wrote a rousing manifesto, calling on the socialist movement to rally to the book, which he called "the *Uncle Tom's Cabin* of wage slavery. It is alive and warm. It is brutal with life. It is written of sweat and blood, and groans and tears." I offered a "Sustainer's Edition," price $1.20, postpaid, and in a month or two I took in four thousand dollars—more money than I had been able to earn in all the past five years. Success always went to my head, and I became drunk, thinking it was going to be like that the rest of my life; and so I could found a colony, or start a magazine, or produce a play, or win a strike—whatever might be necessary to change the world into what it ought to be.

In this case the first thing I did was to buy a saddle horse for a hundred and twenty-five dollars. It wasn't as reckless as it sounds because the horse could also be driven to the buggy, and I had to have some form of exercise to help the poor stomach that apparently was not equal to keeping up with the head. Also I had to have some way to get into town quickly, because I now had a business on my hands and had to be sending telegrams and mailing proofs. I had a printing firm in New York at work putting *The Jungle* into type. Then, just as the work was completed, someone suggested that I offer the book to Doubleday, Page and Company. So I found myself in New York again, for a series of conferences with Walter H. Page and his young assistants.

This publisher and editor played an important part in American history, so I will tell what I saw of him. He was extremely kind and extremely naïve; being good himself, he believed that other people were good; and just as he was swallowed alive by Balfour and other British Tories during World War I, so he was very nearly swallowed by the Chicago packers. Anxious not to do anybody harm in such a good and beautiful world, he submitted the proofs of *The Jungle* to James Keeley, managing editor of the Chicago *Tribune* and a highly honorable gentleman, who sent back a thirty-two page report on the book, prepared, so Keeley avowed, by one of his reporters, a disinterested and competent man. I sat down to a luncheon with the firm, at which this report was produced, and I talked for two or three hours, exposing its rascalities. I persuaded the firm to make an investigation of their own, and so they sent out a young lawyer, and the first person this lawyer met in the yards was a publicity agent of the packers. The lawyer mentioned *The Jungle*, and the agent said, "Oh, yes, I know that book. I read the proofs of it and prepared a thirty-two page report for James Keeley of the *Tribune*."

X

The young lawyer's report upheld me, so Doubleday, Page agreed to bring out the book, allowing me to have a simultaneous edition of my own to supply my "sustainers." The book was published in February 1906, and the controversy started at once. The answer of the packers appeared in a series of articles by J. Ogden Armour in the *Saturday Evening Post*, whose editor was Armour's former secretary, George Horace Lorimer. The great packer did not condescend to name any book, but he referred in dignified fashion to the unscrupulous attacks upon his great business, which was noble in all its motives and turned out products free from every blemish. I remember reading this canned literature in Princeton, and thinking it over as I rode my new saddle horse back to the farm. I was boiling, and automatically my material began to sort itself out in my mind. By the time I got home, I had a reply complete, and sat down and wrote all through the night; the next morning I had an eight-thousand-word magazine article, "The Condemned Meat Industry."

I took the first train for New York, and went to *Everybody's Magazine*, which had just electrified the country with Thomas W. Lawson's exposure of Wall Street methods. I figured they would be looking for something new, and I asked to see the publisher of the magazine—realizing that this was a matter too important to be decided by a mere editor. I saw E. J. Ridgway and told him what I had, and he called in his staff of editors. I read them the article straight through and it was accepted on the spot, price eight hundred dollars. They stopped the presses on which the May issue of the magazine was being printed, and took out a story to make room for mine. Two lawyers were summoned, and once more I had to go over my material line by line, and justify my statements.

It was dynamite, no mistake. Bob Davis, of *Munsey's Magazine*—how I blessed him for it!—had introduced me to a wild, one-eyed Irishman who had been a foreman on Armour's killing beds and had told under oath the story of how the condemned carcasses, thrown into the tanks to be destroyed, were taken out at the bottom of the tanks and sold in the city for meat. The Armours had come to him, and offered him five thousand dollars to retract his story; by advice of a lawyer he accepted the money and put it in the bank for his little daughter, and then made another affidavit, telling how he had been bribed and why. I had both these affidavits; also I had the court records of many pleas of guilty that Mr. Armour and his associates had entered in various states to the charge of selling adulterated meat products. It made a marvelous companion piece to Mr. Armour's canned literature in the *Saturday Evening Post*.

The article in *Everybody's* was expected to blow off the roof. But alas, it appeared on the newsstands on April 20, and April 19 was the date selected by the Maker of History for the destruction of San Francisco by earthquake and fire. So the capitalist news agencies had an excuse for not sending out any stories about "The Condemned Meat Industry!" I have met with that sort of misfortune several times in the course of my efforts to reach the public. In 1927 I traveled all the way across the continent in order to make war on the city of Boston for the suppression of my novel, *Oil!*; and just as I set to work, Lindbergh landed in America after his flight to France! For a couple of weeks there was nothing in the American newspapers but the "lone eagle" and the advertisements.

XI

However, *The Jungle* made the front page a little later, thanks to the efforts of the greatest publicity man of that time, Theodore Roosevelt. For the utilizing of Roosevelt in our campaign, credit was claimed by Isaac F. Marcosson, press agent for Doubleday, Page and Company, in his book, *Adventures in Interviewing*. If I dispute his exclusive claim, it is because both of us sent copies of the book to the President, and both got letters saying that he was investigating the charges. (Roosevelt's secretary later told me that he had been getting a hundred letters a day about *The Jungle*.) The President wrote to me that he was having the Department of Agriculture investigate the matter, and I replied that that was like asking a burglar to determine his own guilt. If Roosevelt really wanted to know anything about conditions in the yards, he would have to make a secret and confidential investigation.

The result was a request for me to come to Washington. I was invited to luncheon at the White House, where I met James R. Garfield, Francis E. Leupp, and one or two other members of the "tennis cabinet." We talked about the packers for a while; said "Teddy": "Mr. Sinclair, I bear no love for those gentlemen, for I ate the meat they canned for the army in Cuba." Presently he fell to discussing the political situation in Washington. At this time *Cosmopolitan* was publishing a series of articles called "The Treason of the Senate," by the novelist David Graham Phillips, which revealed the financial connections and the reactionary activities of various Senators. (The articles were basically sound, though I had the impression that Phillips, whom I knew rather well, was longer on adjectives than on facts.) The President called the roll of these traitors, and told me what he knew about each one. I sat appalled—what, after all, did Theodore Roosevelt know about me? I was a stranger, a young socialist agitator, from whom discretion was hardly to be expected; yet here was the President of the United States discussing his plans and policies, and pouring out his rage against his enemies—not even troubling to warn me that our talk was confidential.

I was so much amused by his language that when I left the White House, the first thing I did was to write out, while I remembered it, his words about Senator Hale of Maine, whom he called "the Senator from the Shipbuilding Trust." If you want to get the full effect of it, sit at a table, clench your fist, and hit the table at every accented syllable: "The most in-*nate*-ly and es-*sen*-tial-ly mal-*e*-vo-lent *scoun*-drel that *God Almight-y ev*-er *put* on *earth!*" I perceived after this session the origin of what the newspapermen of Washington called "the Ananias Club." I was assumed to know that the President's words were not meant to be quoted; and if I broke the rule, "Teddy" would say I was a liar, and the club would have a new member.

A curious aspect of this matter: it was only a few weeks later that Roosevelt made his famous speech denouncing the "muckrakers." The speech named no names but was generally taken to refer to David Graham Phillips on account of his "Treason of the Senate" articles; and this gave great comfort to the reactionaries. Yet Phillips in his wildest moment never said anything against the Old Guard senators more extreme than I had heard Roosevelt say with his own lips at his own luncheon table. Needless to say, this experience did not increase my respect for the game of politics as played in America.

I was sent to see Charles P. Neill, labor commissioner, and James Bronson Reynolds, a settlement worker, the two men who had been selected to make the "secret and confidential" investigation. I talked matters out with them, promised silence, and kept the promise. But when I got back to Princeton, I found a letter from Chicago telling me it was known that the President was preparing an investigation of the yards and that the packers had men working in three shifts, day and night, cleaning things up. I found also waiting for me a business gentleman with dollar signs written all over him, trying to interest me in a proposition to establish an independent packing company and market my name and reputation to the world. This gentleman haunted my life for a month, and before he got through he had raised his bid to three hundred thousand dollars in stock. I have never been sure whether it was a real offer, or a well-disguised attempt to buy me. If it was the latter, it would be the only time in my life this had happened; I suppose I could consider that I had been complimented.

XII

Roosevelt's commissioners asked me to go to Chicago with them; but I have never cared to repeat any work once completed. I offered to send a representative to put the commissioners in touch with the workers in the yards. For this I selected two socialists whom I had come to know in the "local" in Trenton, Ella Reeve Bloor and her husband. Mrs. Bloor had five small children, but that never kept her from sallying forth on behalf of the cause. She was a little woman, as tireless as a cat; the war converted her to Bolshevism, and her five children became active communist workers, and she herself became "Mother Bloor," gray-haired, but hardy, and familiar with the insides of a hundred city jails. I paid the expenses of her and her husband for several weeks, a matter of a thousand dollars. You will find me dropping a thousand here and a thousand there, all through the rest of this story; I can figure up seventy-five of them, all spent on causes—and often spent before I got them.

The commissioners obtained evidence of practically everything charged in *The Jungle*, except that I was not able to produce legal proof of men falling into vats and being rendered into pure leaf lard. There had been several cases, but always the packers had seen to it that the widows were returned to the old country. Even so, there was enough to make a terrific story if it got into the newspapers. It had been Roosevelt's idea to reform the meat-inspection service, and put the bill through Congress without any fuss. But the packers themselves prevented this by their intrigues against the bill. Finally, with the tacit consent of the commission, I put the New York *Times* onto the track of Mr. and Mrs. Bloor, and the whole story was on the front page next day. So Roosevelt had to publish the report, and the truth was out.

I moved up to New York and opened an amateur publicity office in a couple of hotel rooms, with two secretaries working overtime. I gave interviews and wrote statements for the press until I was dizzy, and when I lay down to sleep at two o'clock in the morning, my brain would go on working. It seemed to me that the walls of the mighty fortress of greed were on the point of cracking; it needed only one push, and then another, and another. In the end, of course, they stood without a dent; the packers had lost a few millions, but they quickly made that up by advertising that their products were now guaranteed pure by the new government inspection service. A year later Mrs. Bloor went back, this time with a reporter from the New York *Herald*. They worked in the yards for many weeks and found all the old forms of graft untouched. Their story was killed by James Gordon Bennett, as I have related in *The Brass Check*.

In the midst of all this there came to my aid a powerful voice from abroad. The Honorable Winston Churchill, thirty-two years of age, was a member of Parliament and a journalist with a large following. He published a highly favorable two-part article on *The Jungle* in an English weekly with the odd name of P.T.O.— the initials, with the first two reversed, of the editor and publisher, T. P. O'Connor. (Because O'Connor was an Irishman, you say it "Tay Pay O.") I quote the first and last paragraphs of Churchill's articles, which ran to more than five thousand words.

When I promised to write a few notes on this book for the first number of Mr. O'Connor's new paper, I had an object—I hoped to make it better known. In the weeks that have passed that object has disappeared. The book has become famous. It has arrested the eye of a warm-hearted autocrat; it has agitated the machinery of a State department; and having passed out of the sedate columns of the reviewer into leading articles and "latest intelligence," has disturbed in the Old World and the New the digestions, and perhaps the consciences, of mankind. . . .

It is possible that this remarkable book may come to be considered a factor in far-reaching events. The indignation of millions of Americans has been aroused. That is a fire which has more than once burnt with a consuming flame. There are in the Great Republic in plentiful abundance all the moral forces necessary to such a purging process. The issue between Capital and Labour is far more cleanly cut to-day in the United States than in other communities or in any other age. It may be that in the next few years we shall be furnished with Transatlantic answers to many of the outstanding questions of economics and sociology upon whose verge British political parties stand in perplexity and hesitation. And that is, after all, an additional reason why English readers should not shrink from the malodorous recesses of Mr. Upton Sinclair's "Jungle."

In the fifty-six years that have passed, Winston Churchill has become one of the most famous names in history. I am pleased by what he said about my book. But I cannot help wondering if he would have written as freely if I had dealt with the horrors I saw in the slums of London seven years later, or of conditions in the mining towns of which I learned from John Burns, who represented the miners in Parliament.

I had now "arrived." The New York *Evening World* said, "Not since Byron awoke one morning to find himself famous has there been such an example of world-wide celebrity won in a day by a book as has come to Upton Sinclair." *The Jungle* was being translated into seventeen languages, and was a best seller in America and in Great Britain for six months. Photographers and reporters journeyed to Princeton, hired hacks and drove out to my farm, and the neighbors who had been selling me rusty machinery and broken-down mules suddenly discovered that I had "put them on the map." Editors wrote or telegraphed commissions, and I was free to name my own price. My friend William Dinwiddie, sent by the New York *Evening World* to get me to write something for them, first got me to sign a contract at five cents a word, and then said: "Sinclair, the first thing you need to learn is to charge." So I doubled my price to the next paper—and might just as well have quadrupled it.

How did it feel to be famous? I can truly say that it meant little to me personally. I got few thrills. I had suffered too much and overstrained whatever it is that experiences thrills. If I had been thinking about my own desires, I would have taken the first train to the wilderness and never come back to crowds and excitement; but I stayed, because "fame" meant that newspapers and magazines would print a little bit of what I wanted to say, and by this means the wage slaves in the giant industries of America would hear some words in their own interest.

XIII

In the third chapter of this narrative, I mentioned one "Jonesy," a city inspector of fruit who was the hero of "Jerome's lemon story." I promised to tell another tale about this Jonesy, and here is the place where it comes in.

I had made some examination of the slaughterhouses in and near New York, and stated in a newspaper article that conditions in them were no better than in Chicago. This aroused the head of New York City's health department, who denounced me as a "muckraker," and challenged me to produce evidence of my charges. The reporters came on the run; and to one of them, who happened to be a friend, I made a laughing remark: "It happens that I know a certain inspector of fruit, a subordinate of the health commissioner's, who manages to keep a motorcar and a mistress on a salary of a couple of thousand dollars a year. How do you suppose he does it?" The remark was not meant for publication, but it appeared in next morning's paper.

At about ten o'clock that evening, a reporter called me on the phone at my hotel. Said he: "I want to give you a tip. The commissioner is taking you up on that statement about the city fruit inspector who keeps a motorcar and a mistress. He knows who the man is, of course, but he figures that you won't dare to name him because he's a friend of your family's. So he is writing you a letter, calling you a liar, and daring you to name the man. He has sent the letter to the papers, and I have a copy of it."

There was a pretty kettle of fish! As matters actually stood, I had no legal evidence of Jonesy's graft—only the word of Jonesy's family, the frequent family jokes. It would have been awkward to name him—but still more awkward to let a Tammany politician, who happened to be Jonesy's boon companion, destroy the work I was trying to do.

I called Jonesy's home on the phone, and his wife—whom I

knew—told me he was out. I tried his club, and several other places, and finally called the wife again. I explained that it was a matter of the greatest urgency and that I could think of only one thing to do: would she please give me the telephone number of her husband's mistress?

So at last I got my victim on the phone and spoke as follows: "The commissioner has sent to the newspapers a letter challenging me to name the fruit inspector who is a grafter. I didn't intend for this to be published, and I'm sorry it happened, but I refuse to let the commissioner brand me before the public and destroy my work. If his challenge is published, I shall name you."

The tones of Jonesy were what in my dime novels I had been wont to describe as "icy." Said he: "I suppose you know there are libel laws in this country." Said I: "That's my lookout. I think I know where I can get the proofs if I have to. I'm telling you in advance so that you may stop the commissioner. Call him at once and tell him that if that letter is published, I shall name you, and name him as your friend and crony."

What happened after that I never heard. I only know that the letter did not appear in any New York newspaper.

XIV

Roosevelt sent me a message by Frank Doubleday: "Tell Sinclair to go home and let me run the country for a while." But I did not accept the advice. I broached to *Everybody's Magazine* the idea of a series of articles exposing the conditions under which children worked in industry. They thought this a promising idea and agreed to use a series of eight or ten such articles. Alas, being new at the game, I omitted to tie them down with a contract. I took Mrs. Bloor and went down to the glass factories of southern New Jersey in the heat of midsummer, and I spent my time watching little boys of ten and twelve working all night in front of red-hot furnaces. One story I remember: an exhausted child staggering home at daybreak, falling asleep on the railroad tracks, and being run over by a train. I lived in the homes of these workers, I talked with them and ate their food, and in later years I put some of them into my books. Always the critics say—

without knowing anything about it—that I "idealize" these characters. I can only say that if there is any finer type in the world than the humble workingman who has adopted brotherhood as his religion and sacrifices his time and money and often his job for his faith, I have not encountered it.

I went next to the Allegheny steel country, the real headquarters of American wage slavery in those old days. What I wrote horrified *Everybody's*, and they changed their minds about my series. So I had to rest, whether I would or not.

It was high time; for one of my teeth became ulcerated, and I had a painful time, wandering about the city of Trenton on a Sunday, trying in vain to find a dentist. After two nights of suffering I went to a dentist in New York, had the tooth drilled through, and for the first time in my life nearly fainted. Afterward I staggered out, went into the first hotel I saw, and got a room and fell on the bed. It happened to be a fashionable hotel, and this gave great glee to the newspapers, which were pleased to discover signs of leisure-class follies in a socialist.

There is a saying among women that every child costs a tooth. With me it read: every crusade costs a tooth. Of course this wasn't necessary; it was not merely overwork but ignorance of diet, the eating of white flour and sugar and other denatured foods, and pouring into the drain pipe the mineral salts from fruits and vegetables. But I did not know anything about all this; my college education, which had left out socialism, and money, and love and marriage, had also left out diet and health. Instead of such things, I had learned what a *hapax legomenon* is, and a *pons asinorum*, and a *glyptocrinus decadactylus*—and was proud of possessing such wisdom.

Another activity during that summer and autumn of 1906 was an effort to turn *The Jungle* into a play. Arch and Edgar Selwyn were playbrokers at this time and suggested Edgar's wife as my collaborator. Margaret Mayo afterward wrote a highly successful farce-comedy, *Baby Mine*, but *The Jungle* was something different, and I fear we made a poor dramatization. We had a manager who was thinking of nothing but making money, and some slapstick comedians put in dubious jokes that I, in my innocence, did not recognize until I heard the gallery tittering. The play came to New York for six weeks and lost money—or so I was told by the managers, with whom I had invested three thousand dollars.

Concerning *The Jungle* I wrote that "I aimed at the public's heart, and by accident I hit it in the stomach." I helped to clean up the yards and improve the country's meat supply. Now the workers have strong unions and, I hope, are able to look out for themselves.

6

Utopia

I

THREE winters spent upon an isolated farm had taken all the romance out of the back-to-nature life for a young author. The roads were either deep with mud or cut with the tracks of sleighs, so that the only place to walk was up and down in a field, along the lee side of a fence. Also, four summers had taken the romance out of agriculture as an avocation for a literary man. The cows broke into the pear orchard and stuffed themselves and died; the farmhands who were brought from the city got drunk and sold the farm produce for their own benefit. "Away from nature!" became the slogan.

The young writer, who had been close to starving for the past five or six years, now had thirty thousand dollars, in hand or on the way, and it was burning holes in all his pockets. He had never heard of such a thing as investing money, and would have considered it an immoral thing to contemplate. He wanted to spend his money for the uplifting of mankind, and it was characteristic of him that even in the matter of getting a home he tried to combine it with the solving of a social problem, and with setting an example to his fellowmen.

As a socialist Thyrsis of course believed in co-operation, and regarded the home as the most ancient relic of individualism. Every person had, or sought to have, his own home, and there lived his own little selfish life, wasteful, extravagant, and reactionary. It did not occur to Thyrsis that not every home might be as unhappy as his own; if anyone had suggested the idea to him, he would have said that no one should be happy in a backward way of life, and he would have tried to make them unhappy by his arguments.

His plan was to establish a co-operative home, to demonstrate its practicability and the wider opportunities it would bring. There was nothing revolutionary about this idea; it was being practiced in many parts of America—only people were doing it without realizing what they were doing. Up in the Adirondacks were clubs where people owned the land in common and built individual cabins, or rented them from the club, and had a common kitchen and dining room; they ran their affairs, as all clubs are run, on a basis of equality and democracy. Only the members didn't use these radical phrases and made no stir in the newspapers.

Thyrsis, for his part, had to make a stir in the papers, else how could he find anybody to go into a club with him? He knew but few persons, and only two or three of these were ready for the experiment. How could others be found? It might have been done by personal inquiry, but that would have been a slow process; when Thyrsis wanted anything, he wanted it at once. Being a modern, up-to-date American, he shared the idea that the way to get something was to advertise. So he wrote an article for the *Independent* (June 4, 1906), outlining his plan for a "home colony" and asking to hear from all persons who were interested. Soon afterward he rented a hall, and announced in the newspapers that a series of discussion and organization meetings would be held.

II

Many persons came; some of them serious, some of them cranks, some of them both. The process of sorting them out was a difficult one, and was not accomplished without heart-burning. There is no standard test for cranks, and there were some with whom Thyrsis could have got along well enough but who were not acceptable to the rest of the group. There were some who quietly withdrew—having perhaps decided that Thyrsis was a crank.

Anyhow, the new organization came into being. A company was formed, stock issued, and the world was invited to invest. In this, as in other reform schemes, Thyrsis found that it was possible to raise about one tenth of the money, and necessary to put up the rest out of one's own pocket. A search was begun for a suitable building; and real-estate agents came swarming, and broken-down hotels were inspected and found unsuitable. Finally there came better tidings; some members of the committee had stumbled upon a place with the poetical name of Helicon Hall.

It stood on the heights behind the Palisades, overlooking Englewood, New Jersey, just above the Fort Lee ferry from New York. It had been a boys' school, and there was a beautiful building planned by an aesthetic-minded pedagogue who hoped that boys could be civilized by living in dignified surroundings and by wearing dress suits every evening for dinner. There were two or three acres of land, and the price was $36,000, all but ten thousand on mortgage. Thyrsis, of course, knew nothing about real estate, what it was worth, or how one bought it; but the sellers were willing to teach him, and in a day or two the deal was made.

So, from November 1, 1906, to March 7, 1907 (at three o'clock in the morning, to be precise), the young dreamer of Utopia lived according to his dreams. Not exactly, of course, for nothing ever turns out as one plans. There were troubles, as in all human affairs. There was a time when the co-operative mothers of the Helicon Home Colony charged that the head of the children's department had permitted the toothbrushes to get mixed up; there was a time when the manager in charge of supplies forgot the lemons, and it was necessary for Thyrsis to drive to town and get some in a hurry. But in what home can a writer escape such problems?

III

The most obvious success was with the children. There were fourteen in the colony, and the care they received proved not merely the economics of co-operation but also its morals; our children lived a social life and learned to respect the rights of

others, which does not always happen in an individual home.
There was a good-sized theater in the building, and this became
the children's separate world. They did most of their own work
and enjoyed it; they had their meals in a dining room of their
own, with chairs and tables that fitted them, food that agreed
with them and was served at proper hours. Now and then they
assembled in a children's parliament and discussed their problems, deciding what was right and what wrong for them. There
was a story of a three-year-old popping up with "All in favor say
aye!"

There was one full-time employee in this children's department, the rest of the time being contributed by the various mothers at an agreed rate of compensation. Many persons had
laughed at the idea that mothers could co-operate in the care of
children, but as a matter of fact our mothers did it without serious trouble. There were different ideas; we had some believers
in "libertarian" education, but when it came to the actual working out of theories from day to day, we found that everyone
wanted the children to have no more freedom than was consistent with the happiness and peace of others.

I recall only one parent who was permanently dissatisfied.
This was a completely respectable and antisocialistic lady from
Tennessee, the wife of a surgeon, who was sure that her darlings
had to have hot bread every day. So she exercised her right to
take them to an individual home. She also took her husband, and
the husband, in departing, tried to take our dining room maid as
his mistress, but without success. This, needless to say, occasioned sarcastic remarks among our colonists as to socialist versus capitalist "free love."

It was generally taken for granted among the newspapermen
of New York that the purpose for which I had started this colony
was to have plenty of mistresses handy. They wrote us up on that
basis—not in plain words, for that would have been libel—but
by innuendo easily understood. So it was with our socialist colony as with the old-time New England colonies—there were
Indians hiding in the bushes, seeking to pierce us with sharp
arrows of wit. Reporters came in disguise, and went off and wrote
false reports; others came as guests, and went off and ridiculed
us because we had beans for lunch.

I do not know of any assemblage of forty adult persons where a higher standard of sexual morals prevailed than at Helicon Hall. Our colonists were for the most part young literary couples who had one or two children and did not know how to fit them into the literary life; in short, they were persons with the same problem as myself. Professor W. P. Montague, of Columbia, had two boys, and his wife was studying to be a doctor of medicine. Maybe, as the old-fashioned moralists argued, she ought to have stayed at home and taken care of her children; but the fact was that she wouldn't, and found it better to leave the children in care of her fellow colonists than with an ignorant servant.

But it was hard on Montague when persons came as guests, attended our Saturday-night dances, and went off and described him dancing with the dining-room girl. It happened that this was a perfectly respectable girl from Ireland who had been a servant at our farm for a year or two; she was quiet and friendly and liked by everybody. Since none of the colony workers were treated as social inferiors, Minnie danced with everybody else and had a good time; but it didn't look so harmless in the New York gutter press, and when Montague went to Barnard to lecture the young ladies on philosophy, he was conscious of stern watchfulness on the part of the lady dean of that exclusive institution. Minnie, now many times a grandmother, lives in Berkeley, California, and writes to me now and then.

Montague came to us innocent of social theories and even of knowledge. But presently he found himself backed up against our four-sided fireplace, assailed by ferocious bands of socialists, anarchists, syndicalists, and single taxers. We could not discover that we made any dent in his armor; but presently came rumors that in the Faculty Club of Columbia, where he ate his lunch, he was being denounced as a "red" and finding himself backed up against the wall by ferocious bands of Republicans, Democrats, and Goo-goos (members of the Good Government League). Of course the palest pink in Helicon Hall would have seemed flaming red in Columbia.

IV

There were Professor William Noyes, of Teacher's College, and his wife, Anna, who afterward conducted a private school. There were Edwin Björkman, critic, and translator of Strindberg, and his wife, Frances Maule, a suffrage worker. There were Alice MacGowan and Grace MacGowan Cooke, novelists. There was Michael Williams, a young writer, who became editor of the *Commonweal*, the Catholic weekly. I count a total of a dozen colonists who were, or afterward became, well-known writers.

There came to tend our furnaces and do odd jobs two runaway students from Yale named Sinclair Lewis and Allan Updegraff; we educated them a lot better than Yale would have done you may be sure. "Hal" and "Up" both wrote novels, but Up was better known as a poet. Hal became the most successful novelist of his time. When he came to Helicon Hall, he was very young, eager, bursting with energy and hope. He later married my secretary at the colony, Edith Summers, a golden-haired and shrewdly observant young person whose gentle voice and unassuming ways gave us no idea of her talent. She eventually became Mrs. Edith Summers Kelly, author of the novel *Weeds*; and after the tumult and shouting have died, this is one of the books that students will be told to read as they are now told to read *Evangeline* and *Hermonn and Dorothea*. I corresponded with Hal Lewis to the end of his life, but I saw him only once in his later years—sad ones, ruined by alcohol.

We had a rule among our busy workers that nobody came to any other person's room except by invitation; so everyone had all the privacy he wanted. When your work was done, and you felt like conversation, there was always someone by the four-sided fireplace or in the billiard room. In the evenings there were visitors, interesting persons from many parts of the world. John Dewey came occasionally, as the guest of Montague. Dewey was perhaps the best-known professor at Columbia in my time, and he exercised tremendous influence upon American education, though his ideas have often been misunderstood to the point of caricature. Personally, he was a most kind and gracious gentleman. Another visitor was William James, who was perhaps the greatest of American psychologists and certainly the ablest of that time. He was open-minded and eager in the investigation of psychic phenomena, and I remember vividly sitting with him at a table watching an old lady with a ouija board. I had never seen this object before, but the old lady held it for a good and trusted friend. She held a pencil or pen in her hand and went into a sort of trance, while some force moved her hand over the board from letter to letter. In Dewey's presence her hand moved and spelled out the sentence "Providence child has been carried to bed." We took this sentence to our faithful member named Randall, who owned a small business in Providence, Rhode Island, and had a wife and child there. He went to the telephone immediately and was told that the child was ill with pneumonia.

Another guest I remember was John Coryell, an anarchist, who earned his living in the strangest way—he was Bertha M. Clay, author of the sentimental romances that all servant maids then read, and may still read. Sadakichi Hartmann, the art critic came and was one of the few who were not welcome; he sent a postcard in advance, "Sadakichi Hartmann will arrive at six P.M." and there he was, on time, but unfortunately drunk, and his companion, Jo Davidson, the sculptor, was not able to control him. When the time came for departure, he didn't want to depart but insisted on sleeping on the cushioned seats in front of our fireplace. We had to turn him out in the snow, and the next day he wrote a letter to the papers about us, and there was quite a furor.

During these months at the colony I wrote *The Industrial Republic*, a prophecy of socialism in America. I have never reprinted this book because of the embarrassing fact that I had prophesied Hearst as a radical president of the United States. He really looked like a radical then, and I was too naïve to imagine the depths of his cynicism and depravity. When in the effort to become governor of New York he made a deal with Tom Murphy, the boss of Tammany, whom he had previously cartooned in prison stripes, I wanted to tear up my book. Incidentally, I had prophesied socialism in America in the year 1913; instead we had two world wars and the Russian Revolution—and I fear that more world wars and more revolutions stand between us and a truly democratic and free society. The world is even worse than I was able to realize; but I still cling to my faith in the methods of democracy.

V

The Helicon Home Colony came to an end abruptly, at three o'clock on a Sunday morning. The first warning I received of its doom was a sound as of enormous hammers smashing in the doors of the building. I was told afterward that it was superheated air in plastered walls, blowing out sections of the walls. I smelled smoke and leaped out of bed.

My sleeping room was in a tower, and I had to go down a ladder to my study below; there was a door, leading to a balcony, which ran all the way around the inside of a court, three stories above the ground. I opened the door, and a mass of black smoke hit me—it seemed really solid, with heavy black flakes of soot. I shouted fire, and ran out on the balcony and up to the front, where there was a studio made over into sleeping quarters for eight or ten of our colony workers. I ran through this place, shouting to awaken the sleepers, but got no response; apparently everybody had got out—without stopping to warn me! The next day, I learned that one man had been left behind—a stranger who had been working for us as a carpenter; he had been drinking the night before and paid for it with his life.

When I came back from the studio to the balcony, the flames were sweeping over it in a furious blast. If I live to be a hundred, I shall never forget that sensation; it was like a demon hand sweeping over me—it took all the hair from one side of my head and a part of my nightshirt. I escaped by crouching against the wall, stooping low, and running fast. Fortunately the stairs were not yet in flames, so I got down into the central court, which was full of broken glass and burning brands, not very kind to my bare feet. I ran to the children's quarters and made sure they were all out; then I ran outside, and tried to stop the fall of two ladies who had to jump from windows of the second story. Harder to stop the fall of human bodies than I would have imagined!

We stood in the snow and watched our beautiful utopia flame and roar, until it crashed in and died away to a dull glow. Then we went into the homes of our fashionable neighbors, who hadn't known quite what to make of us in our success but were kind to us in our failure. They fitted us out with their old clothes—for hardly anyone had saved a stitch. I had the soles of my feet cleaned out by a surgeon, and was driven to New York to stay with my friends, the Wilshires, for a couple of days. An odd sensation, to realize that you do not own even a comb or a toothbrush—only half a nightshirt! Some manuscripts were in the hands of publishers, so I was more fortunate than others of my friends.

Two or three days later I was driven back to Englewood to attend, on crutches, the sessions of the coroner's jury. So I learned what the outside world had been thinking about our little utopia. They not only thought it a "free-love nest," but the village horse doctor on the jury thought we had set fire to it ourselves, to get the insurance. Also, and worse yet, they thought we had arranged our affairs in such a way that we could beat the local tradesmen out of the money we owed them. It was a matter for suspicion that we had got ropes, to serve as fire escapes, shortly before the fire; they blamed us for this, and at the same time they blamed us because we had made insufficient preparations—although they had made no objection to the same conditions existing in a boys' school for many years. In short, we did not please them in any way, and everything they said or insinuated went on to the front pages of the yellow newspapers of the country.

Every dollar of the debts of the Helicon Home Colony was paid as soon as my feet got well, which was in a week or two. Likewise all those persons who were left destitute were aided. I bought myself new clothes and looked around to decide what to do next. If I had had the cash on hand, I would have started the rebuilding of Helicon Hall at once; but we had long negotiations with insurance companies before us, and in the meantime I wanted to write another novel. I took my family to Point Pleasant, New Jersey, rented a little cottage, and went back to the single-family mode of life. It was like leaving modern civilization and returning to the dark ages. I felt that way about it for a long time, and made efforts at another colony in spite of a constantly increasing load of handicaps.

VI

We employed an honest lawyer and made an honest statement of the value of our property. The insurance companies then cut it by one third and told us that if we were not satisfied, we could sue, which would mean waiting several years for our money. I learned too late that this is their regular practice; to meet it, you double the value of your claim. You must have a *dis*honest lawyer.

We could not afford to wait, for many persons were in distress, and I was unwilling to see them suffer even though they had no legal claim upon me or the company. We settled the insurance matters and sold the land for what it would bring; after the mortgage holders were paid, I had a few thousand dollars left from the thirty thousand *The Jungle* had earned. My friend Wilshire was in trouble with his gold mine just then, and as he had loaned me money several times, I now loaned some to him; that is, I invested it in his mine, and he wrote me a letter agreeing to return it on demand. But his affairs thereafter were in such shape that I never did demand it. And that was the end of my first "fortune."

However, I did not worry; I was going to make another at once—so I thought. Having portrayed the workers of America and how they lived, I was now going to the opposite end of the scale—to portray the rich, and how they lived. There had come many invitations to meet these rich; there were intelligent ones among them, like "Robbie" Collier, Mrs. "Clarrie" Mackay, and Mrs. "Ollie" Belmont; there were some who were moved by curiosity and boredom, and some even with a touch of mischief. The suggestion that I should write *The Metropolis* came first from a lady whose social position was impregnable; she offered me help and kept her promise, and all I had to do in return was to promise never to mention her name.

I refer to this matter because, in the storm of denouncement that greeted *The Metropolis*, the critics declared that it was less easy to find out about "society" than about the stockyards. But the truth is that I had not the slightest trouble in going among New York's smart set at this time. Many authors had stepped up the golden ladder, and my feet were on it. My radical talk didn't hurt me seriously; it was a novelty, and the rich—especially the young ones—object to nothing but boredom. Also there are some of the rich who have social consciences, and are aware that they have not earned what they are consuming. You will meet a number of such persons in the course of this story.

The reason why *The Metropolis* is a poor book is not that I did not have the material but that I had too much. Also, I wrote it in a hurry, under most unhappy circumstances. The career of a novelist is enough for one man, and founding colonies and starting reform organizations and conducting political campaigns had better be left to persons of tougher fiber. It took me thirty years to learn that lesson thoroughly; meantime I lost the reading public that *The Jungle* had brought me.

I did my writing about smart society in a shack that had walls full of bedbugs. I made cyanogen gas, a procedure almost as perilous to me as to the bugs. I worked through the spring and summer, and when the New York *Herald* offered me my own price to make another investigation of the stockyards, I resisted the temptation and turned the job over to Ella Reeve Bloor. The result was a great story "killed," as I have previously mentioned.

I was having my customary indigestion and headaches, the symptoms of overwork that I would not heed. Also, in the middle of the summer, Corydon suffered an attack of appendicitis that very nearly ended the troubles between us. A country doctor diagnosed her illness as menstrual, and when, after several days, I called a surgeon from New York, he said it was too late to operate. So there lay my youthful dream of happiness, at the gates of death for a week or two. I had then an experience that taught me something about the powers of suggestion, which are so close to magical; I saved Corydon's life, and she knew it, and told me so afterward.

I literally pulled her back through those gates of death. She was lying in a semistupor, completely worn out by pain that had lasted more than a week; she had given up, when she heard my voice. I did not pray for her—I did not know how to do that—

but I prayed *to* her, urging her to live, to keep holding on; and
that voice came to her as something commanding, stirring new
energies in her soul. When modern psychotherapists state
that we die because we want to die, I understand exactly what
they mean.

Corydon was taken to the Battle Creek Sanitarium to recuperate, accompanied by her mother and an elderly surgeon
friend. How easy it is for human beings to accumulate needs!
Four summers back Corydon and Thyrsis had lived with their
baby in a tent in the woods and had thought themselves fortunate to have an income of thirty dollars a month assured them;
but now Corydon needed sixty dollars a week to stay at a leisure-
class health resort, and half as much for her mother's board, and
a private physician into the bargain. The child had to have a
nursemaid, and a relative to take care of him in the Point Pleasant cottage; while the father had to flee to the Adirondack
wilderness to get away from the worry and strain of it all! Such
is success in America, the land of unlimited possibilities.

VII

To one of the most remote lakes in the Adirondacks I portaged
a canoe, found a deserted open camp, stowed my duffle, and set
to work to finish *The Metropolis*. My only companions were blue-
jays and squirrels by day, and a large stout porcupine by night.
I lived on rice, beans, prunes, bacon, and fish—no fresh fruit or
vegetables—and wondered why I suffered from constipation and
headaches. I was beginning to grope around in the field of diet
reform and decided that beans, rice, and prunes were not the
solution to my problem!

To the lake came a party of young people, a dozen of them,
evidently wealthy, with guides and expensive paraphernalia.
They had a campfire down the shore and sang songs at night,
and the lonely writer would paddle by and listen in the darkness,
and think about his sick wife, who also sang. Then one afternoon
several of the young men came calling; one of the party had got
into a bee's nest and was badly stung. Did I have anything to
help? They invited me to join them at their campfire. I did so,

and met a jolly party, and chatted with several pretty girls. One of them, sitting next to me, asked what I did, and I admitted that I wrote books. That always interests people; they think it is romantic to be a writer—not knowing about the constipation and the headaches.

I always tried to avoid giving my name, because I had come to know all possible things that people would say to the author of *The Jungle*. But these people asked the name, and when I gave it, I became aware of some kind of situation; there was laughing and teasing, and finally I learned what I had blundered into—the girl at my side was a daughter of the head of J. Ogden Armour's legal staff!

We fought our battles over again, and I learned, either from this girl or from someone in the party, that Mr. Armour had been shut up with his lawyers for the greater part of three days and nights, insisting upon having me indicted for criminal libel, and hearing the lawyers argue that he could not "stand the gaff." I suppose that must have happened in more than one office since I started my attack on American big business. The secret is this: you must be sure that the criminal has committed worse crimes than the ones you reveal. I have been sued for libel only once in my life, and that was when an eccentric lady pacifist named Rosika Schwimmer took exception to my playful account of her activities; this incident I will tell about later.

The Metropolis was done, and the manuscript shipped off to Doubleday, Page and Company. Meantime I went over into Keene Valley and paid a visit of a week or two to Prestonia Mann Martin, wealthy utopian, who for many years had turned her Adirondack camp into a place of summer discussions—incidentally making her guests practice co-operation in kitchen and laundry. Her husband was an Englishman, one of the founders of the Fabian Society. When I met them, they were both on the way toward reaction; Prestonia was writing a book to prove that we had made no progress in civilization since the Greeks.

Both she and her husband became good, old-fashioned tories; the last time I met him was just before World War I, and we got into an argument over the results to be expected from woman suffrage. "Anyhow," said he, "it's not worth bothering about, because neither you nor I will ever see it." I offered to wager that he would see it in New York State within ten years, and John Martin thought that was the funniest idea he had ever heard. But he saw it in about five years.

At this camp was James Graham Stokes, then president of our Intercollegiate Socialist Society. World War I came, and he began drilling a regiment in one of the New York armories, preparing to kill any of his former comrades who might attempt an uprising. His wife, Rose Pastor, at one time a cigar worker in New York, had tried with gentle patience to fit herself into the leisure-class world. When the war came, she gave it up and became a Bolshevik, and her marriage went to wreck.

Also at the camp was Harriet Stanton Blatch, suffragist, and Edward E. Slosson, whom I had met as one of the editors of the *Independent*. He became a well-known popularizer of science and started the Science Service. We had much to argue about.

VIII

Doubleday, Page and Company declined *The Metropolis*. They said it wasn't a novel at all and urged me to take a year to rewrite it. I had further sessions with Walter H. Page and observed that amiable gentleman again believing what other people told him. The bright young men in his business office were certain that New York society wasn't as bad as I portrayed it; when I told them what I knew, I observed a certain chill. I attributed it to the fact that their magazine, the *World's Work*, was edited and published in New York, and its revenue came from the advertising of banks and trust companies that I exposed in my book. It was one thing to tell about graft in Chicago, a thousand miles away, and another to tell about it in one's own financial family. Doubleday, Page had made a fortune out of *The Jungle* and used it to become rich and reactionary. I bade them a sad farewell.

The *American Magazine*, then owned and run by reformers, read the manuscript and agreed to feature parts of it as a serial. I left the book manuscript with Moffat, Yard and Company, and went out to join my wife at the Battle Creek Sanitarium. I stayed there for three weeks or so and tried their cure. I listened to Dr. W. K. Kellogg set forth the horrors of a carnivorous diet, and as a result I tried vegetarianism for the next three years. I felt better while I was taking treatments at the "San," so I thought I had solved my problem of how to overwork with impunity.

Michael Williams, one of our Helicon Hall colonists, now out of a job, came out to the "San" to write it up for some magazine, and he and I saw a great deal of each other at this time. Mike was a Canadian of Welsh descent who had had a hard life, beginning as porter in a big department store, and contracting both tuberculosis and the drink habit. He had cured himself of the latter and was trying to cure himself of the former by Battle Creek methods. Incidentally, he was an ardent socialist, and a writer of no little talent; I thought he would serve the cause and was glad to help him. We devised a brilliant scheme for a vacation and a book combined; we would get a couple of covered wagons and take our two families across the continent on a tour, living the outdoor life and seeing America close at hand. A "literary caravan" we would call it, "Utopia on the Trek." The *American Magazine* fell violently for the idea and promised to make a serial out of our adventures.

But that was a summer plan, and it was now November. We decided to take our families to Bermuda for the winter, and there write a book about our health experiences. Moffat, Yard were very keen about *The Metropolis* and its prospects; I, remembering the advice of my newspaper friend that I should "learn to charge," extracted an advance of five thousand dollars on royalty account. So the path of life stretched rosy before Mike and me. We would have a two-family utopia amid the coral reefs of Bermuda; I would pay the bills, and Mike would repay me out of his future earnings. "It will be a debt of honor," he said, proudly, and repeated it every now and then.

We went to New York, the first stage of our journey, just in the wake of a great event. Wall Street had been in the midst of a frenzy of speculation, but "somebody asked for a dollar," and there was the panic of 1907. I have told in *The Brass Check* the peculiar circumstances under which I came to get the inside story of this event. Suffice it here to say that I had the biggest news story ever sprung in America, certainly at any rate in my time. I was able not merely to charge but to prove that the elder Morgan had deliberately brought on that panic as a means of putting the independent trust companies out of business. The *American Magazine* editors wanted the story and signed a contract for it, but in the course of two or three weeks they got cold feet and begged me to let them off, which I did.

IX

Behold Mike and me in a fairyland set with jewels, in the remotest part of the Bermudas, far from the maddening crowd of tourists. The house is white limestone, set upon a rocky shore overlooking a little bay, behind which the sun sets every evening. Out on a point in front of us stands an old ruin of a mansion, deserted, but having a marvelous mahogany staircase inside so that we can assure the children it was once the home of a pirate chief. The water is brilliant azure, shading to emerald in the shallows; over it flies the man-o'-war bird, snow-white, with a long white feather trailing like a pennant. The sun shines nearly always. There is a tennis court, surrounded by a towering hedge of oleanders in perpetual blossom. There are roses, and a garden in which a colored boy raises our vegetarian vegetables. The house is wide and rambling, with enough verandas so that both halves of this two-family utopia can sleep outdoors.

Mike is working on his autobiographical novel—it was published under the title of *The High Romance*. I am writing *The Millennium*, a play, and we write our health book together—I won't tell you the name of that, having changed my ideas to some extent. I have brought a secretary with me, and Mike has half her time, the salary being added to that "debt of honor" of which we keep a careful account. There is a Swedish governess who takes care of my son and the two Williams children impartially; also Mike's wife has an elderly friend to assist her. There is Minnie to do the housework for all of us—Irish Minnie who danced with the college professors at Helicon Hall. Our utopia contains a total of twelve persons, and my five thousand dollars exactly suffices for the fares and the six months' expenses.

Then *The Metropolis* is published and sells eighteen thousand copies, barely justifying the advance; so there are no more royalties, and I am stuck in a strange land, without money to get the family home! Mike volunteers to go to New York and find a publisher for the health book, our common property; he will get an advance and remit me half. He goes, and places the book with the Frederick A. Stokes Company; he collects an advance and puts it all into his own pocket—and I am stuck again!

I borrow money from somebody and come home. Mike and his family go to California, and he takes up his old drinking habits and gets another hemorrhage; the next thing I hear, he has sought refuge in the religion of his childhood. He told all that in *The High Romance*; Saint Theresa came to him, and proved her presence by making him smell a rose as he was walking down the street. That was a miracle, and by it Mike knew he was one of the elect. That any hypnotist could have worked a hundred such miracles—could have caused Mike to smell all the flowers that bloom in the spring, tra-la-la—that had nothing to do with the case.

X

So ended my attempt to raise up and train a new socialist writer. It is an ugly story to tell on a man—the only mean story in this amiable book, you may note. Nothing could hire me to tell it—except for a later development, which you have still to hear.

Ten years passed, and Mike was all but forgotten. I started a magazine and in it published *The Profits of Religion*, dealing with the churches by the method of economic interpretation. Mike, being now a champion of Roman Catholicism—his publishers were introducing him as "one of the most influential lay Catholics of America"—sallied forth to destroy my book. That was all right; I grant every man a right to disagree with me—the more the merrier, it is all advertising. But Mike found his task difficult, for the reason that my statements in *The Profits of Religion* are derived from Catholic sources—devotional works, papal decrees, pastoral letters, editorials in church papers—everything with the holy imprimatur, *nihil obstat*.

So, instead of attacking the book, Mike chose to attack its author. He accused me of being a writer for gain, and headed his review with the title "A Prophet for Profit"! I have heard that charge many times, but it did seem to me there was one person in

America who was barred from making it—and that was my old friend and pensioner, Michael Williams. Since he made it, and published it, it seems to me that the consequences are upon his own head. And that is why I tell the story here. I never saw him again, and never will—for he is dead.

XI

The satiric comedy *The Millennium*, which I had in my suitcase, made a hit with the leading stage impresario of that time, David Belasco. He agreed to produce it on an elaborate scale in the course of the coming winter. He was fighting the "trust" and had two big theaters in New York, where he put on two big productions every year. But after keeping me waiting for a year, and making many promises, he suddenly made peace with his enemies; he then wanted small shows that could be put on the road, so he threw over *The Millennium* and produced *The Easiest Way*, by Eugene Walter, which had only eight characters. So vanished one more of those dreams that haunted me for ten years or more—earning a lot of money and starting another colony.

I got an advance from a publisher, and took my family to Lake Placid in the Adirondacks, rented a little camp, and settled down to the task of weaving into a novel my story of how the elder J. P. Morgan had caused the panic of the previous autumn. *The Moneychangers* was the title. It was to be a sequel to *The Metropolis*. I was planning a trilogy to replace the one that had died with *Manassas*. My plans were still grandiloquent.

When I was gathering material for the book, Lincoln Steffens introduced me to two of my most valuable informants: Samuel Untermyer and James B. Dill. Dill had been the most highly paid corporation lawyer in Wall Street, and had recently been appointed Chief Justice of the Supreme Court in New Jersey. So he was free and could talk; and the stories he told me you wouldn't believe. I will tell only one. He took me out to his home in New Jersey to spend the night, and when we came into the dining room, he said, "Make a note of this table and that window with the double French doors, I will tell you a story about them."

This was the story. There was a lawsuit involving several million dollars, and Dill came into possession of a document that would decide the case. He wanted to make certain that this document could not be stolen. He was certain that a desperate attempt would be made to steal it, so he put two or three typists to work all day, and they made a total of twenty-one copies; he sent his office employees out to rent safe-deposit boxes in various banks in and around Wall Street. He sealed the copies in twenty-one envelopes, and one of them contained the original document. He alone knew which bank got the original. He took one of the copies out to his home that evening and said to his butler, "The house will be burglarized tonight, but don't pay any attention to it. I want them to get what they come for."

He set the sealed envelope on the corner of his dining-room table; sure enough, the next morning he found that the French windows had been opened and the envelope taken.

When he reached his office in the morning he called up the firm of the other side in the case and said, "By now you know what we have; our terms are two and one-half million dollars"—or whatever the amount was—and they settled on that basis. I used the story in one of my novels and, of course, everybody said it was preposterous; but it was told to me by James B. Dill.

The Moneychangers did not come up to my hopes, mainly because of the unhappy situation in which I was living. My health made continuous application impossible. I beg the reader's pardon for referring to these matters, but they are a factor in the lives of authors. I am fortunate in being able to promise a happy ending to the story—I mean that I have solved the problem of doing my work and keeping entirely well. I will tell the secrets in due course—so read on!

For recreation I climbed the mountains, played tennis, and swam in the lake. I slept in an open camp under the pine trees and conformed to all the health laws I knew. We had Irish Minnie with us, and also a woman friend of Corydon's, a young student whom she had met at Battle Creek, very religious, a Seventh-day Adventist. Corydon was trying various kinds of mental healing, and I was hoping for anything to keep her happy while I went on solving the problems of the world.

For myself I had good company that summer; a man whom I had met two years before, at the time *The Jungle* was published. An Englishman twelve years older than I, he had come to

New York and sent me a letter of introduction from Lady War-
wick, our socialist countess. H. G. Wells was the traveler's name,
and I had been obliged to tell him that I had never heard of him.
He sent me his *Modern Utopia,* inscribing it charmingly, "To the
most hopeful of Socialists, from the next most hopeful." I found
it a peerless book, and wrote him a letter that he accepted as "a
coronation." I had him with me that summer in the Adirondacks
by the magic of eight or ten of his early romances, the most delightful books ever made for a vacation. *Thirty Strange Stories*
was one title, and I smiled patronizingly, saying that a man could
write one strange story or maybe half a dozen—but thirty! Yet
there they were, and every one was strange, and I knew that I
had met a great imaginative talent. Since then I have heard the
highbrow critics belittle H. G. Wells; but I know that with Bernard Shaw he constituted a major period in British letters.

The Moneychangers was published, and my revelations made a
sensation for a week or two. The book sold about as well as *The
Metropolis,* so I was ahead again—just long enough to write another book. But it seemed as if my writing days were at an end;
I was close to a nervous breakdown, and had to get away from a
most unhappy domestic situation and take a complete rest. Corydon wanted to have an apartment of her own in New York, and
solve her own problems. My friend Gaylord Wilshire now had a
gold mine, high up in the eastern slope of the Sierra mountains;
also George Sterling, the poet, was begging me to come to Carmel and visit him; so I set out over the pathway of the argonauts
in a Pullman car.

7

Wandering

It was my first trip across the American continent; and I stopped first in Chicago, to visit the stockyards after four years. There was a big hall, and a cheering crowd—the socialists having got up a mass meeting. In front of the platform sat a row of newspaper reporters, and I told them of the New York *Herald's* investigation of conditions in the presumably reformed yards. The investigation had been made a year before, and nothing about it had appeared in the Chicago press. A good story, was it not?—I asked the reporters at the press tables, and they nodded and grinned. Yes, it was a good story; but not a line about either story or meeting appeared in any capitalist paper of Chicago next morning.

The next stop was Lawrence, Kansas, to meet the coming poet of America, as I considered him. He was a student at the state university, and I had discovered his verses in the magazines and had written to him; he had sent me batches of manuscript and poured out his heart. A real genius this time—one who wrote all day and all night, in a frenzy, just as I had done. He had gone to the university a bare-footed tramp, and now slept in an attic over a stable, wrapped in a horse blanket. He was so eager to meet me that he borrowed money, bought a railroad ticket, and boarded my train a couple of hours before it reached Lawrence; we had lunch in the diner—the first time in the poet's life, he assured me.

When we got to town, I was escorted about and shown off, and begged to talk to a group of the students and even a professor or two. It was a great hour for the "box-car poet"; I being an object of curiosity, and he being host and impresario. We went for a walk in the country, and he told me his troubles. He had never had anything to do with a woman, but here the girls flirted with him—none of them in earnest, because he was a poor devil, and poetry was a joke compared with money. Now and then he was on the verge of suicide, but he'd be damned if he'd give them that much satisfaction. Such was Harry Kemp in his far-off day of glory; I was thirty, and he twenty-five, and the future was veiled to us both. So eager was he for my time that he borrowed more money and rode another two or three hours on the train with me.

Denver, and Ben Lindsey, judge of the Children's Court; a new idea and a new man. I watched the court at work and sat in at a session of the Judge's friends in the YMCA. He was in the midst of one of those political fights that came every year or two, until finally the "beast" got him. He revealed to me that he had written an account of his war with the organized corruption of Denver. I took the manustcript, read it on the train, and telegraphed *Everybody's Magazine* about it; they sent out Harvey O'Higgins and so got another big serial, "The Beast and the Jungle."

The book was afterward published by Doubleday, Page and Company, and withheld from circulation—the same trick they played upon Theodore Dreiser, but never upon Upton Sinclair, you can wager! If there should ever be another crop of muckrakers in America, here is a tip they will find useful: put a clause into your contract to the effect that if at any time the publisher fails to keep the book in print and sell it to all who care to buy it, the author may have the right to the use of the plates, and print and sell an edition of his own. That makes it impossible for the publisher to "sell you out"; the would-be buyer, when he reads that clause, will realize that he is buying nothing.

A day in Ogden, Utah, with a horseback ride up the canyon; and one in Reno, Nevada, walking for hours among the irrigation ditches in the hills, and then, in the evening, watching the gambling—it was a wide-open town even in those days. A curious two-faced little city, with a fine state university, and a fashionable tone set by several hundred temporary residents from the East, seeking divorces. The Catholics and the fundamentalists of America have combined to force men and women to live together when they want to part; so here were the lawyers and the politicians of this little mining town getting rich, by selling deliverance to the lucky few who could afford a few weeks' holiday. Corydon was talking of joining this divorce colony, so I looked the ground over with personal interest.

II

A day's journey on the little railroad that runs behind the Sierras, through the red deserts of Nevada. In the little town of Bishop, California, the Wilshires met me, and we rode saddle horses up to the mine, eighteen miles in the mountains. A high valley with Bishop Creek running through, towering peaks all about, and cold, clear lakes—the first snows of the year were falling, and trout had quit biting, but I climbed the peaks, and ate large meals in the dining room with the miners. The camp was run on a basis of comradeship, with high wages and plenty of socialist propaganda; we slept in a rough shack and in the evenings discussed the mine with the superintendent and foreman and assayer. These were old-time mining men, and they were of one accord that here was the greatest gold mine in America. You could see the vein, all the way up the mountainside, and down in the workings you could knock pieces off the face and bring them up and have them assayed before your eyes.

But alas, there were complications in quartz mining beyond my understanding. Most of the vein was low-grade, and it could only be made to pay if worked on a large scale. Wilshire did not have the capital to work it in that way, and in the effort to get the money, he bled himself and thousands of readers of his magazine who had been brought to share his rosy hopes. I stood by him through that long ordeal, and know that he did everything —except to turn the mine over to some of the big capitalist groups that sought to buy it and freeze out the old stockholders. Ultimately, of course, the big fellows got it.

Socialists ought not to fool with money-making schemes in

capitalist society. I have heard that said a hundred times, and I
guess it is right; but there is something to be noted on the other
side. The socialists of America have never been able to maintain
an organ of propaganda upon a national scale; the country is too
big, and the amount of capital required is beyond their resources.
The *Appeal to Reason* was a gift to them from a real-estate spec-
ulator with a conscience, old J. A. Wayland—may the managers
of the next world be pitiful to him. (His enemies set a trap for
him, baited with a woman; he crossed a state line in her company, which is a prison offense in our pious America, and when
he got caught, he blew out his brains.) *Wilshire's Magazine* was
a gift from a billboard advertising man with a sense of humor.
So long as his money lasted, we all took his gift with thanks; if
his gold-mining gamble had succeeded, we would all have made
money, and had a still bigger magazine, and everything would
have been lovely. But my old friend Gay died in a hospital in
New York, all crippled up with arthritis. I missed his fertile mind
and his sly, quiet smile.

III

On to Carmel, a town that boasts more scenery to the square
mile than any other place I know; a broad beach, bordered by
deep pine woods and flanked by rocky headlands; at one side a
valley, with farms, a river running through it and mountains beyond. Fifty years ago the place was owned by a real-estate spec-
ulator of the Bohemian Club type; that is to say, a person with
the art bug who would donate a lot to any celebrity who would
confer the honor of his presence. Needless to say, George Sterling, the Bohemian Club's poet laureate, had his pick of lots, and
a bungalow on a little knoll by the edge of a wood remote from
traffic and "boosting."

George was at this time forty, but showed no signs of age. He
was tall and spare, built like an Indian, with a face whose resemblance to Dante had often been noted. When he was with the
roistering San Francisco crew he drank, but when he was alone
he lived the life of an athlete in training; he cut wood, hunted,
walked miles in the mountains, and swam miles in the sea. A
charming companion, tenderhearted as a child, bitter only

against cruelty and greed; incidentally a fastidious poet, aloof and dedicated.

His friend Arnold Genthe gave me the use of a cottage, and there I lived alone for two or three months of winter, in peace and happiness unknown to me for a long time. I had been reading the literature of the health cranks, and had resolved upon a drastic experiment; I would try the raw-food diet, for which so much was promised. I ate two meals a day, of nuts, fruits, olives, and salad vegetables; the only cooked food being two or three shredded-wheat biscuits or some graham crackers. The diet agreed with me marvelously, and for the entire period I never had an ache or pain. So I was triumphant, entirely overlooking the fact that I was doing none of the nerve-destroying labor of creative writing. I was reading, walking, riding horseback, playing tennis, meeting with George and other friends; if I had done that all my life I might never have had an ache or pain.

In Oakland was the Ruskin Club, an organization of socialist intellectuals, who wanted to give a dinner and hear me make a speech. George and I went up to town, and George stopped in the Bohemian Club, and stood in front of the bar with his boon companions; I stood with him and drank a glass of orange juice, as is my custom. Then we set out for the ferry, George talking rapidly, and I listening in a strange state of uncertainty. I couldn't understand what George was saying, and I couldn't understand why. It wasn't until we got to Oakland that I realized what was the matter; my California Dante was drunk. When we got to the dinner, someone who knew him better than I took him off and walked him around the block and fed him bromo-seltzers; the socialist poem he had written for the occasion had to be read by someone else.

I went back to Carmel alone, feeling most sorrowful. I was used to my poor old father getting drunk, and some of my other men relatives, but this was the first time I had ever seen a great mind distorted by alcohol. I wrote George a note, telling him that I was leaving Carmel because I could not be happy there. George came running over to my place at once, and with tears in his eyes pleaded forgiveness. He swore that he had had only two drinks; it was because he had taken them on an empty stomach. But I knew that sort of drinker's talk, and it did not move me. Then he swore that if I would stay, he would not touch another drop while I was in California. That promise I accepted, and he kept it religiously. Many a time I have thought my best service to letters might have been to stay right there the rest of my days!

That Ruskin Club dinner was a quaint affair. Frederick Irons Bamford, assistant librarian of the Oakland Public Library, had organized the group and ran it with a firm hand. I think he must have been a Sunday-school superintendent before he came into the socialist movement; he shepherded the guests in just that way, telling us exactly what to do at each stage, and we did it with good-natured laughter. There were songs printed for us to sing, each at the proper moment; there were speeches, poems, announcements in due order. "And now," said our shepherd, "we will have ten minutes of humor. Will some one kindly tell a funny story?"

A man arose, and said, "I will tell you a story that nobody can understand." The two or three hundred banqueters pricked up their ears, of course, and prepared to meet the challenge. I have tried out this "story that nobody can understand" on several audiences, and it always "goes," so I give you a chance at it. Said the man at the banquet: "I wish to explain that this is not one of those silly jokes where you look for a point but there is no point. This is a really funny story, and you would laugh heartily if you could understand it, but you can't. I will ask you, if you are able to see the point, to raise your hand, so that we can count you." He told the story, and a silence followed; all the people craned their necks to see if there was any hand up. Finally several did go up, I forget how many. We all had a good laugh, and it was really ten minutes of humor. The story was as follows:

Mrs. Jones goes into her grocer's and asks for a dozen boxes of matches. Says the grocer: "Why, Mrs. Jones, you had a dozen boxes of matches yesterday!" Says Mrs. Jones: "Oh, yes, but you see, my husband is deaf and dumb, and he talks in his sleep."

Raise your hand!

IV

Tramping the hills and forests and beaches of Carmel, riding horseback over the Seventeen Mile Drive, there began to haunt my brain a vision of a blank-verse tragedy; the story of a child of the coal mines who is adopted by rich people and educated, and finally becomes a leader of social revolution. The first act was set in the depths of the mine, a meeting between the rich child and the poor one, a fairy scene haunted by the weird creatures who people the mine boy's fancy as he sits all day in the darkness, opening and closing a door to let the muleteams through. The second act was to happen in utopia, being the young hero's vision of a world in which he played the part of a spiritual leader. The third act was in the drawing room of a Fifth Avenue mansion, whose windows looked out upon the street where the hero leads the mob to his own death.

The verses of this to me marvelous drama would come rolling through my mind like breakers on the Carmel strand; but in the interest of health I put off writing them, and soon they were gone forever. I suppose it is natural that I should think of this drama as the greatest thing I ever had hold of—on the principle that the biggest fish is the one that got away. Curiously enough, the main feature of the second act was to be an invention whereby the hero was to be heard by the whole world at once. Such was my concept of utopia; and now, more than half a century later, the people of my home town sit all evening and listen to the wonders of the Hair-Again Hair Restorer, and the bargains in Two-Pants Suits at Toots, the Friendly Tailor; every now and then there is a "hookup" of a hundred or two stations, whereby all America sees and hears the batterings of two bruisers; or maybe the Jazz-Boy Babies, singing; or maybe the "message" of some politician seeking office.

My rest came to an end, because a stock company in San Francisco proposed to put on my dramatization of *Prince Hagen,* and the newspaper reporters came and wrote up my "squirrel diet" and my views on love and marriage, duly "pepped up"—though I don't think we had that phrase yet. I thought there ought to be a socialist drama in America, and I sat down and wrote three little one-act plays, which required only three actors and no scenery at all. Feeling so serene in my new-found health, I resolved to organize a company and show how it could be done. I made a deal with the head of a school of acting to train my company, going halves with him on the profits; and for two or three

weeks I had all the comrades of the Bay cities distributing hand-
bills, announcing our world-beating dramatic sensation.

One of these plays was *The Second-Story Man.* It was later
published in one of the Haldeman-Julius Little Blue Books;
every now and then some actor would write and tell me it was
"a wonder," and would I let him do it in vaudeville? He would
get it ready, and then the masters of the circuit would say nix on
that radical stuff. The second play was a conversation between
"John D" and "the Author" on a California beach, having to do
with socialism and John D's part in bringing it nearer—by
putting all the little fellows out of business. The third play, *The
Indignant Subscriber,* told about a newspaper reader who lures
the editor of his morning newspaper out in a boat in the middle
of a lake, makes him listen for the first time in his life, and ends
by dumping him overboard and swimming away. In production,
the "boat" was made by two chairs tied at opposite ends of a
board; the editor sat in one chair, and the indignant subscriber
in the other, and the oars were two brooms. The comedy of row-
ing out into the middle of an imaginary lake while admiring the
imaginary scenery was enjoyed by the audience, and when the
editor was dumped overboard, a thousand social rebels whooped
with delight.

The plays were given seven or eight times, and the theaters
were packed; the enterprise was, dramatically speaking, a success; but, alas, I had failed to investigate the economics of my
problem. The company had engagements for only two or three
nights in the week, whereas the actors were getting full salaries.
Distances were great, and the railway fares ate up the receipts.
If I had started this undertaking in the Middle West where the
company could have traveled short distances on trolley cars, and
if I had done the booking in advance so as to have a full sched-
ule, there is no doubt that we could have made a success. As it
was, the adventure cost me a couple of thousand dollars.

V

Letters from Corydon informed me that our son had celebrated his winter in New York by being laid up with tonsillitis;
also, Corydon herself had not found joy in freedom, and was

ready to live according to her husband's ideas for a while. David Belasco was promising to produce *The Millennium* in the following autumn, so I telegraphed Corydon to join me in Miami, Florida. I took a train to Galveston, Texas, and from there a steamer to Key West.

My squirrel diet was difficult to obtain on trains, and perhaps I had overworked on my dramatic enterprise—anyhow, on the steamer across the Gulf of Mexico I developed a fever. I remember a hot night when it was impossible to sleep in the stateroom. I went out on deck and tossed all night in a steamer chair, having for company a member of the fashionable set of one of our big cities—I forget which, but they are all alike. A man somewhat older than I, he had just broken with his wife and was traveling in order to get away from her; he had a bottle in his pocket, and the contents of others inside him, enough to unlimber his tongue.

He told me about his quarrel with his wife, every word that she had said and every word that he had said; he told me every crime she had ever committed, and some of his own; he poured out the grief of being rich and fashionable in a big American city; he told me about the fornications and adulteries of his friends— in short, I contemplated a social delirium with my own half-delirious mind. The element of phantasmagoria that you find in some of my books may be derived from that night's experience, in which fragments of fashionable horror wavered and jiggled before my mind, vanished and flashed back again, loomed colossal and exploded in star showers, like human faces, locomotives, airplanes, and skyscrapers in a futurist moving-picture film.

At Key West I was taken off the steamer and deposited in a private hospital, where I stayed for a week; then, somewhat tottery, I met Corydon and our son at Miami, and we found ourselves a little cottage in a remote settlement down the coast, Coconut Grove. It was April, and hot, and I basked in the sunshine; I took long walks over a white shell road that ran straight west into a flaming sunset, with a forest of tall pine trees on each side. Incidentally, I slapped innumerable deer flies on my face and hands and legs. I do not know if they call them that in Florida—maybe they don't admit their existence; but deer fly was the name in the Adirondacks and Canada for those little flat devils, having half-black and half-white wings, and stinging you like a needle.

We went swimming in a wide, shallow bay, warm as a bathtub; you had to walk half a mile to get to deep water, and on the soft bottom lay great round black creatures that scooted away when you came near. I wondered if it would be possible to catch one, but fortunately I did not try, for they were the disagreeable sting rays or stingarees. (Having become a loyal Californian, it gives me pleasure to tell about the entomological and piscatorial perils of Florida.) The owner of a big beach-front place tried to sell it to us for five or six thousand dollars, and we talked of buying it for quite a while. I suppose that during the postwar boom the owner sold it for a million or two, and it is now the site of a twenty-story office building full of tenants.

In Coconut Grove, as in Carmel, there was a "literary colony." I met some of them, but remember only one: a figure who walked the white shell roads with me, tall, athletic, brown, and handsome as a Greek statue—Witter Bynner, the poet. Corydon, smiling, remarked, "Bynner is a winner." That compliment, from a qualified expert, I pass on to him, in exchange for the many fine letters he has written to me about my books. He is eighty now—and I am eighty-four.

I think it was during these six weeks that I wrote *The Machine*, the play that forms a sequel to *The Moneychangers*. An odd sort of trilogy—two novels and a play! But it was the best I could do at the time. I saw a vision of myself as a prosperous Broadway dramatist, a licensed court jester of capitalism. But the vision proved to be a mirage.

VI

For the summer of 1909 I rented a cottage on the shore at Cutchogue, near the far end of Long Island; beautiful blue water in front of us, and tall shade trees in the rear. I was carrying on with my raw-food diet, and my family also was giving it a trial. To aid and abet us we had a household assistant and secretary who was an even less usual person than myself. Dave Howatt was his name. He was fair-haired and rosy-cheeked and he nourished his great frame upon two handfuls of pecans or al-

monds, two dishes of soaked raw prunes, and a definite number
of ripe bananas every day—it may have been a dozen or two, I
cannot remember. This blond Anglo-Saxon monkey romped with
my son, oversaw his upbringing, typed my letters, and washed
and soaked the family prunes. A youth after my own heart—
vegetarian, teetotaler, nonsmoker, pacifist, philosophical anarchist, conscientious objector to capitalism, dreamer, and practitioner of brotherhood—Dave had been at Bernarr Macfadden's
Physical Culture City, and had known Harry Kemp since boyhood. Now Dave is living in Cuba, and at last report was loving
it.

But alas for idealistic theories and hopes—the diet that had
served me so marvelously on the shore of the Pacific played the
dickens with me on the shore of the Atlantic. The difference was
that now I was doing creative writing, putting a continuous
strain upon brain and nerves, and apparently not having the
energy to digest raw food. Dave Howatt, in his role of guide and
mentor, thought my indigestion was due to my evil habit of including cooked breadstuff in the diet, so for a while I changed
from a squirrel to a monkey. Then he thought I ate too much, so
I cut the quantity in half, which reduced the size of the balloon
inside me; but it left me hungry all the time, so that when I
played tennis, I would have to stop in the middle and come home
and get a prune.

Under these trying conditions I wrote another book, endeavoring to put the socialist argument into a simple story, which
could carry it to minds that otherwise would never get .it. I
aimed at the elemental and naïve, something like *The Vicar of
Wakefield* or *Pilgrim's Progress*. The border line between the
naïve and the banal is difficult to draw, and so authorities differ
about *Samuel the Seeker*. Some of my friends called it a
wretched thing, and the public agreed with them. But on the
other hand, Frederik van Eeden, great novelist and poet in his
own language, wrote me a letter of rapture about *Samuel*, considering it my best. Robert Whitaker, pacifist clergyman who
committed the crime of taking the sixth commandment literally
and spent several months in a Los Angeles jail during World
War I, came on a copy of the book at that time, and he
also judged it a success. The publishing firm of Bauza in Barce-

lona, desiring to issue an edition of my novels, saw fit to lead off with *Samuel Busca la Verdad*. So perhaps in the days of the co-operative commonwealth the pedagogues will discover a new classic, suitable for required reading in high schools!

VII

By the end of the summer my health was too bad to tell about, and I had got my thoughts centered on a new remedy, a fast cure. I had been reading *Physical Culture* magazine, and I wrote to Bernarr Macfadden, who was then running a rival institution to the Battle Creek Sanitarium. He invited me to bring my family and let him have a try at my problem.

Athlete, showman, lecturer, editor, publisher, and health experimenter—I could make B. M. the subject of an entertaining essay, but there is not space here. To the high-brows he was a symbol of the vulgarity and cheapness of America. And it won't help for me to defend him, because I may also be on that list. I merely state what Macfadden did for me—which was to teach me, free, gratis, and for nothing, more about the true principles of keeping well and fit for my work than all the orthodox and ordained physicians who charged me many thousands of dollars for not doing it. Believe me, I went to the best there were in every field, and while some of them had mercy on a writer, others treated me like a millionaire. I number many doctors among my friends, and the better they know me, the more freely they admit the unsatisfactory state of their work. Leo Buerger, a college mate who became a leading specialist in New York, summed the situation up when I mentioned the osteopaths, and remarked that they sometimes made cures. Said my eminent friend: "They cure without diagnosing, and we diagnose without curing."

My visit to Macfadden took place in 1909—back in the dark ages, before the words "preventive medicine" had ever been joined together. I had asked doctor after doctor to advise me how to keep well, and not one of them seemed to know what I was talking about; they attempted to cure my sickness, and then they sent me away to go on doing the things that had brought the sickness on. The secrets of natural living were the property of a little group of adventurous persons known as "health cranks";

and it has been my pleasure to watch the leading ideas of these
"cranks" being rediscovered one by one by medical authority,
and so made known to the newspapers and the public. It was not
Dr. Auguste Rollier of Switzerland who invented the sun cure;
no indeed, the semilunatics of Physical Culture City were going
around in breechclouts, men and women getting themselves
arrested by rural constables, before ever the word *Nacktkultur*
was imported.

The same thing is true of vitamins, and of the evils of denatured foods, and the importance of bulk in the diet—we knew all
that before Sir Arbuthnot Lane ever addressed a medical congress. As to fasting, I stood the ridicule of my medical friends for
twenty years, and then in the files of the *Journal of Metabolism*
I found the records of laboratory tests upon humans as well as
dogs proving that the effect of a prolonged fast is a permanent
increase in the metabolic rate—which is the same thing as re-
juvenation, and exactly what we "health cranks" have claimed.

VIII

At Macfadden's institution in Battle Creek were perhaps a
hundred patients, faithfully trying out these eccentricities. They
fasted for periods long or short; I met one man who went to fifty-
five days, attempting a cure for locomotor ataxia—he was beginning to walk, in spite of all the dogmas. Later I met a man who
weighed nearly three hundred pounds, who fasted over ninety
days, which is the record so far as I know. This was before suffragettes and hunger strikes, and it was the accepted idea that a
human being would starve to death in three or four days.

After the fast we went on a thing known as a milk diet, absorb-
ing a glass of fresh milk every half hour, and sometimes every
twenty minutes, until we had got up to eight quarts a day. The
fasters sat around, pale and feeble in the sunshine, while the
milk drinkers swarmed at the dairy counter, and bloomed and
expanded and swapped anecdotes—it was a laboratory of ideas,
and if you had a new one, no matter how queer, you could find
somebody who had tried it, or was ready to try it forthwith.
When you came off the milk diet, you might try some odd combination such as sour milk and dates. In the big dining room you

were served every sort of vegetarian food. There were dark rumors that the smell of beefsteaks was coming from Macfadden's private quarters. I asked him about it, and he told me he was trying another experiment.

I met him again when he was sixty; still of the same experimental disposition, he wanted to know what I had learned in twenty years. He then owned a string of magazines and newspapers, I don't know how many, and I would not venture to imagine how many millions they brought him every year, or the number of his blooming daughters—I think there were eight in a photograph on his desk. He still had his muscles of steel, and would take two packs of cards, put them together, and tear them in half before your eyes. He had been a weakling in his youth, had built up that powerful frame, and would put on bathing trunks and come out on a platform and show it to people; very vulgar, of course—no "ethical" medico would dream of doing it. But it caused great numbers of men and women to take an interest in their health, and it set up resistance to those forces of modern civilization that were destroying the body.

My personal experience has been told in a book, *The Fasting Cure*, so I will merely say that I took a fast of ten or twelve days, and then a milk diet of three weeks, and achieved a sense of marvelous well-being. My wife did the same, and we became enthusiasts. I took a second fast of a week or so, and when I left the place I had gained about twenty pounds, which I needed. But I did not keep it, for as soon as I left the sanitarium I started on a new book.

IX

Harry Kemp came to see us in Battle Creek; he was on his way back to college after a summer's work on the oreboats of the Great Lakes. He had a suitcase full of manuscripts, an extra shirt, and a heart bubbling over with literary excitements. He met Corydon for the first time and found her interesting; Corydon, for her part, was maternal to a forlorn poet.

The fates wove their webs, unguessed by any of us. It happened that at the Kellogg Institution, just down the street, there was a young lady from the Delta district of Mississippi—she had accompanied her mother and a cousin who were undergoing treatment. Mary Craig Kimbrough was the name of the young lady, and one day when she was walking with her cousin, the cousin remarked, "Would you like to meet an author? There goes Upton Sinclair with his wife." Said the haughty young lady, "I don't think he would interest me." But the cousin insisted. "Oh, come on, I met him the other day, and he's not so bad as he looks."

She called the author from across the street, introductions were exchanged, and we chatted for a few minutes. The propagandist author, being just then excited over fasting, and having no manners or tact or taste or anything of that sort, informed an extremely proud young Southern belle that she was far too thin and needed a fast and a milk diet. It was the first time in her whole life that a man had ever addressed her except in the Southern mode of compliment.

I invited her and her cousin and her mother to come over to Macfadden's that evening, where I was to give an outdoor talk. They came; and I was in a jovial mood, telling of the many queer ideas I had tried out in my search for health. The audience rocked with laughter when I set forth how, in the course of my first fast, I had walked down a hill from the institution, and then didn't have the strength to climb back. No one was more amused than the young lady from Mississippi.

I remember that we took a walk up and down the piazza of the sanitarium, while this most sedate and dignified person— then twenty-five years of age—confided to me that she was troubled in her mind and would appreciate my advice. She revealed that she found herself unable to believe what she had been taught about the Bible. This was a source of great distress to her, and she didn't know quite what to think of herself. Had I ever heard of anyone similarly afflicted?

I assured her with all necessary gravity that I had heard of such cases. This was a relief to her; there were few such persons in the Mississippi Delta, she declared. The development of her faithlessness had become a cause of anguish to her family; her mother would assemble the ladies of all the local churches in her drawing room, and the straying sheep would be called in and compelled to kneel down with them, while one after another they petitioned the Deity for the salvation of her soul. When they had finished, they would look at the fair sheep, and wait to see the effect of their labors; but so far the medicine had failed.

I assured the young lady that I also was a lost soul, and gave her the names of an assortment of books—T. H. Huxley's essays among them. She duly bought them all, and when she got home, a brother discovered her reading them and took them away to his law office, where only men could be corrupted by them. He himself soon gave up his faith.

X

For the winter I took my family to the single-tax colony at Fairhope, Alabama, on Mobile Bay. Since I could not have a colony of my own, I would try other people's. Here were two or three hundred assorted reformers who had organized their affairs according to the gospel of Henry George. They were trying to eke out a living from poor soil and felt certain they were setting an example to the rest of the world. The climate permitted the outdoor life, and we found a cottage for rent on the bay front, remote from the village. Dave Howatt was with us again; having meantime found himself a raw-food wife, he lived apart from us and came to his secretarial job daily.

I was overworking again; and when my recalcitrant stomach made too much trouble, I would fast for a day, three days, a week. I was trying the raw-food diet, and failing as before. I was now a full-fledged physical culturist, following a Spartan regime. In front of our house ran a long pier, out to the deep water of the bay. Often the boards of this pier were covered with frost, very stimulating to the bare feet, and whipped by icy winds, stimulating to the skin; each morning I made a swim in this bay a part of my law. (Says Zarathustra: "Canst thou hang thy will above thee as thy law?")

Among the assorted philosophies expressed at Fairhope was the cult of Dr. J. H. Salisbury, meat-diet advocate; I read his book. Let me remind you again that this was before the days of any real knowledge about diet. Salisbury was one of the first regular M.D.'s who tried experiments upon himself and other human beings in order to find out how particular foods actually affect the human body. He assembled a "poison squad" of healthy young men, fed them on various diets, and studied the ailments they developed. By such methods he thought to prove that excess of carbohydrates was the cause of tuberculosis in humans. His guess was wrong—yet not so far wrong as it seems. It is my belief that denatured forms of starch and sugar are the predisposing cause of the disease; people live on white flour, sugar, and lard, and when the body has become weakened, the inroads of bacteria begin.

Anyhow, Salisbury would put his "poison squad" on a diet of lean beef, chopped and lightly cooked, and cure them of their symptoms in a week or two. He had a phrase by which he described the great health error, "making a yeastpot of your stomach." That was what I had been doing, and now, to the horror of my friend Dave Howatt, I decided to try the Salisbury system. I remember my emotions, walking up and down in front of the local butchershop and getting up the courage to enter. To my relief, I caused no sensation. Apparently the butcher took it quite as a matter of course that a man should purchase a pound of sirloin.

I had been a practicing vegetarian—and what was worse, a preaching one—for a matter of three years; and now I was a backslider. My socialist comrade, Eugene Wood, happened to be spending the winter in Fairhope, and he wrote a jolly piece about "America's leading raw-food advocate who happens just now to be living upon a diet of stewed beefsteaks." I had to bow my head, and add crow to my menu!

XI

In Fairhope was the Organic School, invention of Mrs. Marietta Johnson. It was then a rudimentary affair, conducted in a couple of shacks, but has since become famous. Our son, David, then eight years old, attended it. His education had been scattery, with his parents moving from a winter resort to a summer resort. But he had always had the world's best literature and had done the rest for himself. Fairhope he found to his taste; we had a back porch and a front porch to our isolated cottage, and he would spread his quilt and pillow on the former, and I would spread mine on the latter, and sleep outdoors every night on the floor. I asked if he minded the hard surface, and his reply belongs to the days of the world's divine simplicity. "Oh, Papa, it's fine! I like to wake up in the night and look at the moon, and listen to the owl, and pee!"

I tried the experiment of fasting while doing my writing; a marvelous idea, to have no stomach at all to interfere with creative activity! A comedy sprang full-grown into my brain, and I wrote it in two days and a half of continuous work—a three-act play, *The Naturewoman*. I record the feat as a warning to my fellow writers—don't try it! During a fast you are living on your nerves and cannot stand the strain of creative labor. When I finished, I could hardly digest a spoonful of orange juice.

The Naturewoman, like all my plays, had no success. It was published in the volume *Plays of Protest* a couple of years later, and had no sale. Not long thereafter, the students of Smith College, studying drama under Samuel Eliot, gave it in New York, and these emancipated young ladies found it charmingly quaint and old-fashioned; they played it in a vein of gentle farce. Apparently it never occurred to them that the author might have meant it that way. I have frequently observed that an advocate of new ideas is not permitted to have a sense of humor; that is apparently reserved for persons who have no ideas at all. For fifty-six years I have been ridiculed for a passage in *The Jungle* that deals with the moral claims of dying hogs—which passage was intended as hilarious farce. The New York *Evening Post* described it as "nauseous hogwash"—and refused to publish my letter of explanation.

Corydon had come to Fairhope for a while, and then had gone north on affairs of her own; it had been arranged that she was to get a divorce from me. I thought that a novel about modern marriage that would show the possibility of a couple's agreeing to part, and still remaining friends, would be interesting and useful. So I began *Love's Pilgrimage*. In the spring I came north and took up my residence in another single-tax colony, at Arden, Delaware, founded and run by Frank Stephens, a sculptor of Philadelphia; a charming place about twenty miles from the big city, with many little cabins and bungalows scattered on the edge of the woods. Frank was glad to have me come—and alas, a year and a half later he was gladder to have me go! For the Philadelphia newspapers found me out, and thereafter, in the stories that appeared about Arden, socialism was more prominent than single tax, and I was more prominent than the founder. This was my misfortune, not my fault. I wanted nothing but to be let alone to write my book; but fate and the editors ruled otherwise.

XII

No bungalows being available in the neighborhood, I rented a lot and installed my ménage in three tents. Corydon, feeling it not yet convenient to get her divorce, occupied one of the tents, on a strictly literary basis. David had a troop of children to run all over the place with, and I had the book in which I was absorbed. It was turning out to be longer than I had planned—something that has frequently happened to my books.

The single-tax utopia, technically known as an enclave, had been founded by a group of men who were sick of grime, greed and strain, and fled away to a legend, the Forest of Arden. Some had a few dollars and could stay all the time; others went up to Philadelphia and were slaves in the daytime. On Saturday evenings they built a campfire in the woodland theater, sang songs and recited, and now and then gave *Robin Hood* or *Midsummer Night's Dream*. On holidays they would get up a fancy pageant and have a dance in the barn at night, and people would actually have a good time without getting drunk. One anarchist shoemaker was the only person who drank in Arden, so far as I know, and he has long since gone the way of drinkers.

Personally, I was never much for dressing up—not after the age of six or so, when my mother had made me into a baker boy for a fancy-dress party. But I liked to watch others more free of care; also I liked to have young fellows who would play tennis in the afternoon. There was Donald Stephens, son of the founder, and there were several of the children of Ella Reeve Bloor. One of these, Hal Ware, was my opponent in the finals of a tournament—I won't say how it turned out! After the Russian Revolution, Hal went over in charge of the first American tractor unit; an odd turn of fate, that a dweller in the Forest of Arden should carry to the peasants of the steppes the dream of a utopia based upon machinery! Don Stephens served a year in the Delaware state prison as a conscientious objector to war, and then helped at the New York end of the Russian tractor work.

Also there was a young professor of the University of Pennsylvania, Scott Nearing—a mild liberal, impatient with my socialistic theories. Did my arguments make any impression on him? I never knew; but in time he was kicked out of the university, and then he traveled beyond me and called me the only revolutionist left in the Socialist Party. There was Will Price, Philadelphia architect, genial and burly—what a glorious Friar Tuck he made, or was it the Sheriff of Nottingham? No doubt he sits now in the single taxers' heaven, engaged in a spirited debate with William Morris over the former's theory of a railroad right of way owned by the public, with anybody allowed to run trains over it! Will had the misfortune to fall in love with my secretary, and she was in love with someone else; a mixup that will happen even in utopia.

Corydon was corresponding with the young lady from the Delta district of Mississippi—who had fasted and gained weight, according to my recommendation. She had then gone home, taking along a "health crank" nurse; she had put her father and mother on a fast, and to the horror of the local doctors, had cured them of "incurable" diseases. Now this Miss Kimbrough was writing a book, *The Daughter of the Confederacy*, dealing with the tragic life story of Winnie Davis, daughter of Jefferson Davis. Winnie had fallen in love with a Yankee, had been forced to renounce him, and had died of a broken heart. Judge Kimbrough had been Mrs. Davis' lawyer, and had fallen heir to the Davis heirlooms and letters. Mary Craig Kimbrough now wrote that she needed someone to advise her about the book, and Corydon went south to help her with the manuscript.

David and I put a stove in our tents and prepared to hibernate in the snowbound Forest of Arden. How many of the so-called necessities men can dispense with when they have to! Once I was asked to drive a youthful guest a couple of miles in a car, so that he might find a barber and get a shave; I was too polite to tell this guest that I had never been shaved by a barber in my life. In New York I heard another young man of delicate rearing

Priscilla Harden Sinclair

Upton Beall Sinclair, Sr.

Upton Sinclair at the age of eight

Upton Sinclair at twenty-seven, when he was writing The Jungle

THE CHICAGO SCANDALS.

The Novel which is Making History.

By WINSTON SPENCER CHURCHILL, M.P.

In the first of these articles Mr. Winston Churchill gives a graphic word-picture of scenes and characters of "The Jungle," Upton Sinclair's novel which is making history. It was this book that stirred President Roosevelt into insisting on an inquiry into the charges brought by its author against the packing industry of Chicago, charges which have given rise to the now notorious "Meat Scandals," and have been endorsed by the report of the American Government's Commissioners published the other day after Mr. Churchill's article was written.

When I promised to write a few notes on this book for the first number of Mr. O'Connor's new paper, I had an object—I hoped to make it better known. In the weeks that have passed that object has disappeared. The book as become famous. It has arrested the eye of a warm-hearted autocrat; it has agitated the machinery of a State department; and having passed out of the sedate columns of the reviewer into leading articles and "latest intelligence," has disturbed in the Old World and the New the digestions, and perhaps the consciences, of mankind.

I.

Mr. Upton Sinclair is one of that active band of reformers, comprising some men of very great gifts and

by society to Mr. Upton Sinclair. And there is, unhappily, good reason to believe—scarcely, indeed, any reason to doubt—that a very considerable body of undeniable and easily ascertainable truth sustains the charges that are made. Mr. Upton Sinclair has done for the "packers" what Mr. Henry Lloyd did some years ago in "Wealth against Commonwealth" for the Standard Oil Trust. The mood and the motive of both books are the same; but in one respect Mr. Sinclair's method has a great advantage over his forerunner. "Wealth against Commonwealth" was a laborious compilation. "The Jungle" is a human tragedy.

II.

The thread on which all is strung is the gradual ruin, moral and physical, of a strong, brave, honest man. We are introduced abruptly to a family of Lithuanian peasants who have migrated to Chicago. The family is numerous. All relationships and all ages are included. There is Jurgis the hero, a mighty man, a Titan among workers. There is Ona, the girl to whom he is pledged, and for whose sake the great adventure of the ocean voyage has been made. There are her father and aunt, and his brother and his sister Marija, and four or five small children of varying ages. All the grown-ups are thrifty, industrious, simple Lithuanian folk who, having massed their savings, have sailed for the

Winston Churchill reviews The Jungle

George Bernard Shaw at Ayot-St. Lawrence, about 1913

Mary Craig Sinclair and Upton Sinclair in Bermuda, 1913

George Sterling, his wife, Carrie, and Jack London

Mrs. Kate Crane-Gartz

Sergei Eisenstein,
about 1933

Upton Sinclair during the EPIC campaign, 1934

Upton Sinclair and Harry Hopkins, 1934

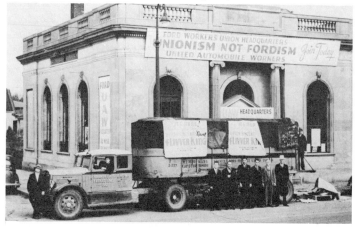

Flivver King *in Detroit, 1937*

*Upton Sinclair, about 1960, with
autographed picture of Albert Einstein*

MILTON K. BELL

Upton Sinclair standing before his home in Monrovia, California

May Hard Sinclair and Upton Sinclair, 1962

Upton Sinclair with seventy-nine of the books he has written

lament the fact that the servant did not always remember to draw the water for his bath; I was tempted to narrate how I bathed every morning of that winter in Arden with water in a tin washbasin and a newspaper spread upon a tent floor. I remember our Christmas turkey, which we hung up outside in the cold; we cooked it joint by joint, hung by a wire inside the little round wood stove. Nobody's turkey ever tasted better.

When Mitchell Kennerley accepted *Love's Pilgrimage,* and paid me an advance of twelve hundred and fifty dollars, I decided to build a house on my single-tax lot at the edge of the Forest of Arden. Frank Stephens was the builder, and I didn't hold it against him that, like all other builders, he underestimated the cost. It came to twenty-six hundred dollars and kept me scratching for quite a while. I was contributing articles to *Physical Culture* at a hundred and fifty dollars a month, which provided my living.

The little two-story cottage was completed early in the spring of 1911. It was painted brown on the outside, and stained on the inside. There was a living room in front with an open fireplace and a chimney that smoked. High on the wall, a shelf ran all the way round and held most of my books. In the rear was one small bedroom, and a still smaller kitchen, plus a bathroom without plumbing. Upstairs was an attic that I planned some day to make into two rooms. We moved in, feeling most luxurious after the tents. Next door was a one-room cabin belonging to Scott Nearing; I rented it for a study, and so had everything of a material nature that a man of letters could desire.

The Forest of Arden turned green again, and put flower carpets on its floor, and the tennis court was rolled and marked, and everything was jolly. The young people were preparing *The Merchant of Venice,* and the Esperantists of America held a convention in the big barn; I studied that language for three weeks, and when I went to supper at the inn I would say, "*Mi desiras lo puddingo*"—at least that is the way I recall it after fifty years. I was writing a sequel to *Love's Pilgrimage,* which I completed but have never published.

Unknown to me, the fates had been weaving a net about my life; and now they were ready to draw it tight. Corydon wrote that Mary Craig Kimbrough was coming to New York to talk with a publisher who had read her life of Winnie Davis, and that she, Corydon, was coming with her. Also there came a letter from Harry Kemp, saying that he was finishing at the university, and was then going to "beat" his way east and visit Arden. George Sterling was on his way from California to New York—he too was to be tied up in that net!

There was an odd development, which served as a sort of curtain raiser to the main tragedy. A little discussion club got into a dispute with George Brown, the anarchist shoemaker. The club members were accustomed to hold meetings in the outdoor theater, and Brown would come and air his opinions on the physiology of sex. The women and girls didn't like it. They asked him to shut up, but he stood on the elemental right of an anarchist to say anything anywhere at any time. He broke up several meetings—until finally the executives of the club went to Wilmington and swore out a warrant for his arrest for disturbing the peace.

That, of course, brought the newspaper reporters, and put my picture in the papers again. I had had nothing to do with the discussion club or with the arrest of Brown, but I lived in Arden and was part of the scenery. The anarchist was sentenced to five days on the rockpile at the state prison; he came back boiling with rage and plotting a dire revenge: he would have all the members of the baseball team arrested for playing on Sunday, and *they* would have a turn on the rockpile! He would add Upton Sinclair, who had been playing tennis on Sunday, and thus would punish Arden by putting it on the front page of every newspaper in America. He carried out this scheme, and eleven of us were summoned to court, and under a long-forgotten statute, dating from 1793, were sentenced to eighteen hours on the rockpile. This made one of the funniest newspaper stories ever telegraphed over the world—you may find the details in *The Brass Check* if you are curious. What the anarchist shoemaker did not realize, and what nobody else realized, was that he was setting the stage and assembling the audience for the notorious Sinclair-Kemp divorce scandal. The fates were against me.

8

Exile

=====================================

I

THE story of Corydon and Thyrsis comes now to its painful climax. They had been married for eleven years, and for the last seven or eight had realized that they were mismated. They talked much of divorce, and according to accepted conventions, Corydon was the one to get it. But the world made divorce difficult and placed handicaps upon a divorced woman; so Corydon kept hesitating, taking one step forward and two steps back.

If this story belonged to Thyrsis alone, he would tell it all, on the theory that the past is past and never returns, and the only use we can make of blunders is to help others in avoiding them. But the story is Corydon's also, and Corydon found herself a new husband and a new life, and has long since retired from the limelight.

Thyrsis, an unhappily married man, bore among his friends the reputation of being "puritanical"; a onetime virtue that now ranks as a dangerous disease. About the bedside of the patient gather the psychoanalysts and up-to-the-minute "intellectuals"; they take his temperature, or lack of it, and shake their heads anxiously over his subnormal condition. Jack London was much worried about Thyrsis and wrote warning letters; but in the course of time, Jack's own theories brought him to a situation where he could not have his wife and another woman at the same time, and so he voluntarily removed himself from the world. Then Frank Harris took over the case of Thyrsis and prescribed for the patient a tempestuous love affair. No man can become a great novelist without one, it seems, nor can a modern autobiography be worthy of suppression by the police unless it contains several adulteries per volume.

Let the fact be recorded that Thyrsis was capable of falling in love, and if he did not do it frequently, it was because he had so many other matters on his mind. There is a story having to do with this period, which ought to be told because of the satisfaction it will bring to the lovers of love, and to those who dislike the puritanical Thyrsis and will be pleased to see him "get his."

It was the winter of 1910–11, when Corydon had gone south, having once more decided upon a divorce. Thyrsis was a free man, so he thought—and, incidentally, a lonely and restless one. He was thirty-two at this time, and went up to New York to attend a gathering in Carnegie Hall, where the Intercollegiate Socialist Society was acting as host to Victor Berger, socialist Congressman-elect. Thyrsis came early, and in one of the aisles came face to face with a lovely young woman of twenty-one or two, wearing the red badge of an usher. In those observant eyes and that frank open countenance was revealed something he had been seeking for a long time; there was a mental flash, and the two moved automatically toward each other. Said she, without hesitation: "You are Thyrsis?" Said he: "You are Inez Milholland?"

A Vassar girl, with a wealthy father, Inez had joined the Socialist Party and had become an active suffragette—all of which, of course, made a sensation in the newspapers. That evening, after the meeting, Thyrsis went with her to her hotel, and they sat in the lobby conversing until three o'clock in the morning, when the place was deserted by all but the night watchman. What did they not talk about, in the vast range of the socialist and suffrage movements in America, and in England, where Inez had been to school; the people they knew, the books they had read, the events that the future held behind its veil!

"I never met anyone I could talk to so easily," said Thyrsis; and Inez returned the compliment. "But don't fall in love with me," she added. When he asked, "Why not?" she answered, "I am already in love, and you would only make yourself unhappy." Later, she told him that she too was unhappy; it was a married man, and she would not break up another woman's home but would only eat her heart out. Again that old, old story that Heine sings, and for which neither socialists nor suffragists have any remedy!

Es ist eine alte Geschichte
Doch klingt sie immer neu.

Inez desired to meet Berger, and he came next morning. The three of us went for a drive and had lunch at the Claremont. We spent the afternoon walking in the park, then had dinner at the hotel, and spent the evening together, solving all the problems of human society. It was another intellectual explosion, this time *à trois*. Said the socialist Congressman: "Thyrsis, if it wouldn't be that I am a family man, I would run away with that girl so quick you would never see her once again." Thyrsis repeated that to Inez, who smiled and said, "He is mistaken; it is not like that."

Thyrsis disregarded the sisterly advice that had been given to him. He fell in love—with such desperate and terrifying violence as he had never conceived possible in his hard-working, sober life. He understood for the first time the meaning of that ancient symbol of the little archer with the bow and arrow. Commonplace as the metaphor seemed, there was no other to be used; it was like being shot—a convulsive pain, a sense of complete collapse, an anguish repeated, day after day, without any respite or hope of it.

He could not give up. It seemed to him that here was the woman who had been made for him, and the thought that he had to lose her was not to be borne. He would go back to Arden and write letters—such mad, wild, pain-distracted letters as would satisfy the most exacting intellectual, the most implacable hater of Puritans! Inez afterward assured him that she had destroyed these letters, which was kind of her. She was always kind, and straightforward, saying what she meant, as men and women will do in utopia.

The storm passed, as storms do, and new life came to Thyrsis. Four years afterward he met Inez Milholland again. She was now married, and it seemed to Thyrsis that the world had laid its paralyzing hand upon her; she was no longer simple, in the manner of the early gods. Was it that the spell was broken? Or

was it that Thyrsis had an abnormal dislike for fashionable cos-
tumes, large picture hats, and long jade earrings? Another two
years, and Inez, a suffrage politician, came out to California
and broke her heart trying to carry the state for Hughes, on
the theory that he would be more generous to the cause than
Woodrow Wilson. This was supposed to be strategy, but
to Thyrsis it seemed insanity. In any case, what a melancholy
descent from the young ardors of the Intercollegiate Socialist
Society! She died of exhaustion.

II

The story of Corydon and Thyrsis comes to an end in the year
1911. George Sterling was coming from California, Harry Kemp
from Kansas; Mary Craig Kimbrough was in New York to consult
with a publisher, and Corydon had come with her.

George Sterling, the day of his arrival, came to call upon
Corydon in her father's home. There he met the young lady from
Mississippi and promptly fell upon his knees before her, after
the fashion of romantic poets, even after they are forty. She was
pale from a winter's labor over manuscript, and George called
her a "star in alabaster" and other extravagant things that moved
her to merry laughter. Later on, Thyrsis met the couple walking
on the street and stopped to greet them. Said Thyrsis matter-of-
factly: "You don't look well, Craig. Really, you look like a skull!"
George raged, "I am going to kill that man some day!" But Craig
replied, "There is the first man in the world who ever told me
the truth."

George Sterling, an unhappily married man, wanted to marry
Craig. She told him, "I can never love any man." When he demanded to know the reason, she told him that her heart had been
broken by an early love affair at home; she knew she would
never love again. But the poet could not accept that statement;
he began writing sonnets to her—more than a hundred in the
course of the next year. Eighteen years later it was my sad duty
to edit these *Sonnets to Craig* for publication, and they were received by the high-brow literary world with some uncertainty.
They have a fatal defect—it is possible to understand what they
mean. Literary tastes move in cycles, and just now poetry lovers

are impressed by eccentricities of language and punctuation. But the day will come when they care about real feelings, expressed in musical language, and then they will thrill to such lines as these:

> All gracious things, and delicate and sweet,
> Within the spaces of thy beauty meet.

And again:

> Sweet, in this love are terrors that beguile
> And joys that make a hazard of my breath.

And again:

> Stand back from me! Have mercy for a space,
> Lest madness break thine image in my mind!

In connection with this unhappy love affair, there was another curious tangle of circumstances. The girlhood sweetheart of Craig in the Far South had brought to her a poem so sad that it had moved her to tears, and she had carried it ever since in her memory. "The Man I Might Have Been" was its title—the grief-stricken cry of those who fall into the trap of John Barleycorn. Now here was the author of that poem, in love with the same woman; and both the unhappy suitors—the Southern boy and the crowned poet of California—were fated to end their lives by their own hands, and those of John Barleycorn.

Thyrsis was invited up to New York to give advice about the life of Winnie Davis. It was April and happened to be warm, so he wore tennis shoes because they were comfortable; to make up for this informality he added kid gloves—which seemed to Mary Craig Kimbrough of Mississippi the funniest combination ever heard of. She said nothing, being the soul of politeness; but her lively red-brown eyes took in everything. She was learning about these strange new creatures called radicals, and their ideas, some of which appeared sensible and others crazy. Watching Thyrsis, she thought, "The funny, funny man!" She watched him, thinking the same thought for a matter of half a century; but she did not always have to be polite about it.

Corydon, Thyrsis, and Craig settled themselves in the little cottage on the edge of the Forest of Arden. Springtime had come,

and the Arden folk were giving *Midsummer Night's Dream*;
Corydon was Titania, in yellow tights and a golden crown. At
this juncture came Harry Kemp, having completed another year
at the University of Kansas; he was lugging two suitcases full of
books and manuscripts, plus an extra blue shirt and a pair of
socks. There was a girl at Arden who was a lover of poetry, and
Thyrsis, fond matchmaker, had the idea that the poet might become interested in this girl. But the fates had other plans, and
were not slow to reveal them. Corydon was interested in the
poet.

It was during this time that Harry Kemp wrote a sonnet to
Thyrsis and handed it to him with the words, "You may publish
this some day." It will not be ranked as a great sonnet, but it is
curious as a part of the story; so, after Harry's death, his permission is accepted.

> Child, wandering down the great world for a day
>   And with a child's soul seeing thru and thru
>   The passing prejudice to Truth's own view.
> Immortal spirit robed in mortal clay,
>   Striving to find and follow the one way
>   That is your way, none other's—to be true
> To that which makes a sincere man of you!
> Still be yourself, and let tongues say their say!
>
> Still fling the seed with daring hand abroad,
>   And, then, mayhap, the Race to come will be
> Gladdened, with ripened fruit and bursting pod
> Of Love, and Brotherhood, and Liberty—
> Open to Nature and Her Laws from God
>   As spreading gulfs lie open to the Sea!

III

Corydon went to New York, to the apartment of her mother
and father, which was vacant in the summer. Harry followed
her; and then came Thyrsis, and the great divorce scandal
burst upon the world. It was made by the newspapers, so the
story had to be told in *The Brass Check*. There seems no good
reason to repeat it here; suffice it to say that Thyrsis found him-

self presented in the capitalist press as having taught his wife free love and then repudiated her when she took him at his word. The newspapers invented statements, they set traps, and betrayed confidences—and when they got through with their victim, they had turned his hair gray.

Corydon and Harry fled from the storm. But after a few days they came back; and then there were interviews of many columns, and Sunday-supplement pages with many pictures, in the course of which the great American public learned all about Thyrsis' dietetic eccentricities and his objections to coffee and cigarettes. Corydon caused vast glee to the New York smart set by describing her life partner as "an essential monogamist"; those who read and laughed did not remember that only last week they had read that he was a "free lover." As a matter of fact, neither the writers nor the readers knew what was meant by either term, so the incongruity did not trouble them.

Thyrsis filed suit for divorce in New York state, which is ruled by Catholic laws, administered by Catholic judges. If in his writings you find a certain acerbity toward the Catholic political machine, bear in mind these experiences, which seared into a writer's soul scars never to be effaced. The Catholic judge appointed a "referee" to hear testimony in the case, and this referee, moved by stupidity plus idle curiosity, asked Thyrsis questions concerning his wife's actions that under the New York law the husband was not permitted to answer. But the referee demanded that they be answered, and what was Thyrsis to do? He answered; so the Catholic judge had a pretext upon which to reject the recommendation of his referee.

The court and the referee had between them several hundred dollars of Thyrsis' hard-earned money, which, under the law, they were permitted to keep—even though Thrysis got no divorce He filed another suit and paid more money, and waited another three or four months, in the midst of journalistic excursions and alarms. Another referee took testimony, and this time was careful to ask only the exactly prescribed questions; in due course another decision was handed down by another Catholic judge, who had also been "seen" by parties interested. This time the decision was that Thyrsis had failed to beat up his wife, or to choke or stab or poison her, or otherwise manifest masculine resentment at her unfaithfulness; therefore he was suspected of "collusion," and the application was again denied. Of course the judge did not literally say that Thyrsis should have behaved in those violent ways; but that was the only possible implication of his decision. When a husband was fair and decent, desiring his dissatisfied wife to find happiness if she could—that was a dangerous and unorthodox kind of behavior, suggestive of "radical" ideas. Men and women suspected of harboring such ideas should be punished by being tied together in the holy bonds of matrimony and left to tear each other to pieces like the Kilkenny cats.

In February 1912 Thyrsis took his son and departed for Europe, traveling second-class in a third-class Italian steamer; sick in body and soul, and not sure whether he was going to live or die, nor caring very much. He had managed to borrow a little money for the trip, and he had a job, writing monthly articles for *Physical Culture Magazine* for a hundred and fifty dollars each. As a writer of books he was destroyed, and nobody thought he would ever have a public again. Mitchell Kennerley, publisher of *Love's Pilgrimage*, remarked, "If people can read about you for two cents, they are not going to pay a dollar and a half to do it." *Love's Pilgrimage* had been published a month or two before the divorce scandal broke and had started as a whirlwind success—selling a thousand copies a week. The week after the scandal broke, it dropped dead, and the publisher did not sell a hundred copies in a year.

IV

Springtime in Florence! *"Kennst du das Land wo die Citronen bluehn?"* Could any man walk under Tuscan skies in March and fail to be happy? George D. Herron had a villa on the slopes towards Fiesole, where he lived in what peace he could find; Thyrsis spent a couple of weeks with him, and talked over old times and the state of the world, with the great cataclysm of World War I only two years and a half in the future. Carrie Rand Herron played Schumann's *Widmung* in the twilight—and for her a death by cancer was even nearer than the war.

Was Thyrsis happy? In truth, he hardly knew where he was

or what he was doing. Places and events went by as if in a dream, and nothing had meaning unless it spoke of pain and enslavement, in America as in Italy. The grim castle of Strozzi was an incarnation in stone of the Beef Trust or the Steel Trust. Crowds of olive-skinned starving children with sore eyes, peering out of doorways of tenements in the back streets of Florence, were simply Mulberry Row in New York. Galleries full of multiplied madonnas and crucified martyrs spoke of Tammany Hall and its Catholic machine, with Catholic cops twisting the arms of socialist working girls on the picket line; Catholic archbishops striding down the aisle of a hall commanding the police to arrest women lecturers on birth control; Catholic judges sitting on the bench in black silk robes, punishing socialist muckrakers for being too decent to their erring wives.

Milan: a great city, with many sights, but for Thyrsis only one attraction—a socialist paper in an obscure working-class quarter, with an editor who was translating Thyrsis' books. And then Switzerland, with towering snow-clad mountains and clear blue lakes—and another socialist editor. Then Germany, and one of the Lietz schools, a new experiment in education, where Thyrsis had arranged to leave his son: a lovely spot on the edge of the Harz Mountains, with a troop of merry youngsters living the outdoor life. Nearby were miles of potatoes and sugar beets, with Polish women working in gangs like Negro slaves. There was another school in Schloss Bieberstein, for the older boys, fine strapping fellows, bare-legged and bare-armed, hardened to the cold, and ready for the slaughter pits; in three years most of them would be turned into manure for potatoes and sugar beets.

Then Holland, where Frederik van Eeden had undertaken to help Thyrsis get the freedom that was not to be had in New York. A lawyer was consulted and put the matter up to the startled judges of the Amsterdam courts. Under the Dutch law, the husband was not required to prove that he had beaten or choked or poisoned his wife; he might receive a divorce on the basis of a signed statement by the wife, admitting infidelity. But what about granting this privilege to a wandering author from America? How long would he have to remain a resident of Holland in order to be entitled to the benefit of civilized and enlightened law? The judges finally agreed that they would admit this one American to their clemency—but never again! Amsterdam was not going to be turned into another Reno!

V

A visit to England. Gaylord Wilshire was living in Hampstead, endeavoring to finance his gold mine in London. The great coal strike was on, and Tom Mann, editor of a syndicalist newspaper, was sent to jail for six months. Wilshire, who by now had come to despair of political action for the workers, leaped into the breach, and he and Thyrsis got out several issues of the paper —the contribution of the latter consisting of a debate in which he opposed the leading idea of the editor. Apparently that satisfied the London police, for the eccentric Americans were allowed to argue without molestation. The newspaper reporters came swarming, and it was a novel experience for Thyrsis to give interviews and read next morning what he said, instead of how he looked and what he ate and how his wife had run away with a "box-car poet."

Some things he liked in England, and some not. A ghastly thing to see the effect upon the human race of slow starvation continued through many centuries! Here were creatures distorted out of human semblance; swarms of them turning out on a bank holiday to play, having forgotten how to run, almost how to walk; shambling like apes, drooping like baboons, guffawing with loud noises, speaking a jabber hardly to be understood. They lay around on Hampstead Heath, men and women in each others' arms, a sight new to an American. Whether they were drunk or sober was difficult for a stranger to tell.

The miners' strike committee held its meetings in the Westminster Hotel; and just across the way were the Parliament buildings, and labor members to welcome a socialist author. John Burns took Thyrsis onto the floor of the House to hear the debate on the settlement of the coal strike, a full-dress affair reported all over the world; Asquith versus Balfour, or rather both of them versus the working masses of Britain. This was what capitalism considered statesmanship—this hodgepodge of cant and cruelty, bundled in a gray fog of dullness. Thyrsis sat in a sacred seat, where no visitor was supposed to be, and gazed upon rows of savages in silk hats, roaring for what little blood was left in the veins of half-starved miners' families. He clenched his hands until his nails made holes in his skin.

When the great lawyer Asquith was in the midst of his sophistries, the young American could stand no more; he half rose from his seat, with his mouth open to say what he thought of these starvers of British labor. Half a dozen times he rose, with words starting from his throat, and half a dozen times he sank back again. They would have arrested him, no doubt, and his protest would have been heard. But it would also have gone to Amsterdam, where the polite judges had still to decide the problem of the custody of Thyrsis' son!

Thyrsis went out and visited Westminster Abbey, where he was swept by a storm of horror and loathing; wandering among marble tombs and statues of ruling-class killers and the poets and men of genius who had betrayed the muse to Mammon. High-vaulting arches, lost in dimness; priests in jeweled robes, and white-clad choirs chanting incessant subjection; a blaze of candles, a haze of altar smoke, and mental slaves with heads bowed in their arms—the very living presence of that giant Fear, in the name of which the organized crimes of the ages have been committed. Here was the explanation of those swarms on Hampstead Heath, deprived of human semblance; here was the meaning of pettifogging lawyers and noble earls and silk-hatted savages shouting for the lifeblood of starving miners; here was the very body and blood of that Godhead of Capitalism—

> Great Christus-Jingo, at whose feet
> Christian and Jew and Atheist meet!

VI

Miss Mary Craig Kimbrough came traveling. It was natural that a young lady from Mississippi should desire to see art galleries and meet celebrities in England; and if she came as the guest of an earl and a countess, that would surely be respectable according to Mississippi standards. It so happened that the noble earl was a bit of a radical and had had his own marital scandal. He had gone to Reno, Nevada, and got himself divorced from an unsatisfactory marriage; then, upon his remarriage in England, his peers had haled him before them, convicted him of bigamy, and sentenced him to six months in jail.

A tremendous uproar in its day, but it had been many days ago; the English nobility are a numerous family, which Mississippi could hardly be expected to keep straight. Craig's father had the general impression, held by every old-fashioned Southern gentleman, that the English nobility are a depraved lot; but on the other hand, Craig's mother knew that they are socially irresistible. She proved it whenever, at a gathering of the local chapter of the United Daughters of the Confederacy, she was asked for news about her daughter who was visiting the Countess Russell in London.

"Aunt Molly" was a plump little Irish lady, the warmest hearted soul that ever carried a heavy title. She had had her own divorce tragedy, and her warm Irish heart was with Thyrsis. She had published two or three novels, and for writing purposes had a retreat, an ancient cottage on the edge of a village not far from Eton. It was so low that you had to stoop to get through the doorway, and its chimney had smoked for at least three hundred years; but it was newly plastered inside, and furnished with antiques and bright chintzes. Here Aunt Molly brought her protegée, and Thyrsis came from Holland to collect local color for the new novel, *Sylvia*, which he was making out of Craig's tales of her girlhood in the Far South. In after years the heroine would stop in the middle of an anecdote, look puzzled, and say, "Did that really happen to me? Or is it one of the things we made up for *Sylvia?*"

One glimpse of the British aristocracy at home. The novel Thyrsis was writing dealt with a splendid young Harvard millionaire, one of whose friends remarks that he deliberately cultivated the brutal manners of the British upper classes toward their social inferiors. Craig was distressed by this, insisting that it couldn't be true; finally it was agreed that Aunt Molly should be the arbitrator. The problem was submitted, and this high authority laughed and said, "Well, look at Frank!" She went on to tell anecdotes portraying the bad manners of his lordship, her husband; also of his uncles and his cousins, Lord This and the

Marquis of That and the Duke of Other. Craig subsided, and the sentence stands as it was written.

Thyrsis, himself, walking along the road in his everyday clothes, saw a fancy equipage drive up and halt, while the occupants asked him the way to a certain place; having been politely answered, the lady and gentleman drove on without so much as a nod of thanks. On another occasion, while walking, he attempted to ask the way of a gentleman out for a constitutional, and this person stalked by without a sound or a glance. Mentioning this experience to a conventional Englishman, Thyrsis received the following explanation: "But if one entered into talk with any stranger who hailed him on the road, one might meet all sorts of undesirable persons!"

VI

To Aunt Molly's home in London came H. G. Wells, and with the countess' half-dozen tiny white dogs dancing in their laps, the two social philosophers compared their views on the state of the world. Wells had now come to the conclusion it would take about three hundred years to get socialism, which to Thyrsis seemed the same as being a die-hard tory. Wells took him to lunch at the New Reform Club, and as they were leaving the dining room, he stopped and whispered that Thyrsis now had an opportunity to observe the Grand Khan of Anglo-American literature, Henry James, eating a muttonchop. On the landing halfway down the stairs they ran into Hilaire Belloc, who held them with half an hour of brilliance. He exhibited an amazing familiarity with the medieval world and its manifold futilities. It was like an exhibition of a million dollars' worth of skyrockets and pyrotechnical set pieces; when it was over, you went away with nothing.

Also Thyrsis met Frank Harris, possessor of a golden tongue. Harris would talk about Jesus and Shakespeare in words so beautiful that only those masters could have matched it; but in the midst of his eloquence something would turn his thoughts to a person he disliked, and there would pour from the same throat such a stream of abuse as might have shocked a fallen archangel. Harris invited the young author to lunch at an expen-

sive hotel and spent four or five pounds on the occasion; politeness forbade Thyrsis to hint his feelings of distress at such a
demonstration. He would not partake of the costly wines, and
could have lived for a couple of weeks on such an expenditure.
Not long after this, Harris published in a magazine his solution
of all the problems of health—which was to use a stomach
pump, get rid of all you had eaten, and start over again.

Then Bernard Shaw. For eight or nine years Thyrsis had followed our modern Voltaire with admiration, but also with some
fear of his sharp tongue. When he met him, he discovered the
kindest and sweetest-tempered of humans, the cleanest, also; he
had bright blue eyes, a red-gold beard turning gray, and the face
of a mature angel. The modern Voltaire motored Thyrsis out to
his country place and gave him a muttonchop or something for
lunch, while he himself ate ascetic beans and salad, and admitted sadly that his periodic headaches might possibly be due to
excess of starch, as Thyrsis suggested. To listen to G. B. S. at
lunch was exactly like hearing him at Albert Hall or reading one
of his prefaces; he would talk an endless stream of wit and
laughter, with never a pause or a dull moment.

After lunch they walked to see the old church. Not even a
modern Voltaire could imagine a visitor from America failing to
be interested in looking at the ruins of an old church! On the
way they came to a sign warning motorists that they were passing a school. Thyrsis asked, "Where is the school?" His host
laughed and explained, "This is England. The school was moved
some years ago, but we haven't got round to moving the sign
yet. The motorists slow up, and then, just after they have got up
speed again they come to the school."

Years back, Thyrsis had met May Sinclair, then visiting in
New York. Those were the days of *The Divine Fire*—does anyone remember that novel? Thyrsis had sent it to Jack London,
who wrote that if he could write one such story, he would be
willing to die. Now in London, Thyrsis went to see May Sinclair
at her studio, and listened while she received another visitor to
tea and asked him questions. It was a shy youth, a shop assistant
in London, who had been invited because May Sinclair was writing a book about such a person and wished to know what hours
he worked, what his duties were, and so on. One could guess

that the poor youth had never been in such company before, and never would be again.

The class lines are tightly drawn in that tight little island. May Sinclair told me a little story about H. G. Wells, who had begun life as a shop assistant; talking to Wells about the novel she was writing, she asked him some question about the dialect of a shop assistant. Wells flushed with annoyance and said: "How should *I* know?" Thyrsis thought that was a dreadful story, so dreadful that he covered his face with his hands when he heard it. May Sinclair was distressed, because she hadn't meant to gossip—she hadn't realized how this anecdote would sound to an American socialist.

VIII

Thyrsis went back to Holland, which was supposed to be his residence. He was not deceiving the honorable judges of the Amsterdam courts—he really did mean to live in Holland, where everybody was so polite and where, alone of all places in Europe, they did not give you short change, or coins made of lead. It was an unusually cold and rainy summer—the peasants of France were reported to be gathering their hay from boats. Thyrsis sat in a little room, doing his writing by a wood stove, and waiting in vain for the sun to appear. His friend Van Eeden took him walking and pointed out the beautiful effects of the tumbled clouds on the horizon. "These are the clouds that our Dutch painters have made so famous!" But Thyrsis did not want to paint clouds, he wanted to get warm.

Craig came to Holland, and Dr. Van Eeden and his wife introduced her to staid burgomasters' wives, who were as much thrilled to meet the granddaughter of American slave owners as she was to meet Dutch dignitaries. Because Van Eeden had been through a divorce scandal in his own life, he could sympathize with the troubled pair. An odd fact, that all the friends who helped him through these days of trial—the Herrons in Italy, the Wilshires and Russells in England, the Van Eedens in Holland —had been through the divorce mill.

Frederick van Eeden was at this time in his fifties, the best-known novelist and poet of his country. But the country was too small, he said—it was discouraging to write for only seven million people! He had had a varied career—physician, pioneer psychotherapist, then labor leader and founder of a colony like Thyrsis; he lived on the remains of this colony, a small estate called Walden. His beard was turning gray, but his mind was still omnivorous, and he and his young American friend ranged the world in their arguments.

Van Eeden's wife was a quiet woman, young in years but old in fashion, the heroine of Van Eeden's *Bride of Dreams*; she sat by and did her sewing and seemed a trifle shocked when the young lady from Mississippi ventured to poke fun at the ideas of her lord and master. Her two little children were lacking altogether in American boisterousness; their utmost limit of self-assertion was to stand by Thyrsis' chair at suppertime, and watch him with big round eyes while he ate a fig, and whisper "Ik ok!"—that is, "Me, too!" Thyrsis found the Dutch language a source of great amusement, and he evolved a rule for getting along; first say it in German, and if that is not understood, say it in English, and if that is not understood, say it halfway between.

Van Eeden took Thyrsis to Berlin, where they visited a young German poet, Erich Gutkind, who under the pen name of Volker had published an ecstatic book that Van Eeden expected to outmode Nietzsche. A charming young Jewish couple—Thyrsis called them the *Gute Kinder*, and sometimes the *Sternengucker*, because of the big telescope they had on the roof of their home. Van Eeden and Gutkind were on fire with a plan to form a band of chosen spirits to lead mankind out of the wilderness of materialism; Thyrsis brought tears into the young rhapsodist's eyes by the brutality of his insistence that the sacred band would have to decide the problem of social revolution first.

All three of these men saw the war coming, and the problem of what to do about it occupied their thoughts. Thyrsis had written a manifesto against war, calling on the socialist parties of the world to pledge themselves to mass insurrection against it. He had found sympathy among socialists in England and France, but very little in Germany. Karl Kautsky had written that the agitation of such a program would be illegal in Germany—which apparently settled it with him and his party. Thyrsis now spent a day with Kautsky and his wife and son—

die heilige Familie, as their enemies dubbed them. He debated the problem with Suedekum, with Fischer, with Ledebour and Liebknecht; the latter two escorted him about the Reichstag and took him to lunch—in a separate dining room where Social Democratic members were herded, apart from the rest! Ledebour and Liebknecht were sympathetic to his program, but could not promise any effective action, and what they told him had much to do with Thyrsis' decision to support the Allies in 1917.

IX

Yes, the war was not far away. Military men with bristling mustaches were strutting about, jostling ordinary folk out of the way, staring over the heads of the men, and into the faces of women. "Papa, why do they twist their mustaches into points?" inquired David, eleven years old, and the answer was, "It is to frighten you." "But it doesn't frighten me," said the little boy. However, it frightened his father, so that he removed his son from the German school to one in England.

The *Gute Kinder* took their guests driving to see the sights of Berlin, including the monstrous statues of the Sieges Allee. Thyrsis thought he had never seen anything so funny since the beginning of his life. He found something funnier to say about each one—until his host leaned over and signaled him to be quiet, pointing to the cab driver up in front. More than once it had happened that a ribald foreigner, daring to commit *lèse-majesté* in the hearing of a Prussian ex-soldier, had been driven to the police station and placed under arrest.

Thyrsis was invited to meet Walter Rathenau. He had never heard the name, but his friends explained that this was the young heir of the great German electrical trust; he went in for social reform and wrote bold books. They were driven to the Kaiserlicher Automobil Klub, a gorgeous establishment, with footmen in short pants and silk stockings. There was a private dining room and an elaborate repast, including plovers' eggs, a dish of which Thyrsis had never heard and which proved to be dangerous in practice, since you never knew what you were going to find when you cracked a shell. Thereafter the irreverent strangers always referred to Rathenau as *Kiebitzei.*

They united in finding him genial but a trifle overconfident—
an attitude that accompanies the possession of vast sums of
money and the necessity of making final decisions upon great
issues. Van Eeden was a much older man who had made himself
a reputation in many different fields—yet he did not feel so
certain about anything as he found this young master of elec-
tricity and finance. However, there is this to be added: it is the
men who know what they think who are capable of action. Walter Rathenau would no doubt have made over German industry
along more social and human lines if the reactionaries had not
murdered him.

X

The Dutch divorce was granted, in pleasant fashion, without
Thyrsis having to appear in court. Craig, who was back in England under the wing of her earl and countess, now wished to
return to Mississippi to persuade her parents to let her marry a
divorced man; Thyrsis also wished to go, having a new novel to
market. These were the happy days before the passport curse,
so it was possible to travel incognito and land in New York without newspaper excitement. In the interest of propriety, the pair
traveled on separate steamers. Craig came on the *Lusitania*, ship
of ill fate for her as for others; in a stormy December passage
she was thrown and broke the bones at the base of the spine,
which caused her suffering for many years, and made a hard task
yet harder for her.

The siege of the family began. The father was a judge and
knew the law—at least he knew his own kind, and took no stock
in a piece of engraved stationery from Amsterdam that he could
not read. "Daughter, you cannot marry a married man!" That was
all he would say; and the answer, "Papa, I have made up my
mind to marry him!" meant nothing. She would spend her nights
weeping—an old story in her life. She was his first child, and
her portrait, a beautiful oil painting, hung in the drawing room;
when she went away to New York again, he put this portrait up
in the attic.

Thyrsis, meantime, was interviewing publishers—an old story
in *his* life. Mitchell Kennerley had no use for *Sylvia*—it was not

in the modern manner. Thyrsis' fate was to wander from one publisher to another—since he would not obey the rules of their game. Literary works were turned out according to pattern, stamped with a trademark, and sold to customers who wanted another exactly like the last. A new publisher came forward, an old-fashioned one; but apparently the buyers of old-fashioned novels distrusted the Thyrsis label. *Sylvia* sold only moderately, and the sequel, *Sylvia's Marriage*, hardly sold at all. Two thousand copies in America and a hundred thousand in Great Britain —that was a record for a prophet in his own country!

It was a time of stirring among the foreign-born workers in America, and Thyrsis and other young enthusiasts thought it was the beginning of the change for which they prayed. There was a strike of silkworkers in Paterson, New Jersey, and the intelligentsia of Greenwich Village made weekend pilgrimages for strike relief and oratory. Leading the strike were Bill Haywood, grim old one-eyed miners' chief from the Rockies; Elizabeth Gurley Flynn, who had begun her rebel career as a high-school girl in New York; Carlo Tresca, his face and body scarred by the bullets of his masters' gunmen; Joe Ettor and Arthur Giovannitti, fresh from a frame-up for murder in Massachusetts. Helping them, and at the same time studying them for copy, were budding young novelists such as Leroy Scott and Ernest Poole; a dramatist, Thompson Buchanan, who was later to employ his knowledge in the concoction of anti-Bolshevik nightmares; and John Reed, war correspondent, whose bones were destined to lie in the Kremlin in less than ten years.

They besought Thyrsis to join them; he yielded to the temptation, and once more saw the busy pencils of the newspaper reporters flying. Did they make up the false quotations themselves, or was their copy doctored in the office? Impossible to say; but Thyrsis saw himself quoted as advising violence, which he had never done in his life. He filed the clippings away, and filed the rage in his heart. It was still six years to the writing of *The Brass Check*.

A terrible thing to see tens of thousands of human beings starved into slavery, held down by policemen's clubs and newspaper slanders. The young sympathizers were desperate, and in the hope of moving the heart of New York, they planned the

"Paterson Pageant"—to bring two thousand silkworkers to the stage of Madison Square Garden and give a mass performance of the events of the strike, with special emphasis on speeches and singing. Over this scheme a group of twenty or thirty men and women slaved day and night for several weeks, and bled their pocketbooks empty—and then saw the New York papers hinting that they had stolen the money of the strikers! Two things out of that adventure will never pass from memory: first, the old warehouse in which rehearsals were held, and John Reed with his shirt sleeves rolled up, shouting through a megaphone, drilling those who were to serve as captains of the mass; and second, the arrival of that mass, two thousand half-starved strikers in Madison Square Garden rushing for the sandwiches and coffee!

XI

The elderly Judge in Mississippi would not change his decision once given; but the ladies of the family were more pliable, and by springtime it had become plain to them that they could not break the bonds that held their daughter to the dreaded socialist muckraker. Two of them came to New York on a pilgrimage to see what sort of man it might be that had woven this evil spell. The mother was a lady who refrained from boasting of being the seventh lineal descendant of that Lady Southworth who had come to Massachusetts to marry the second colonial governor; but who allowed herself a modest pride as founder of the Christian (Disciples) church of her home town and sponsor of no one knew how many monuments to Confederate heroes throughout the South. With her came a greataunt, one of the few "strong-minded women" the state of Mississippi had produced; she had gone to California, and become a schoolteacher, and married a pioneer, General Green, who was known as the "father of irrigation" and had left her a newspaper, the Colusa *Sun*, to manage.

These two reached New York in a state of trepidation hardly to be comprehended by irreverent intellectuals. Oh, fortunate chance that the socialist muckraker had been born close to Mason and Dixon's line, and had so many Virginia ancestors he could talk about! Actually, there were cousins who were cousins of cousins! His mother had taught him exactly how to use a knife and fork; his bride-to-be had taught him that gloves do not go with tennis shoes! For these reasons, plus a lawyer's assurance that the divorce was valid in the United States, it was decided that there should be a wedding.

But surely not in New York, swarming place of reporters! Let it be in some decent part of the world, where family and good breeding count! Mississippi was impossible, because the Judge forbade it; but in Virginia there were cousins who would lend the shelter of their name and homestead. So the party took a night train—one amused but attentive muckraker and three Southern ladies on the verge of a nervous crisis, seeing a newspaper reporter in every sleeping-car berth. "Oh, the reporters! What will the reporters say!" Thyrsis heard this for a week, until he could stand it no more and suddenly exploded in a masculine cry: "Oh, *damn* the reporters!" There followed an awe-stricken silence—but in their secret hearts the two elderly ladies were relieved. It was a real man, after all!

Fredericksburg, scene of the slaughter of some fifteen thousand Yankees. The old-maid cousins knew Craig, because she had been sent to them to recuperate after dancing seasons; they now welcomed this romantic expedition with open arms. There was a tremendous scurrying about, and the respectable mother set out to persuade the pastor of her respectable kind of church to officiate. But, alas, that dread stigma of a divorce! Thyrsis had to seek out an Episcopal clergyman and persuade him. Having been brought up in that church, he knew how to talk to such a clergyman; having been the innocent party in the divorce, he had under the church law the right to be remarried.

But the clergyman required evidence that Thyrsis had been the innocent party; so the would-be bridegroom came back to the hotel to get the divorce certificate. As it happened, in the hurry of packing, the proper document had been overlooked; instead, there was another and subsequent document, giving Thyrsis the custody of his son. It was in the Dutch language, and the author, who was no Dutchman, took it and translated it, with the elderly clergyman looking over his shoulder. Somehow the legal formulas became confused, and a certificate of custody underwent a mysterious transmogrification—it became a certificate of divorce based on the wife's admitted infidelity.

The Episcopal proprieties having thus been satisfied, the clergyman put on his glad robes, and there was a ceremony in an ancient family garden by the banks of the swiftly flowing Rappahannock, with the odor of violets and crocuses in the air, and a mother and a greataunt and several old-maid cousins standing by in a state of uncertain romance. As for the bride and groom—the world had battered them too much, and they could hardly squeeze out a tear or a smile. Thyrsis had even forgotten the ring, and with sudden tears his mother-in-law slipped her own wedding ring from her finger into his hand. Apart from this lapse, and the single "damn," he played his part perfectly. He promised to love, honor, and obey—and did so for a total of forty-eight years thereafter.

At home in Mississippi sat the elderly Judge, having been forewarned of the event and waiting for the storm to break. The telephone rang: the Memphis *Commerical Appeal*—or perhaps it was the New Orleans *Times-Picayune*. "Judge Kimbrough, we have a dispatch from Fredericksburg, Virginia, saying that your daughter has married Upton Sinclair." "Yes, so I understand." "The dispatch says that the husband is an advocate of socialism, feminism, and birth control. Does your daughter share her husband's ideas on these matters?" Said the Judge: "My daughter does not share *any* of her husband's ideas!" And so the interview went out to the world.

9

New Beginning

I

THE fates who deal out marriages seldom chose two more different human personalities for yoking together. Craig was all caution and I was all venture. She was all reticence, and I wanted to tell of my mistakes so that others could learn to avoid them. Craig would have died before she let anyone know hers. When she got some money she wanted to hide it like a squirrel; when I got some I wanted to start another crusade, to change a world that seemed to me in such sad shape. Craig agreed about the shape, but what she wanted to do was to hide us from it. This duel was destined to last for forty-eight years.

My mother and hers had proudly produced their family trees, and behold, we were both descended from the same English king. We had traveled by different routes: Craig's ancestor, Lady Southworth, had come to Massachusetts to be married to the colonial governor, William Bradford; mine had come to Virginia and entered the Navy. One of my ancestors had been a commander in the Battle of Lake Huron in the War of 1812, and his son, Captain Arthur Sinclair, my grandfather, had commanded one of the vessels with which Admiral Perry opened up Japan. That grandfather, three uncles, and several cousins had fought in the Confederate States Navy. Craig's great-grandfather had been appointed by President Jefferson the first surveyor general of the Territory of Mississippi. So those two mothers had got along conversationally, and Mama Kimbrough had good news to take back to Leflore County.

The youngest Kimbrough daughter, Dolly, was at a school in Tarrytown, on the Hudson, and I escorted Mama Kimbrough there. On the way she set out to make a Christian out of me, and I was so attentive that we went an hour past our station; we had to get out and wait for a train to take us back. We found Dolly in bed, blooming in spite of an appendix operation. By the time we returned to New York I had been able to persuade Mama that my socialism was just Christian brotherhood brought up to date; also Mama had decided that a trip to Europe with Craig and me would be educational for Dolly.

II

The first place we visited was Hellerau, in Germany, where the Dalcroze School was holding its annual spring festival. Hellerau means "bright meadow." Rising from that meadow was a temple of art, and we witnessed a performance of Gluck's *Orpheus*, represented in dance as well as in music. It was one of the loveliest things I had ever seen, and a quarter of a century later I used it for the opening scene of *World's End*—the world's beginning of Lanny Budd. The young Lanny met on the bright meadow—as we ourselves had met—Bernard Shaw with his golden beard outshining any landscape. I had already had lunch at his home in London and at his country home; he welcomed us, and our joy in the Dalcroze festival was confirmed by Britain's greatest stage critic. He was always so kind, and the letters he wrote me about the Lanny Budd books helped them to win translation into a score of foreign languages.

We traveled to David's school and collected him. We had lunch in a restaurant in Dresden. I ordered an omelet in my most polished German, and very carefully specified that I did not want pancakes. "*Kein Mehl,*" I said several times, but they brought us pancakes; when we refused to accept them and tried to leave the restaurant, they would not let us out. Our train was due so we had to pay, and I bade an unloving farewell to Germany—just a year before World War I.

We went to Paris, and there rented an apartment for a couple of weeks. When we were ready to pay our bill, the proprietress pulled a rug from under the bed and accused us of having spilled grease on it. We had had no grease, and hadn't even seen the rug; but when we refused to pay for the damage, the woman called in a policeman—I think he was the tallest man I ever saw in uniform. He told us we would have to pay or we could not leave. It was a "racket," of course, but there was nothing we could do; so to France also we bade an unloving farewell. When World War I came, we weren't quite sure which person we wanted most to have punished—the German restaurant proprietor or the French virago and tall policeman.

III

We went to England, where nobody ever robbed us. We settled in the model village of Letchworth, built by co-operatives. I had acquired from Mrs. Bernard Shaw the right to make a novel out of a drama by the French playwright Eugène Brieux, called *Damaged Goods*, dealing with venereal disease. I wrote that novel and got an advance from the publisher, and so we had a pleasant summer. I played tennis at the club, and in a middle-aged bachelor girl found the first female antagonist who could keep me busy. I have forgotten her name, but I remember that whenever I got in a good shot she would exclaim, "Oh, *haught!*"

Also I remember an outdoor socialist meeting at which I addressed an audience of co-operators, speaking from the tail of a cart along with dear, kind George Lansbury, member of Parliament and leader of the left-wing socialists.

We moved into London for a while, and there the lady from the Mississippi Delta met more strange kinds of people—among them Mrs. Pethick Lawrence, Sylvia Pankhurst, and other suffrage combatants. Craig's sister Dolly had met them too, and we learned, somewhat to our dismay, that Dolly had carried into the National Art Gallery a hatchet concealed under her skirt. Known suffragettes, when they tried to go in, were searched; but the guards didn't know Dolly, and it was a simple matter for her to retire to the ladies' room and pass the hatchet. What would Chancellor Kimbrough, president of two banks in Mississippi, have said if a newspaper reporter had called him up and told him that his youngest daughter had been arrested for passing a hatchet!

While I renewed my acquaintance with my socialist friends, it was Craig's pleasure to go out on the streets and watch the people. At home the servants had been black; here they had white skins but even so were like another race. The educated classes were gracious and keen-minded; but the poor seemed to be speaking a strange language. What did "Kew" mean? Every shop assistant said it when you handed her money; and once when Craig and I were going down into "the Tube," two male creatures rushed past us in the midst of a hot argument. We caught one shouted sentence, "Ow, gow an' be a Sowshalist!"

I had a curious experience in London with Jessica Finch, who was the owner and director of a fashionable American school for young ladies, just off Fifth Avenue in New York. Her prices were staggering, and admission had to be arranged years in advance. She was an ardent suffragist and a socialist as determined as myself; she taught these two doctrines to her pupils, and when they went home for Christmas vacation, the Intercollegiate Socialist Society moved into her school to hold its annual convention.

When Craig had first met me in New York, I had taken her to one of these conventions, and she had met a youth named Walter Lippmann, founder and president of the Harvard chapter of that organization. Walter was interested now to meet a young lady from the Far South, and began at once to further his education. "What is the economic status of the Negro in Mississippi?" Craig, with her red-brown eyes twinkling, replied, "I didn't know he had any."

Jessica was in the habit of taking a bevy of her pupils abroad at the end of each school year, and they were all snugly ensconced in the palatial home of London's great department-store proprietor, Harry Gordon Selfridge. Jessica laughingly assured me that she had a Rembrandt in her bedroom and that every one of the girls had a hundred thousand dollars' worth of pictures on her walls. Jessica loved to talk, and there was plenty to talk about; the suffragettes and the British socialist movement and the prospect of a world war. It must have been two or three o'clock in the morning when we parted. Craig and I saw her several years later in New York. She was married to J. O'Hara Cosgrave, onetime editor of *Everybody's Magazine* and later editor of the New York *Sunday World*.

The happy summer passed. *Damaged Goods* was coming out, and I had to be in New York. Craig's blessed mother, much against the judgment of the Judge, allowed Dolly to stay in London to become a paying guest at the Wilshires' and attend the Dalcroze School of Eurythmics. My David was placed in one of the progressive schools near the city.

As I have already said, Craig had written some tales of her Southern girlhood; and I had stolen them from her for a novel to be called *Sylvia*. *Damaged Goods*, both the play and novel, had filled my mind with the subject of venereal disease, something considered unmentionable in those days. I now decided to use the material from *Sylvia* for a novel on that theme, and we settled down in a little apartment to finish it. We had long arguments of course. Craig was herself Sylvia, and she thought she knew what Sylvia would do and say. I had to agree; but I thought I knew what the public would want to read. If anybody had been in the next room while we were arguing they would surely have thought that World War I had already broken out.

IV

We decided to transfer the battleground to Bermuda for the winter. We found one of those little white cottages built of blocks carved out from coral. Craig had had enough of social life to last all her days, she said; all she wanted was to sit in the shade of a palm tree and decide what she believed about life. In the afternoon I would mount a bicycle and ride down to the Princess Hotel and play tennis with a captain of the British Army, stationed nearby.

A former young woman secretary of mine had married a Bermuda planter, and they would come for us in a carriage—no autos permitted in those days—and take us to a home completely surrounded by onions and potatoes. At night the planter took me out on Harrington Sound in a flat-bottomed boat; holding a torch we would look into the clear water, and there would be a big green lobster waiting to be stabbed with a two-pronged spear.

It was in Bermuda that we had an experience Craig delighted to tell about. Walking along the lovely white coral road, we stopped at a little store to buy something to eat. Looking up, my eyes were caught by familiar objects on shelves near the ceiling—flat cans covered with dust but with the labels still visible: "Armour's Roast Beef." "What are those cans doing up there?" I asked, and the proprietor replied, "Oh, some years ago a fellow wrote a book about that stuff, and I haven't been able to sell a can since."

V

In the spring of 1914 we came back to New York. The novel, which we called *Sylvia's Marriage*, was finished: the story of a Southern girl who marries a wealthy Bostonian and Harvard man and bears a child blinded by gonorrhea. A terrible story, of course, and an innovation in the fiction of that time. I took the manuscript to Walter Lippmann, who had himself graduated from Harvard and had founded a branch of the Intercollegiate Socialist Society there. He read it, and invited me to lunch at the Harvard Club.

I remember vividly his reaction to my novel. I hadn't thought of him as an ardent partisan of Harvard, but perhaps he was already coming to a more conservative attitude to life. He told me that my picture of a Harvard man was utterly fantastic; no such pretentious snob had ever been seen there, and my portrait was a travesty. I remember one sentence: "It's as preposterous as if you were to portray an orgy in this place." And Walter waved his hand to indicate that most decorous dining room.

I would have been embarrassed had I not known certain facts that, unfortunately, I was not at liberty to mention to my old ISS friend. I thanked him for his kindness, took my departure, and have not met him since.

It was Mary Craig who had provided me with the picture of that august Harvard senior, named Van Tuiver in the novel. What had happened was this. In my little cottage in the single-tax colony of Arden, Craig had met a patron of the colony, a leading paper manufacturer, Fiske Warren. When I left Arden, my secretary, Ellen, had become one of the secretaries to this extremely wealthy and important Bostonian. On his country estate each of his secretaries had a separate cottage of her own, and Ellen had invited Craig to pay her a visit in her cottage. Craig had done so, and Fiske had dropped in now and then in the evening to chat with Craig. He did not invite her to the mansion, and Craig was shrewd enough to guess why and proud enough to be amused. Fiske's wife, Gretchen Warren, was the most august and haughty leader of Boston society, and was not accustomed to receive secretaries socially—or friends of secretaries.

To spare too many details: Craig happened to mention that she was a lineal descendant of that Lady Southworth who had come to Massachusetts to marry Governor Bradford. Fiske went up into the air as if she had put a torpedo under him. He hurried to confirm it in his genealogy books, and then to tell Gretchen about it—with the result that Ellen lost her guest and Craig was moved up to the "big house" (I use the phrase to which Craig was accustomed in Mississippi).

So it had come about that she had met "Van Tuiver"—only of course that was not his real name. Gretchen had invited the top clubmen of eligible age to meet this Southern belle, and Craig had listened to their magnificence. Of course, she was no longer "eligible," being engaged to me, but she was not at liberty to reveal that fact; and she let them spread their glory before her. She had never met this particular kind of arrogance and self-importance, in Mississippi or anywhere else.

So when she came back from the visit she gave me Van Tuiver as a character for our book, with every detail of his appearance, his manner, and his language. And so it was that I was not disturbed by the opinion of Walter Lippmann. Walter's chances of meeting such a man at Harvard had been of the slimmest, for Walter suffered not merely from the handicap of being Jewish but also from having declassed himself by setting up a socialist society. (Never have I forgotten the tone of voice in which the secretary of the Harvard Club answered me when I asked if I could obtain a list of Harvard students in order to send them a circular about the proposed Intercollegiate Socialist Society.

"*Socialist!*" he exclaimed, incredulously; and I got the list elsewhere.)

VI

In New York we had found ourselves a ten-dollar-a-week apartment on Morningside Heights. One evening I went to a meeting at Carnegie Hall alone; Craig, being tired, preferred to sleep. I came back about midnight; and after that she had little sleep, because I told her about the meeting.

Mrs. Laura Cannon, wife of the president of the Western Federation of Miners, had told the story of what came to be known to the world as the Ludlow massacre. In the lonely Rocky Mountains were coal camps fenced in and guarded like medieval fortresses. No one could enter without a pass or leave without another, and the miners and their families were in effect white slaves. Rebelling against such conditions, they had gone on strike and had been turned out of the camps. Down in the valley, with the help of their unions, they had set up tent colonies; after they had held out for several months, the gunmen of the company had come one night, thrown kerosene on the tents, and set fire to them. Three women and eleven children had been burned to death; but the newspapers of the country, including those of New York, had given only an inch or two to the event.

The most important fact about the whole thing was that these coal camps were owned by the Colorado Fuel and Iron Company, a Rockefeller concern. I told my terrified wife what I had decided to do—to take Mrs. Cannon to the office of John D. Rockefeller, Jr., in the morning and ask him to hear her story. If he refused, we would charge him with murder before the American public and organize a group of sympathizers who would put mourning bands around their arms and walk up and down in front of the Standard Oil Building in protest against the company's crime.

I won't try to portray the dismay of my bride of just one year. We had been so perfectly happy and so carefully respectable—and now this horror! "You will all be arrested," she exclaimed. I answered, "Maybe, but they couldn't do anything but fine us, and someone will put up the money." We didn't have it.

Craig couldn't bring herself to say no—not this time. In the morning I set to work to call people who had been at the meeting, and put them to work to call others to the Liberal Club that evening. And, of course, we did not fail to notify the newspapers. Some thirty or forty people assembled—having scented publicity, which "radicals" dearly love. I set forth the proposal and called for the help of those who would agree to a program of complete silence and complete nonresistance. One man, overcome with indignation, called for a program of collecting arms, and I invited him to go into the next room, shut the door, and collect all the arms he wanted.

Craig was willing to be one of the marchers but insisted that she had to have a proper costume. She waited until the department stores opened, and then she got herself an elegant long white cape. When I arrived at nine in the morning, I found no men but four ladies, one of whom had provided herself with a many-colored banner and a loud screaming voice. I invited her to set the banner against the wall of the Standard Oil Company and to stuff her handkerchief in her mouth; we then took up our silent parade in front of the office of Mr. John D. Rockefeller, Jr. (We never saw him, and I learned that he had taken up the practice of coming in by a back door.)

VII

We walked for perhaps five minutes, and then policemen politely told us to walk somewhere else; when we politely refused, they told us that we were under arrest. One of them grabbed me by the arm and started to hustle me, but I said to him very quietly, "Please behave like a gentleman. I have no idea but to go with you." So after that we had a pleasant stroll to the police station, where we found a half-dozen newspaper reporters with their pads of scratch paper and their busy pens.

To the sergeant at the desk I told the story of the Ludlow massacre all over again. It wasn't his business to listen, but it was the reporters' business, and all police sergeants are respectful to reporters. A little later we were put into a patrol wagon and taken to the police court, and again I told the story, this time to the judge. The policeman who had arrested me testified that my conduct had been "that of a perfect gentleman"; whereupon the judge found me guilty of disorderly conduct and fined me three dollars. I declined to pay the fine, and so did the four ladies; so each of us got three days instead of three dollars, and I was led over the "Bridge of Sighs" to a cell in the ancient prison known as The Tombs.

A most interesting experience, because I had as cellmate a young Jewish fellow in for stealing. He was a lively talker and told me all about his art; and of course every kind of knowledge is useful to a novelist sooner or later. This young fellow stole because he loved to. It was a sporting proposition—he pitted his wits against the owners of property in the great metropolis, and he didn't especially mind when he was caught because the charge was always petty theft; apparently they never bothered to compare his fingerprints with previous fingerprints, and he was always a "first offender." He trusted me—I suppose he thought of a socialist as an intellectual and higher type of thief. Anyhow, we were pals, and I was entertained for two days.

I never left the cell, because I had learned about fasting, and when I contemplated prison fare, I decided this was a good time to apply my knowledge. At the end of the second day a message came to me that if I wanted to appeal my sentence I would have to pay a fine; for, obviously, if I served the whole three days I could not sue to get my time back. It was my wife who had sent this information, and she set out to find the court where the one dollar for the third day was to be paid. She has told in *Southern Belle* the delightful story of how she got lost in the several galleries of courtrooms and stopped a gentleman to ask the way to the room where the fine should be paid. The gentleman asked, "What is it for?" and Craig said, "Some idiot of a judge has sent my husband to jail." "Madam," was the reply, "I am that judge." But he told her where to go to pay her dollar.

We kept that demonstration going for a couple of weeks, and Craig met such people as Judge Kimbrough's daughter had never dreamed of meeting in this world—lumberjacks from the mountains, sailors from the harbor, and poor Jewish garmentworkers half-starved in a period of unemployment.

George Sterling, the poet, happened to be visiting in New York. He marched on one side of Craig, with Craig holding his

arm to keep him from making any move when the "slugs" mut-
tered insults at her. ("Slugs" was what Craig called them, groping for a word.) Clement Wood, stenographer and also poet,
marched on the other side. Irish-born novelist Alexander Irvine
and Irish-born suffragette Elizabeth Freeman took charge while
Craig rested, and some rich supporter put up money for a rest
room and feeding station. I went out to Colorado to make publicity there, and to write it; meantime Craig kept things going on
lower Broadway. Clement told her that an agent of the Rockefellers had come to him and offered him money for secret information about our plans and purposes. Since we had no secrets
of any sort, Craig told him to get all the Rockefeller money that
was available.

VIII

A group of students of the Ferrer School, an anarchist institution, came down to march, and later decided to carry the demonstration to the Rockefeller estate in Pocantico Hills. They did
not ask our consent, and we had nothing to do with it—until
they were beaten up for trying to hold a free-speech meeting in
nearby Tarrytown. Then I went up to try to persuade the board
of directors of the town to let us hold a meeting; I carried with
me a letter from Georg Brandes, perhaps the most highly re-
spected literary critic in Europe—but I doubt if the trustees
had heard of him. They turned down our request.

What should turn up then but an offer from a millionaire lady,
whose estate adjoined the Rockefellers', to let us hold a free-
speech meeting in her open-air theater; I went there and made a
speech and was not beaten up. Let would-be reformers make a
note of this item and always have their free-speech meetings on
the property of millionaires.

The time came when all our money was gone, and we went
back to our little apartment on Morningside Heights. A day or
two later our telephone rang. It was the nearby police station
calling to ask Craig if she knew Arthur Caron and if she would
come and identify his body. Caron was a French-Canadian boy
who had been in a strike in Rhode Island and beaten there. After
being beaten at Tarrytown, he and two of his colleagues had set

to work in a tenement-house room to make a bomb, doubtless to blow up the Rockefellers. Instead, they had blown out the top floor of the tenement house, and two of them were killed.

I have often thought what must have been the effect of that event upon the Rockefeller family. There has been an enormous change in their attitude to the public since that time. John D., Jr., went out to his coal mines and danced with the miners' wives and made friends with the angry old Mother Jones; more important, he made a deal to recognize the unions and reform conditions in all the camps of the Colorado Fuel and Iron Company. If you look at the record that his son, the present Nelson A. Rockefeller, is making as governor of New York State, you will see that our lessons were indeed learned by that family.

One curious outcome of that "civil war" of ours had to do with the newspapers. Craig had made friends with some of the reporters, and they had told her how their stories were being mutilated in the office. The New York *Herald* gave us especially bad treatment, making many statements about us that were pure invention. For example, they said that the president of the board of trustees in Tarrytown had denounced my conduct in an angry speech. I went up to see the gentleman, to whom I had been perfectly courteous. He assured me he had made no such statement to anyone—and he gave me a letter to that effect.

That letter was shown to the *Herald*, but they refused publication and even repeated the charge; so I told a lawyer friend to bring a libel suit against them. Then I went back to my writing and forgot all about it. The usual law's delay occurred. Some three years later, to my astonishment, I received a letter from my lawyer telling me that the case had been settled, with the *Herald* paying three thousand dollars' damages!

George Sterling and Clement Wood each got a fine poem out of this experience. George wandered down to the battery and gazed at the Statue of Liberty and asked,

> Say, is it bale-fire in thy brazen hand,
>   A traitor light set on betraying coast
>   To lure to doom the mariner? . . .

And Clement Wood, after collecting his Rockefeller money, wrote a sonnet beginning:

> White-handed lord of murderous events,
> Well have you guarded what your father gained. . . .

Both these poems are in my anthology, *The Cry for Justice*, which I set out to compile as soon as the excitement of the "mourning parade" was over.

IX

We were broke as usual, but the John C. Winston Company of Philadelphia fell for my proposition of a book, *The Cry for Justice: An Anthology of Social Protest*; they advanced a thousand dollars to make possible its compilation. A good friend, Frederick C. Howe, then United States Commissioner of Immigration, offered us the use of a cottage in the hills above Croton-on-Hudson; so we moved out of our ten-dollar-a-week apartment into a fifty-dollar-a-month cottage on the edge of woods that sloped down to the Croton River. In summer the woods were green, and in winter the ground was white, and George Sterling came and chopped down dead trees for firewood. Clement Wood came to be my secretary and to quarrel with me over all the poetry I put into *The Cry for Justice* and all that I left out—including some of his. Vachel Lindsay had come to see us in New York, and his book had set Clement on fire; we would hear him roaring through the forest:

> Or Mumbo-Jumbo, God of the Congo . . .
> Mumbo-Jumbo will hoo-doo you!

Poor dear Vachel! He had been sending me his stuff for two or three years, and I had been praising it; but when I met him he suddenly burst out, to my consternation, "*Oh, you don't like me!*" I had to persuade him that I liked him very much indeed. Clement liked him, and liked Walt Whitman too, but he didn't like Edward Carpenter for two cents. We had fierce arguments, but in the end we got *The Cry for Justice* put together, and it was published and widely reviewed.

Edgar Selwyn and his wife, Margaret Mayo, lived within bicycling distance, and so I had tennis. Isadora Duncan's sister had her dancing school nearby, and we met unusual characters there. Floyd Dell and Robert Minor constituted a little radical colony, and we could go there and solve all the problems of the world, each in his own special way.

As usual, I was on the verge of making a fortune; *The Jungle* was being made into a movie, and I went to watch the procedure in a big warehouse in Yonkers. An odd confusion there—the show was being directed by A. E. Thomas; I took this to be Augustus Thomas and named him as the director, greatly to his surprise. It was a poor picture; the concern went into bankruptcy, and so ended another dream. All I got was the film, and I loaned it to some organization and never got it back. Whoever has it, please let me know!

One incident I remember on the opening night. In the lobby of the theater I found myself being introduced to Richard Harding Davis. He had come back from some expedition and was still wearing khaki. I had read one or two of his books, and had an impression of him as a prince among snobs; but when he heard my name, he held my hand and said, "Ah, now, *you* are a *real* writer. I only write for money." I never saw him again.

I saw the world war coming. I had a friend, J. G. Phelps Stokes, well known in New York as the "millionaire socialist"— you didn't have to be more than moderately rich to receive that title. I learned that his butler was in England and about to return, so I made arrangements for the butler to bring back my son, David. I put the boy in the North Carolina school of C. Hanford Henderson, whose wise and gracious book about education I had read. That left Craig and me free, and at last there came the long-awaited letter from the Judge, inviting us "home."

X

That meant Ashton Hall, on the Mississippi Sound near Gulfport. The family used it only in summer, and we were free to have it eight months of the year. I have a vivid memory of getting off at a little railroad stop in the backwoods: we were the only persons to descend, and there was only one person to meet us—a boy of fourteen dressed in the uniform of a military academy, a boy with gracious manners and a strong Southern brogue.

Such was my first meeting with Hunter Southworth Kimbrough, who was to be our standby for almost half a century. I remember how he insisted on carrying both bags; and today I have only to go to the telephone and call him, and eight hours later he arrives from Phoenix, Arizona, ready to lift all the contents of the house on his sturdy shoulders.

We walked a quarter of a mile or so to the Gulf of Mexico, and there just beyond a sandy-beach drive stood the lovely old house, built of sound timbers before the Civil War. The front stood high above the ground, so there was room underneath to stow sailboats and even buggies. (Jefferson Davis' buggy and his daughter's boat were there.) We went up a wide flight of steps to what was called a gallery, which ran around three sides of the house. On it were big screened cages in which you could hide from the mosquitoes when the wind from the back marshes drove them to the front.

There was a dining room that could seat a score of persons, and two reception rooms with doors that rolled back to make a big room for dancing. Upstairs were four bedrooms, and above that a great attic with a row of beds and cots to accommodate the beaux when they came from New Orleans. That attic was haunted for Craig, because it was there the Judge had hung bunches of bananas to ripen, and Craig's five-year-old sister had climbed up and eaten unripe bananas and died in Craig's arms —this when Craig herself was little more than a child. The mother had been screaming to God while Craig was making the child vomit; but neither effort helped.

There was "Aunt" Catherine, whom I had been hearing about ever since I had met Craig, a half-dozen years previously. Aunt Catherine—all the older Negroes were "Aunt" or "Uncle"—was an ex-slave and happy to tell about "dem days." "Dey wormed us all," she said, "wormed us all good." Which sounded alarming but merely meant the giving of worm medicine. Aunt Catherine's happiness was to fix elaborate meals, and her distress was great when she discovered that I did not want them. She took to wandering off down the beach, visiting the servants in other beach homes. She was elegant in the castoff clothing of Craig's mother and sisters, and I remember her coming down the beach with the wind blowing half-a-dozen colored scarves in front of her. When Craig rebuked her for neglecting her duties, the answer was, "But, Miss Ma'y, *somebody* gotta keep up de repitation of de family—*you* won't do it."

XI

Hunter, in the course of his explorations in Gulfport, picked up a sailor on liberty from one of the ships. He brought the man to the house to cut firewood and perform other labors. He was a Norwegian, a good fellow, and we put him up in one of the rooms in a back building, where the cooking was done and where the Negroes slept on the second floor. Gus, as his name was, quarreled with Catherine, who had contempt for any white man in the position of servant. She neglected to prepare his breakfast early, and Gus burst into her room to scold her. Catherine came to Craig, weeping wildly, "Oh, Miss Ma'y, I done seed a naked white man—never befo' in my life I seed a naked white man!"

The great thing in Craig's life now was the impending visit of her father. Her heart was in her mouth when I came up the steps after a walk, and the Judge was there. We shook hands, he bade me welcome, and I thanked him for the most precious gift I had ever received. He had hated to give it, of course, but all the same I had it, and for keeps. After a little talk I went into the house, and Craig said, "Well, Papa, what do you think of him?" The answer was, "I guess I overspoke myself." Craig told me afterward it was the first time in her life she had heard him make any sort of apology.

He was six feet four, with a little white beard. He was a judge of the Chancery Court, which means that he handled estates and was happy in his duty of protecting the property of widows. Also, he traveled a "circuit" and presided at court in four counties, where he was famous for his way of handling the Negroes who got into trouble. He could be very stern, but he also had a keen sense of humor and knew there was nothing the Negroes dreaded more than to be laughed at. He would propose penalties that would make the audience roar, such as making two husky men who had been fighting kiss each other and make up.

But for good Negroes he had only kindness and understanding. He owned plantations and lands, and some of his land was worked by trusted Negroes on shares. They would come to see him and tell him their needs, and he would sit on the back porch and chat with them, being interested in their minds. He would tell funny stories about them, but he gave serious advice and help when needed. On Christmas Day they all came to have their "dram," and in the evening when there were parties some would play music and be as happy as the dancers.

But don't think that he couldn't be stern, for he had to be. Dreadful things happened. A Negro woman, furious with jealousy, poured boiling grease into her sleeping husband's ear; a woman nurse, jealous of a rival for the position, set fire to the curtains on the balcony where the white children were sleeping. Craig told the story of a Negro meeting in the woods back of her Greenwood home. A fight broke out in the night, and the Judge grabbed his shotgun and rushed out; Mama Kimbrough grabbed his rifle and followed behind—to protect her big six-foot-four husband. He didn't want to shoot any of the Negroes because they were "his." He just waded in, using his shotgun as a club, and scattered them and drove them to their cabins. Such was life on a Mississippi plantation when Craig was a child, three quarters of a century ago. The sight of bleeding Negroes was familiar to her from the beginning of her life, and once she helped to sew on a torn ear.

XII

My aim that winter was to write a novel called *King Coal*, dealing with those labor camps in the Rocky Mountains about which I had learned so much. The first essential for my work was quiet, and the way to get it was to have a tent at a corner of the property remote from the house. A tent must have a platform, so I ordered the necessary lumber and set to work. Nobody at Ashton Hall, white or black, had ever seen a white "gentleman" doing such work, and I damaged my reputation thereby. A colored boy helped me to get the tent up, since that couldn't be done alone. I built a little doorframe for the front and tacked on mosquito netting.

Thereafter, when the wind brought mosquitoes, my technique was as follows: I would dart out from the big house, run as fast as my feet could take me to the tent, brush off the mosquitoes that had already attached themselves, dart inside and fasten the door, then with a flyswat proceed to eliminate all the mosquitoes inside. The size of the tent was eight by ten; so I had three steps east and then three steps west while I thought up the next scene in my story. I would sit down and write for a while on the typewriter, then get up and walk and think some more. So, in the end I had *King Coal*.

The Judge came from Greenwood now and then and took me fishing—always with a Negro man to row the boat and bait our hooks. Brother Willie Kimbrough came, a big laughing stout man, and took me to catch pompano in what was called Back Bay, a sort of deep sound.

Craig's sister Dolly, back from England, came to stay with us; Craig, who disapproved of idleness, assigned her a job. Behind the house stood an enormous arbor of scuppernong grapes, loaded with ripe fruit that it would be a shame to waste. So Dolly put two Negro boys to picking grapes. When they had two big baskets full, they would take them to the trolley, and Dolly would ride into town and arrange with a grocery to buy them. Never before had an occupant of Ashton Hall engaged in trade, and Dolly wept once or twice, then became interested in making pocket money.

Everything was going beautifully, and if it went wrong there was someone to attend to it. I made the mistake of leaving my small possessions, such as fountain pen and cuff links, on my bureau, and one by one these objects disappeared. After searching everywhere I mentioned the matter to the youthful Hunter, who knew exactly what to do. He called a Negro boy, one of the house servants, and said with due sternness, "Empty your pockets." Sure enough, the boy proceeded to shell out all my possessions. Hunter didn't say, "I'll call the police." He said, "Now, you keep out of Mr. Sinclair's room; if I ever hear of you being in there again, I'll skin you alive." Such was "gov'ment" on the Mississippi Sound. I don't know how it is now, but I am able to understand both sides in the racial problem.

XIII

Visitors came to see us—among them Captain Jones. I don't know that I ever heard his first name, but that wasn't necessary as there was only one "Captain Jones" in that world. He had built the Gulfport harbor, also the railroad that connected Gulfport with the North, and also the trolley line that paralleled the road in front of Ashton Hall and carried me into town when I wanted to play tennis at Captain Jones's Great Southern Hotel.

The old gentleman and his wife came to Ashton Hall, and he poured out his heart to us. He was probably the richest man in Mississippi; but nobody loved him, nobody wanted anything but money from him, and some of their ways were wicked and cruel. His railroad, which ran through the desolate "piney woods" of southern Mississippi, was a blessing to everybody along the way; but the miserable piney-woods people, "clayeaters" as they were called, had only one thought—to plunder Captain Jones's railroad. They would cut the wire fence that protected both sides of the track and turn some scrawny old cow onto the railroad right of way; when the creature was struck and killed by a train, they would demand the price of a prize bull in a cattle show.

I was duly sympathetic, of course, and was somewhat embarrassed when a strike of the dockworkers developed in Captain Jones's Gulfport. He had made all the prosperity of that town, and here was one more case of ingratitude. It was embarrassing to me and to the Kimbrough family when the strikers sent a deputation to ask me to speak at a meeting in the largest hall in Gulfport. I had never refused an invitation from strikers, and I wasn't going to begin at the age of thirty-six. I told them I couldn't discuss their particular issues because I didn't know the circumstances and didn't have time to investigate them; but I would tell them my ideas of democracy in industry, otherwise known as socialism, where strikes would be unnecessary because workers would be striking against themselves.

The meeting was duly announced, and the Kimbrough family were too polite to tell me what they thought about the matter. What the wife of Captain Jones thought about it surprised both Craig and me. She called us up and said she would be glad to go to the meeting with us; and would we come to the Great Southern Hotel and have dinner with her before the meeting? Of course we said we would be pleased.

It was Craig's practice to sit in the very back of a hall, where she would be inconspicuous and if possible unrecognized. But Mrs. Jones wouldn't have it that way. She took me by an arm and Craig by an arm, and marched us straight down the center aisle to the front seats in the hall so that everybody would know who had brought us. I have had a number of experiences like that with the very rich, and they have encouraged me to realize that democracy is a real force in America.

XIV

So everything seemed lovely at Ashton Hall, until one tragic day when the roof fell in on us—the moral and spiritual roof. My former wife saw fit to come to Gulfport and bring a lawsuit for the custody of our son. I cannot shirk the telling of this story because it played an enormous part in my life and Craig's; but I tell it as briefly and tactfully as possible. I don't think the lady actually wanted David, but the grandmother did. My former wife is still living, has been married twice, and has children and grandchildren whom I have no desire to hurt. Suffice it to say that her coming created a scandal in Gulfport—one that not even the wife of Captain Jones could mitigate.

David was with us at the time, and I had a secretary, a young man from the North, who considered it a great lark to carry the lad off into the woods and hide him from the courts of Mississippi for a few days. There was a trial with plenty of publicity; the court, presided over by a Catholic judge, awarded six months' custody to me and six months to his mother. To make the painful story short, I took David to California for the first six months; and when the time came for his mother to come and get him, I heard nothing from her—then or afterward.

Judge Kimbrough had made Craig an offer promising her Ashton Hall if she would live there. It was said to be worth a hundred and fifty thousand dollars, and with the development that has come in the past thirty or forty years, the lot alone is probably worth that now. But we couldn't be happy there. A friend had told me about the wonders of southern California, where there were no mosquitoes. I begged Craig to come, and I went ahead to find a home.

10

West to California

It was November of 1915. I wanted to be warm so I went as far south as possible, to Coronado; but it proved not to be so warm. Cold winds blew off the wide Pacific, and the little cottage I rented leaked both wind and rain. I pasted newspapers inside to keep out the wind—which was not very ornamental.

Craig was wretchedly unhappy over the humiliation she had brought to her family, and only time could heal that wound. She told me long afterward that she hadn't been sure she would follow me to California; but her father, who had labored so hard to keep us apart, now kept us together. He said, "Daughter, you must go to your husband." She came, and we had a hard time because George P. Brett of Macmillan rejected *King Coal*. It was a painful, a terrible subject, and I had failed to make the characters convincing. Craig, who agreed with him, wrote to him telling him her ideas and offering to make me revise the manuscript accordingly. Brett said he would read the manuscript again after she had finished.

You can imagine what a hold that gave her in our family arguments. The heroine of my story was a daughter of the mining camps named Mary Burke. I had failed to describe what she looked like; Craig sought in vain to find out from me, because I didn't know. Likewise, Craig insisted that Mary Burke was naked, and thereafter for the rest of our lives the revision of my manuscripts was known as "putting the clothes on Mary Burke."

Anybody who heard us in that little leaky cottage would have been quite sure we were getting ready for a divorce; but we made an agreement about all our quarrels—whenever one of us got too excited, the other would say "Manuscript," and the excitement would diminish.

When the rains stopped, I would go out and meet the idle rich, playing tennis on the courts of the immense and fashionable Coronado Hotel. Craig would never go; she had met enough rich people to last her the rest of her life. But I had to have characters as well as tennis, and I watched the characters playing at polo and other expensive diversions. I wrote a novel about some of these people that has never yet been published—Craig never got around to putting clothes on the characters.

As far as I can recall we had only one visitor that entire winter. Jane Addams wrote that she wanted to see me, and I was surprised and pleased. I had seen a good deal of her in Chicago because I had had my meals at the University Settlement all the time I was getting material for *The Jungle*. What she had come for now was to ask me about Emanuel Julius. Her niece, Marcet Haldeman, had become engaged to marry him, and what sort of man was he? He was editor of the *Appeal to Reason* and had been the means of making *The Jungle* known to the American masses. I am not sure whether I had met him at that time, but I could say that he had a brilliant mind and was, like myself, an ardent socialist.

I may as well complete the story here by saying that the marriage took place; and that after the tragic death of J. A. Wayland, Emanuel Haldeman-Julius bought the *Appeal to Reason* with his wife's money and built up a great publishing business, including many hundreds of titles of the five-cent Little Blue Books that did so much to educate America. But, alas, Julius took up with a secretary, and Marcet divorced him. Julius drowned in his swimming pool, and no one knows whether it was a suicide. The good Jane Addams did not live to see these painful events. A son survives, a good friend.

II

We decided that we wanted to get away from ocean winds; and I had met a tennis professional who lived in Pasadena and who assured me I would find plenty of tennis there. So we made the move and found ourselves a brown-painted, two-story house on Sunset Avenue, a remote part of the town. It was covered with a huge vine of red roses, and roses were as important to Craig as tennis was to me.

The house stood on the edge of a slope, with the valley of the Arroyo Seco to the west. It was unfurnished, so Craig would walk several blocks to the streetcar, ride a couple of miles downtown, and then wander about looking for secondhand furniture shops. That way she got three chairs with ragged upholstery for our living room, two beds for upstairs, and packing boxes for tables and bureaus. We were able to do all those things because Brett had accepted *King Coal* and paid a five-hundred-dollar advance. After that magical achievement, Craig was boss of the family.

Pasadena in the year 1916 was a small town that called itself "City of Roses" and was called by others "City of Millionaires." These last occupied the wide, elegant Orange Grove Avenue, with palaces on both sides and two very elegant hotels for the winter visitors. We had no thought of the rich, and never expected them to have any thought of us in our humble brown cottage overlooking the sunset. The beautiful roses and the sunsets were enough for Craig, and as for me, I had started *The Coal War*, a sequel to *King Coal*, with more about Mary Burke and her clothes. I had learned now!

But wherever there are millionaires there are also socialists—they are cause and effect. The socialists came to see me and invited me to speak at a meeting in support of a proposed cooperative; of course I went. I had found a woman secretary to type my manuscripts—another necessity of my life—and in the course of the evening this lady came to my wife and whispered a portentous sentence: "Mrs. Gartz wants to meet you."

"Who is Mrs. Gartz?" asked Craig; and the awe-stricken secretary replied, "Oh, my dear, she is the richest woman in Pasadena."

Craig said, "Well, bring her here."

The secretary, dismayed, responded, "She said for you to come to her."

The secretary didn't know Craig very well, but she learned

about her right there. "If she wants to meet me," said Craig, "she will come to me." And that was that.

When the meeting was over, the secretary came back, and with her was a large, magnificent lady of the kind that Craig had known all through her girlhood. The lady was introduced; and, of course, she knew another lady when she met one. More especially, she knew a lovely Southern voice and manner; so she asked if she might come to see us, and Craig said that she might. Craig made no apology for her living room that had only three ragged chairs in it—the biggest one for the large rich lady and the other two for Craig and myself.

Mrs. Kate Crane-Gartz was the elder daughter of Charles R. Crane, plumbing magnate of Chicago, dead then for several years. He had been a newspaper celebrity, not only because he was one of the richest men in America but because he differed from most rich men in being talkative and in voicing original opinions. He was particularly down on college education, insisting that it was all wasteful nonsense. He hadn't had one himself, and look where he had got!

Mrs. Gartz was an elegant lady with a haughty manner and a tender heart. She had had many sorrows, which we learned about in the course of time. She had lost two of her children in a theater fire in Chicago. She still had a son and a daughter, both of whom she adored, but they gave her little happiness. She had a soft heart and an overfull purse, and she was preyed upon freely—all that we learned soon. But there was one person who would never prey upon her, and that was Mary Craig Sinclair.

III

This new friend was the most curiously frank person we had ever known. She looked around at our new establishment and said, "Why do you live like this?" "We have to," said Craig, and no more. "Don't your husband's books sell?" demanded the visitor. "They have sold in the past," said Craig, "but he has spent all his money on the socialist movement. He always does that, I'm sorry to say."

Mrs. Gartz obtained our promise to come and see her, also

permission to send her car for us. Then she got into a magnificent limousine and told the uniformed chauffeur to drive her downtown to a furniture store. Early the next morning came a van, and two men unloaded a set of parlor furniture upholstered in blue velvet.

Craig said, "What is this?" One of the men said, "It was ordered. We don't know anything about it." Craig said, "I didn't order it, and I don't want it. Take it back."

So it came about that there was one person in Pasadena whom Kate Crane-Gartz could not merely respect but could even stand a bit in awe of. There was one person she would never dare to humiliate, and one who would come to her luncheon parties wearing unfashionable clothing. So it came about that for something like a quarter of a century Mary Craig Sinclair controlled the purse strings of the richest woman in Pasadena.

The main factor in this, I think, was that for the first time in her life Mrs. Gartz met someone whom she regarded as her social equal and possibly her superior. Craig had not only the loveliest Southern voice, but also had gracious manners, wit, and what is called charm. She could keep a roomful of company in continuous laughter. Both men and women would gather around to hear what she had to say. She had taste, and could look lovely in clothes she found on a bargain counter. She had the strangest imaginable combination of haughtiness and kindness. She had a heart that bled for every kind of suffering except that which was deserved. She was a judge of character, and no pretender could ever fool her.

Most important of all, she had come with my help to understand what was wrong with the world—the social system that produces human misery faster than all the charity in the world can relieve it. She had married me partly because I had taught her that, and now she understood the world better than any person whom Kate Crane-Gartz had ever known.

For many years Craig would never take a cent from Mrs. Gartz for herself. "Give it to the co-operative. Give it to the Socialist Party." For a while Mrs. Gartz was timid about doing that, so she would ask Craig to pass it on, which Craig faithfully did.

The "co-op" had been started by a devoted socialist woman named Tipton, who took in washing while her husband drove a delivery wagon. You can imagine that the first time Mrs. Kate Crane-Gartz showed up at one of the monthly "co-op" bean suppers at the Tipton house it was an event in the history of that City of Millionaires.

Mr. Gartz, who handled his wife's millions, was not long unaware of these developments. He was beside himself with rage; and when for the first time his wife invited us to a supper party at the fashionable Maryland Hotel, he came into the dining room and stood behind my chair and started muttering abuse in a low tone of voice.

Craig had never had to handle a situation like that, but she was equal to all situations. She got up and invited Mr. Gartz to come over to the next table and speak to her. He obeyed, and she pointed out to him that there was only one possible conclusion the public would draw if he persisted in making a public scene with Upton Sinclair. With that terrible threat she scared him; at the same time, with her lovely Southern voice she calmed him down, and he went his way. Once or twice he raved at me in his home, but I had promised not to answer him, and I obeyed.

That situation continued for a matter of twenty years. The daughter, Gloria, sided with her father, and the son, Craney, sided with his mother. Alas, Craney drank, and when he was drinking he was very generous. To pacify him I would accept his gifts and then return them when he was sober. I once returned a Buick car.

IV

I finished *The Coal War*, a story of the great strike through which I had lived in spirit if not in physical presence; but I never published it, for world war had come and no one was interested in labor problems any more. Mrs. Gartz was a pacifist. A federal agent came to investigate her, and Craig had the job of pacifying *him*. "What I want to know is," he said, "is she pro-German, or is she just a fool?" Craig assured him that the latter was the case.

Craney became an Air Force officer and traveled around in a blimp looking for German submarines off the Atlantic coast. I resigned from the Socialist Party in order to support the war; and Mrs. Gartz, a pacifist on her son's account, took a lot of persuading from Craig—who, being a Southerner, had less objection to fighting. At any rate, that was true when the fighting was against the German Kaiser.

My socialist comrades called me bad names for a while, and Craig and Mrs. Gartz argued every time they met. But by that time Craig's influence had become strong enough to keep Mrs. Gartz from getting into jail. We had a lot of fun laughing over the idea of Kitty—as I had come to call her—misbehaving in a jail. I think even Mr. Gartz appreciated what I was doing, and he no longer growled when he saw me in his home.

In 1918 I started the publication of a little socialist magazine to support the American position in the world war. I called it *Upton Sinclair's: For a Clean Peace and the Internation.* (Later the slogan became *For Social Justice, by Peaceful Means if Possible.*) For that, Craig felt justified in letting Mrs. Gartz hand her several government bonds. It was amusing the way the great lady argued with us about what was in the magazine, and at the same time helped to keep it going. Some of my socialist and other friends argued with me. They would write me letters of protest against my supporting the war, and I would put the letters in the magazine and reply to them. The more angry the letters were, the more my readers were entertained. All my life I have had fun in controversy.

My position was, of course, to the left of the government. Indeed, Woodrow Wilson was to the left of his own government, and many of his officials didn't understand his ideas—or disapproved of them when they did understand. When the first issue of the magazine appeared, I applied to the Post Office Department for second-class entry—which was essential, for if I had to pay first-class postage I would be bankrupt at the outset. I had sent copies of the magazine to a number of persons in Washington whom I knew or knew about; and when I got notice that the second-class entry had been refused, I telegraphed to Colonel House. He told me that he was with the President when the telegram was delivered, and he had told the President what was in the magazine and the President approved of it.

As it happened, John Sharp Williams, United States Senator from Mississippi, was Craig's cousin; in her girlhood she had driven him over the shell roads of the Gulf Coast and learned about politics from his humorous stories. I had sent the magazine to him, of course; and now he wrote that he had read it and had taken up the matter of the second-class entry with Postmaster General Burleson, who was also a Southerner. Burleson had a copy of the magazine with the passages that he considered "subversive" marked. Williams said, "I'll undertake to read those passages to Woodrow Wilson, and I'll agree to eat my hat if he doesn't approve every word of them."

So it all worked out very nicely. My little magazine got the second-class entry, and Senator Williams of Mississippi went on wearing his hat.

I published, in all, ten issues of that little magazine. The first issue was April 1918; then I had to skip a month because of the delay with second-class entry. The last issue was February 1920. In all, I built up a subscription list of ten thousand, paid for at one dollar per year. I had five secretaries and office girls wrapping and mailing. Mrs. Gartz would come down and argue with Craig and me—she being an out-and-out pacifist. Her attitude was summed up by James Russell Lowell in two lines of verse—

> Ez fer war, I call it murder—
> There you hev it plain an' flat.

—although I don't think Mrs. Gartz had ever heard of *The Biglow Papers.*

V

Like all the other liberals, radicals, and socialists, I was bitterly disappointed by the settlement to which President Wilson consented in Paris. It seemed to us that our hopes had been betrayed, and it seemed to Mrs. Gartz that her seditious opinions had been vindicated. But nothing made any difference in our friendship, or interrupted the flow of checks to help keep the magazine going.

The checks brought one amusing development before long: the president of Pasadena's biggest bank invited Mrs. Gartz to remove her account from his institution. Whether that had ever happened in the banking world before I do not know. Checks payable to Mary Craig Sinclair were poisonous or incendiary. I might add that in the new bank Craig deposited a thousand-dollar bond that Mrs. Gartz had brought to her personally, in return for some writing Craig had done for her. "Don't let Mr. Sinclair get hold of it," said Mrs. Gartz, "or he'll spend it all on the magazine. Go down to the bank and rent a safe-deposit box and hide it away."

Since Craig could feel that she had earned this bond, she took Mrs. Gartz's advice. Some months later, she went down to the bank to get the bond and discovered that the box was empty. In the normal course of events she would have reported the matter to the head of the bank; but she would have had to tell him where she had got the bond, and she did not care to do that. She took the loss quietly and did not tell her too-generous friend.

While editing and publishing the magazine, I was also writing a new novel based on my experiences in the Socialist Party, of which I had been a member for a couple of decades. I had known all kinds of picturesque characters and types, and heard stories of their adventures. A Socialist Party candidate for vice president, Ben Hanford, had invented the name "Jimmie Higgins" for the humble worker in the party who makes no speeches and gets no honors but does the tiresome jobs of addressing envelopes, distributing literature, and making house-to-house calls to bring his fellow workers to meetings. I took this character for my hero, and started the publication of *Jimmie Higgins* in the magazine.

When in 1919 our Army made its somewhat crazy landing on the shores of the Archangel Peninsula, as a start to putting down the Bolshevik movement in Russia, I decided to change the tone of my novel at the end. So far Jimmie had been a socialist patriot and had loyally gone to war; but now he turned into a malcontent, to be jailed and tortured. I recall that some reviewer in the New York *Times* rebuked me severely for this seditious invention; but it wasn't long afterward that the New York *Times* itself was reporting just such incidents as having happened in the Army at Archangel. When I wrote to the *Times* pointing out these details, my letter was ignored.

In this magazine I had all kinds of fun. I got letters of praise and letters of fury, and published them side by side. The more bad names I was called, the more amusing I found it; and my readers let me know that they too enjoyed it. I sent the magazine to well-known persons, got responses pro and con, and published them. H. G. Wells wrote a gay letter. I published it in facsimile, and somebody wrote asking me please to supply a translation. Socialists denounced me as a renegade; patriots denounced me as a traitor—and I printed the letters along with those of Colonel House, Senator John Sharp Williams, and other patriots of repute.

All this labor was wearing on my brain and my stomach, as well as my purse. Then suddenly I thought of a solution. Emanuel Haldeman-Julius had taken over the *Appeal of Reason* and changed its name to the *Haldeman-Julius Weekly*. He had a circulation of something like half a million, whereas *Upton Sinclair's* had succeeded in getting only ten thousand. I was always lured by a larger audience, and I made him a proposition to merge my magazine with his. He would let me have one full page called "Upton Sinclair's," in which I would say what I pleased. The serial I was writing would fill part of the page, which was newspaper size, and I could supply material similar to the contents of my magazine to fill the rest of the page. So it was agreed, and instead of having a monthly deficit I would have an income of fifty dollars a week. At least it was enough to pay the secretary who was taking my dictation. Also, it was a load off the mind of my overburdened wife; and if any of my subscribers complained, I could remind them that they had never offered to pay my printer's bill.

11

The Muckrake Man

I

FOR all my thinking lifetime I had been making tests of the big-business press of America. Almost everywhere it was on the side of privilege and exploitation, almost nowhere was it alert to the interest of democratic freedom. I had made notes and had envelopes full of clippings, and a head full of memories and a heart full of rage. I decided that I would put all that into a book and use the huge circulation I had got from that four-page Kansas weekly paper.

Seeking a title, I went back to the days of my youth when I had joined in the election campaign against Tammany Hall. William Travers Jerome had told about the wholesale prostitution that was protected because of graft paid to the police department. The "price of a woman's shame" was a brass check purchased at the entrance. Jerome had based his whole campaign upon it, and it struck me that *The Brass Check* was a fine title for a book about the prostitution of the press. I made the term known not merely to all America but to Europe as well, for the book was translated into many languages. It was a book of facts that no one could dispute, because I had saved the clippings, and I verified every story that I told.

It happened that an old friend was spending the winter in a cottage at our fashionable hotel. Samuel Untermyer, whom I had met through Lincoln Steffens, had been the highest-paid corporation lawyer in New York. Now he was an old man, tired

—except for his tongue. He could tell more terrible stories of corruption than anyone I ever knew, and he had told some to me when I visited his home up the Hudson and inspected the orchids that decorated every room.

I took him the manuscript of *The Brass Check*. When he had read it, he said, "Upton, you can't possibly publish that book. It contains a score of criminal libels and a thousand civil suits." I said, "I am going to publish it and take the consequences."

In Hammond, Indiana, I had found a large printing concern that had printed my book, *The Profits of Religion,* and made no objection. Now with some qualms I sent them the bulky "criminal" manuscript. To my surprise they made no comment, but quoted a price and proceeded to send me proofs.

I remember an amusing episode. The elderly treasurer of the company paid a visit to California and asked to see me. He came, and I learned to what I owed the honor. He said, very mildly, that he had recently discovered that I had run up a debt of twenty thousand dollars, and he wondered if I realized how much money that was. I told him that I had never had such a debt in my life hitherto, but that the book was selling well and the money would come in installments; and it did.

The book was published serially in the *Appeal,* and I was really surprised by the result. I had never had so many letters or so many orders. I knew that this time I had a real best seller. When I got the finished books, I gave a copy to my old friend, Gaylord Wilshire, who had made his home in Pasadena. He threw me into a panic when he phoned to tell me that it was inconceivable that the publication of this book would be permitted in America. He urged me to get all my copies distributed at once to socialist and labor groups and bookstores, and tell them to hide the books. I took this seriously and did as he suggested. It was an easy way to get rid of books, but a hard way to make money.

I had to have more paper; when I applied to the wholesalers I was told there was no paper on the market. World War I had caused a shortage of everything. The big concerns had their contracts, of course, and were getting their paper; but there was none left over for a little fellow like the author of *The Brass Check.*

I wrote to every wholesale paper dealer in the United States, but got no response. I took my lamentations into the city of Los Angeles, and there made a surprising discovery. There was a kind of paper called Kraft—otherwise known as plain brown wrapping paper. I could get it in a light weight, and it was possible to read print on it.

Nobody in the world had ever thought to print a book on it; but I got the price for a carload, six thousand dollars, and went back home and laid siege to my old friend, Sam Untermyer. I pointed out to him that I hadn't been arrested, and I hadn't even had a civil suit threatened; so I begged him to lend me six thousand dollars. I made him so ashamed of his misjudgment as a lawyer that he actually wrote me a check. He was quite pathetic when he told me how necessary it was that he should get it back. (He did.)

The book created a tremendous sensation and, of course, no end of controversy. I won't go into the details because the stories are old—and many of the newspapers have learned something about ethics. I venture to think that reporters all over the country read the book and took courage from it. Many of them are now editors, and while they still have to "take policy," they don't take it quite so completely.

I had called upon them to form a union to protect their rights, and this they promptly did—but they preferred to call it a guild, which is more aristocratic. Now the guild has branches all over the country and has had some effect in establishing standards of professional decency. While I was completing this book their New York chapter invited me to come and receive an award.

II

Next book: *The Goose-Step.* In the early spring of 1922 I left my long-suffering wife in charge of my office with an elderly secretary and three or four assistants, while I took a tour all over the United States, going first to the Northwest, then across to Chicago, New York, and Boston, then back through the Middle West and Southwest. I had been through five years of City College and four years of postgraduate work at Columbia, and had come out unaware that the modern socialist movement existed.

So now I meant to muckrake the colleges, showing where they had got their money and how they were spending it. I had jotted down the names of discontented schoolteachers and college professors who had written to me, or whose cases had become known; I visited some thirty cities, and in each of them some educator had assembled the malcontents in his or her home, and I sat and made notes while they told me their angry or hilarious stories.

There were many comical episodes on my tour. The University of Wisconsin had been liberal in the days of Robert LaFollette; but now it had a reactionary president, and I had a lively time with him. I had applied for the use of a hall, and he had already announced that he wouldn't grant it. He referred me to the board of regents, and I had a session with them. I finally got the use of the gymnasium, and the newspaper excitement brought a couple of thousand students to ask me questions for an hour after my talk. The concluding paragraph of my Wisconsin story was as follows:

Next afternoon I met the champion tennis team of the university, and played each of the pair in turn and beat them in straight sets; I was told that the student body regarded this as a far more sensational incident than my Socialist speech. An elderly professor came up to me on the campus next day—I had never seen him before, and didn't know his name; he assured me with mock gravity that I had made a grave blunder—I should have played the tennis matches first, and made the speech second, and no building on the campus would have been big enough to hold the crowd.

From Wisconsin I went on to Chicago, to what I called the University of Standard Oil. The students had a hymn that they sang there:

> Praise God from whom oil blessings flow,
> Praise Him, oil creatures here below,
> Praise Him above, Ye Heavenly Host,
> Praise Father, Son—but John the most.

I interviewed the president there, and he granted me the use of a small hall. When I assured him I would need a larger one, he refused to believe me; so I found myself quite literally packed in, with students climbing into the windows and sitting on the

sills and standing in the corridors. Just outside the hall I had no-
ticed a beautiful quadrangle with lovely soft grass and plenty of
room. I suggested that we all move out onto the grass and that
somebody find me a soapbox to stand on—the classical pulpit
of radical orators. There were loud cheers, and we moved outside. Still more people came running, and I talked to the crowd
for an hour or two and answered questions for an hour or two
more. Everybody had a good time except the Standard Oil president.

The next day I played the tennis champion of that university,
and I have to record that he beat me—but with an effort so
mighty that he split his pants.

III

One of the cities was my birthplace, Baltimore, and one of my
sources there was Elizabeth Gilman, daughter of the founder of
Johns Hopkins University. She filled her home with professors
one day and with schoolteachers the next, and they told me their
troubles.

I have mentioned my friendship with Mencken. It began by
mail; he was a tireless letter writer. There are some two hundred
letters from him in the collection of my papers in the Lilly Library of the University of Indiana. He liked to write little short
notes—he had secretaries and kept them busy. He didn't care
in the least what he said—provided only that it was funny. The
more extravagant, the more fun; and the more seriously you took
it, the still greater fun. When I was in New York, I called at the
American Mercury office, and his conversation was just like his
letters.

Now he had retired, and I visited his home in Baltimore—like
Uncle Bland's, it was one of those brick houses, four stories high,
apparently built a whole block at a time in solid, uniform rows,
each house with three or four white marble steps up to the front
door. Mencken poured out his Jovian thunderbolts for a whole
afternoon. This was the longest time I had with him, and the
most diverting.

Uncle Bland, as I have already related, was the founder and
president of the United States Fidelity and Guaranty Company

and had become one of the most important men in Baltimore
—but he had never met his "Sunpaper" editor. He insisted that I
invite Mencken out to Catonsville, his summer home, for dinner.
For this occasion my cousin Howard Bland sent his wife and
children over to the "big house," and we four men had Howard's
dining room for the evening.

It wasn't a pleasant occasion for me because the other three
spent most of the time discussing the various brands of wines,
brandies, and whiskies. Partly, of course, it was done to "kid"
me. It was the time of prohibition, and Uncle Bland had a tragic
experience to report. He had foreseen the trouble coming and had
a large stock safely locked up in his cellar; but while he was in
his town house for the winter, the cellar door was pried open,
and everything was carted away in the night. Everybody but me
was grieved.

I had shipped home various boxes containing documents. I
came back and for several months labored and wrote *The Goose-
Step*. As usual, I was warned about libel; but, as usual, it did not
happen.

The Goose-Step, a big book, 488 pages, price two dollars, was
published in 1923, and I assure you the college professors read
it—and talked about it, even out loud. I could get paper this
time, and filled all the orders, some twenty thousand copies.
Then I wrote *The Goslings*, 454 pages, price two dollars, telling
about schools of all sorts; the teachers read it, and many had the
courage to write to me. I had given them weapons to fight with,
or perhaps lanterns to light with; anyhow, I have seen changes
in America, and I tell myself I have helped a little to bring them
about.

IV

It was in that period that the American Civil Liberties Union
was started; I joined at once, and attended weekly luncheons of
its directors when I was in New York. Whether we had supported the war or opposed it, we all supported our right to say
what we thought and our willingness to let the other fellow do
the same. Among those I knew best were Roger Baldwin, who
became a civil-liberties hero and devoted his life to the cause;

Oswald Garrison Villard, publisher of *The Nation,* who remained a pacifist even in the face of Kaiser Wilhelm; and B. W. Huebsch, then a publisher on his own, and later editorial head of Viking Press; he was my guide and mentor through the eleven Lanny Budd volumes, about which I shall tell.

Also, there was W. J. Ghent, author of *Our Benevolent Feudalism.* He and I got into an argument over the war in the columns of *The Nation.* The argument got too hot for Villard, and he wouldn't publish my reply; so I paid for a page advertisement in *The Nation* and had my say. I remember Ghent's published comment: "Sinclair has taken the argument into the advertising columns, where I am unable to follow." After that, I was summoned to a luncheon with Villard and Huebsch and very gently asked to call off the war—that is, the Ghent War.

Not long afterward came the founding of the Southern California branch of the ACLU, a drama in which I had the leading role. It began when I tried to read the Constitution of the United States at a meeting on private property that had been organized on behalf of workers who were on strike at San Pedro Harbor. I was arrested after the third sentence. When I got out of jail, I wrote a letter to Louis D. Oaks, chief of police in Los Angeles. It was printed as a leaflet and widely circulated in Los Angeles. It was also printed in *The Nation* of June 6, 1923, along with an editorial note. I'm going to reprint that page from *The Nation,* partly because it tells the story, but mainly because it conveys so vividly the atmosphere of that period and the repression and brutality that went on then—which a new generation might find hard to credit.

In refusing to bow to the police of Los Angeles, who in the harbor strike have been the servile tools of the Merchants' and Manufacturers' Association, Upton Sinclair is strictly and legally a defender of the law against those who would violate it. And it is doubly to his praise that in this case he, a civilian, happens to be defending the law against the men who are sworn and paid to uphold it and have all the power of constituted authority on their side. The facts are undisputed: the police arrested Mr. Sinclair and his associates on *private property,* where they had assembled with the written consent of the owner. The law gives a police officer the right to enter private property only in two cases: if he has a warrant of arrest, or if a felony is actually being committed. Neither of these excuses existed in Los Angeles. The persons interfered with would have been legally justified in dealing with the police as violently as with a thief or kidnapper. We print below Mr. Sinclair's letter to the chief of police of Los Angeles because it is a recital of facts which our readers should know and a nobly patriotic protest which should have their support.

Pasadena, California, May 17, 1923

Louis D. Oaks,
Chief of Police, Los Angeles

Having escaped from your clutches yesterday afternoon, owing to the fact that one of your men betrayed your plot to my wife, I am now in position to answer your formal statement to the public, that I am "more dangerous than 4,000 I.W.W." I thank you for this compliment, for to be dangerous to lawbreakers in office such as yourself is the highest duty that a citizen of this community can perform.

In the presence of seven witnesses I obtained from Mayor Cryer on Tuesday afternoon the promise that the police would respect my constitutional rights at San Pedro, and that I would not be molested unless I incited to violence. But when I came to you, I learned that you had taken over the mayor's office at the Harbor. Now, from your signed statement to the press, I learn that you have taken over the district attorney's office also; for you tell the public: "I will prosecute Sinclair with all the vigor at my command, and upon his conviction I will demand a jail sentence with hard labor." And you then sent your men to swear to a complaint charging me with "discussing, arguing, orating, and debating certain thoughts and theories, which thoughts and theories were contemptuous of the constitution of the State of California, calculated to cause hatred and contempt of the government of the United States of America, and which thoughts and theories were detrimental and in opposition to the orderly conduct of affairs of business, affecting the rights of private property and personal liberty, and which thoughts and theories were calculated to cause any citizen then and there present and hearing the same to quarrel and fight and use force and violence." And this although I told you at least a dozen times in your office that my only purpose was to stand on private property with the written permission of the owner, and there to read the Constitution of the United States; and you perfectly well know that I did this, and only this, and that three sentences from the Bill of Rights of the Constitution was every word that I was permitted to utter—the words being those which guarantee "freedom of speech and of the press, and the right of the people peaceably to assemble, and to petition the government for the redress of grievances."

But you told me that "this Constitution stuff" does not go at the Harbor. You have established martial law, and you told me that if I tried to read the Constitution, even on private property, I would be thrown into jail, and there would be no bail for me—and this even though I read you the provision of the State constitution guaranteeing me the right to bail. When you arrested me and my friends, you spirited us away and held us "incomunicado," denying us what is our clear legal right, to communicate with our lawyers. All night Tuesday, and all day Wednesday up to four o'clock, you and your agents at the various jails and station-houses repeated lies to my wife and my attorneys and kept me hidden from them. When the clamor of the newspaper men forced you to let them interview me, you forced them to pledge not to reveal where I was. You had Sergeant Currie drive us up to Los Angeles, with strict injunctions not to get there before four o'clock—he did not tell me, but I heard another man give the order to him, and I watched his maneuvers to carry it out. It was your scheme to rush us into court at the last moment before closing, have lawyers appointed for us, and have us committed without bail, and then spirit us away and hide us again. To that end you had me buried in a cell in the city jail, and to my demands for counsel the jailers made no reply. Only the fact that someone you trusted tipped my wife off prevented the carrying out of this criminal conspiracy. My lawyers rushed to the jail, and forced the granting of bail, just on the stroke of five o'clock, the last moment.

I charge, and I intend to prove in court, that you are carrying out the conspiracy of the Merchants' and Manufacturers' Association to smash the harbor strike by brutal defiance of law. I was in the office of I. H. Rice, president of this Association, and heard him getting his orders from Hammond of the Hammond Lumber Company, and heard his promise to Hammond that the job would be done without delay. It is you who are doing the job for Rice, and the cruelties you are perpetrating would shock this community if they were known, and they will be punished if there is a God in Heaven to protect the poor and friendless. You did all you could to keep me from contact with the strikers in jail; nevertheless I learned of one horror that was perpetrated only yesterday—fifty men crowded into one small space, and because they committed some slight breach of regulations, singing their songs, they were shut in this hole for two hours without a breath of air, and almost suffocated. Also I saw the food that these men are getting twice a day, and you would not feed it to your dog. And now the city council has voted for money to build a "bull-pen" for strikers, and day by day the public is told that the strike is broken, and the men, denied every civil right, have no place to meet to discuss their policies, and no one to protect them or to protest for them. That is what you want—those are the orders you have got from the Merchants' and Manufacturers' Association; the men are to go back as slaves, and the Constitution of the United States is to cease to exist so far as concerns workingmen.

All I can say, sir, is that I intend to do what little one man can do to awaken the public conscience, and that meantime I am not frightened by your menaces. I am not a giant physically; I shrink from pain and filth and vermin and foul air, like any other man of refinement; also, I freely admit that when I see a line of a hundred policemen with drawn revolvers flung across a street to keep anyone from coming onto private property to hear my feeble voice, I am somewhat disturbed in my nerves. But I have a conscience and a religious faith, and I know that our liberties were not won without suffering, and may be lost again through our cowardice. I intend to do my duty to my country. I have received a telegram from the American Civil Liberties Union in New York, asking me if I will speak at a mass meeting of protest in Los Angeles, and I have answered that I will do so. That meeting will be called at once, and you may come there and hear what the citizens of this community think of your efforts to introduce the legal proceedings of Czarist Russia into our free Republic.

UPTON SINCLAIR

The ending of this episode: We hired a good-sized hall in Los Angeles by the week and held crowded meetings every afternoon and evening. The Southern California branch of the American Civil Liberties Union was formed, and a Congregational minister, Reverend Clinton J. Taft, resigned from his pulpit and served as director for the next twenty years or so. At the end of a couple of weeks the editor of the Los Angeles *Examiner* called me on the telephone and said, "Sinclair, how long is this thing going on?" I answered, "Until we have civil liberties in Los Angeles." "What, specifically, do you mean by that?" he asked, and I said, "For one thing, Chief Oaks must be kicked off the force; and we must have the assurance that there will never again be mass arrests of strikers." The editor said, "You may count upon both these conditions being met." I asked, "What guarantee have we?" He said, "I have talked it over with the half-dozen men who run this town, and I have their word. You may take mine."

So we called off the meetings. A few days later we read in the newspapers that Chief Oaks had been expelled from the force, having been found parked in his car at night with a woman and a jug of whisky. So far as I can recall, there have been no mass arrests of strikers in the past twenty-nine years.

V

Moved by the cruelties I had seen, I indulged myself in the pleasure of writing two radical plays—"radical" was a terrible word in those days. *Singing Jailbirds* portrayed the Industrial Workers of the World, of whom we had met many; they sang in jail and were put "in the hole" for it. They were called "wobblies" because in the early days they had done their first organizing in a restaurant kept by an old Chinaman who could not say IWW but made it "I-wobble-wobble."

I started with that scene, and then had the wobblies in jail recalling the battles they had fought and the evils they had suffered. There was a lot of singing all through, and the play made a hit when it was produced in Greenwich Village by a group of four young playwrights—one of them was Eugene O'Neill and another was John Dos Passos, who now after forty years has evolved from a rampant radical into a rampant conservative. I was writing for Bernarr Macfadden's *Physical Culture* in those days (at $150 per article). I took my boss to the show, and he put up a thousand dollars to keep it going. I, of course, got nothing.

The other play was in blank verse and was called *Hell*. It portrayed the devils as being bored, and amusing themselves by sending a messenger up to earth to create a great deposit of gold and set all the nations to warring over it. (This was just after World War I, of course.) My fastidious friend, George Sterling, was outraged by my verse, but I had a lot of fun. I found myself a solitary spot on the edge of the Arroyo Seco, and there paced up and down composing it and laughing over it. Dear old Art Young made a delightful cover drawing, and I published the play in pamphlet form; I still have copies, and—who can tell?—somebody might produce it before World War III comes and ends all producing.

Joking aside, I hope to live to see it.

VI

The only house we went to in Pasadena was that of Mrs. Gartz. This was a couple of miles up the slope from our home, and occupied a whole block of beautiful grounds, like a park. The house was built around a central court containing palm trees, ornamental plants, and a swimming pool. On the front of the house was a wide veranda and a flight of stone steps. The veranda looked out over the whole of Pasadena, and it was a pleasant place to sit and listen to arguments over the future of mankind.

Every Sunday afternoon Mrs. Gartz would invite some lecturer, and after she met Craig, all these lectures dealt with the so-called radical movement. It appeared that when the very rich become radical they go the whole way. She became far more radical than we were, and it was Craig's function to tone her down; but, alas, this service was not appreciated by Mrs. Gartz's husband, who blamed us for all his troubles. I could tell many funny stories of those meetings in a millionaire's palace with a raging millionaire husband roaming through the rooms, growling and grumbling to himself.

The whole of the class struggle was represented in that tormented home. Wobblies, when they got out of jail, would come and tell Mrs. Gartz their stories; the tears would come into her eyes, and she would write indignant letters to the newspapers—which the newspapers did not print. Also, there were the pacifists of all varieties, and later the communists, who finally "captured" the gullible great lady.

Mrs. Gartz took up the practice of writing to public officials about these outrages against civil liberty, and as her letters were not always coherent she would bring them to Craig to revise. Craig would take occasion to tone them down a bit; so presently she was in charge of all the great lady's public relations. Craig hit upon the idea of publishing a little volume entitled *Letters of Protest*. This made a hit, and thereafter every year there would be a little volume that Mrs. Gartz distributed to everyone on her mailing list. In all there were seven pretty little books, and no doubt they helped somewhat to diminish the stodginess of our millionaire city.

VII

I have given a few glimpses of Mary Craig's skill as a social practitioner. I must also tell a little about her as a homemaker.

To the north of the "brown house" we had bought, there extended seven lots rising slightly to a corner, from which the view over the Arroyo was still more attractive. Craig said nothing to me about her plans, but she bought those lots on installment payments. When I started the magazine it was on our dining-room table; so she went out traveling on foot about the town and found an old house that she bought for a hundred and fifty dollars and had moved onto the lot next to ours. She had a carpenter build a long table, and that was where the magazines were wrapped and prepared for the mail. One little cubbyhole in that house became my office, and several books were written there.

Of course, as the subscriptions came in we had to have still more help. We had no car in those days, but somehow Craig found another house and had it moved and connected up with the first one. Before she got through, she had bought four houses and fitted them in a row on two lots, and bought a fifth house to be wrecked for lumber to join the other houses together. I wrote an article about it in my magazine, *Upton Sinclair's,* and printed a photograph of the houses.

It made a really funny story, because every house was a different color. I described the consternation of the neighbors; but they recovered when the job was finished, for Craig really made a beautiful home of it, with a long porch along the front and, of course, a uniform coat of paint. It was an especially good home for us because Craig could have her room at the south end and I could practice my violin at the north end.

There was an old carpenter named Judd Fuller who worked for Craig, making old houses into new. Many a time I sat on a roof with him, nailing down shingles; and all the time we talked politics, and the state of the world. I tried to make a socialist out of an old-style American individualist, and I learned how to deal with that kind of mind. Some years later I wrote a pamphlet called *Letters to Judd,* and of course made him very proud. I printed something over a hundred thousand of the pamphlet, and with the help of Haldeman-Julius distributed them over the country.

VIII

I decided to muckrake world literature. I had read a mass of it in the one language my mother had taught me, in the three that my professors had failed to teach me—Latin, Greek and German —and in the two I had taught myself—French and Italian. To me literature was a weapon in the class struggle—of the master class to hold its servants down, and of the working class to break its bonds. In other words, I studied world literature from the socialist point of view.

That had been done here and there in spots; but so far as I knew it had not been done systematically, and so far as I know it has not been done since. Of course, *Mammonart* was ridiculed by the literary authorities; and of course I expected that. It was all a part of the class struggle, and I had set it forth in the book. Great literature is a product of the leisure classes and defends their position, whether consciously or by implication. Literature that opposes them is called propaganda. And so it is that you have probably never heard of my *Mammonart.*

I had now studied our culture in five muckraking books: *The Profits of Religion, The Brass Check, The Goose-Step, The Goslings, Mammonart.* After that, I took up American literature, mostly of my own time. I had known many of the writers, and some liked me and some didn't, according to which side they were on. I had published the five earlier books myself—in both cloth and paper; but there were not so many libel suits in the field of literature, so now I found a publisher. From that time on for many years my arrangement was that the publisher had his edition and I had mine, always at the same price. I had a card file of some thirty thousand customers.

I called the new book *Money Writes!* Its thesis was that authors have to eat; in order to get food they have to have money, and for that to happen the publisher has to get more money. So, in a commercial world it is money that decides what is to be written. My discussion of this somewhat obvious truth gave offense to many persons.

IX

When I was working on a book, my secretary had orders never to disturb me. But one day she did disturb me by bringing in a visiting card attached to a hundred-dollar bill. (She judged I would consider that a fair price for an interruption.) I looked at the card and saw the name, King C. Gillette, familiar to all men who use a safety razor. Some years earlier I had noted on the shelves of the Pasadena Public Library two large tomes entitled *World Corporation* and *Social Redemption*. I had taken them down and examined them with curiosity; they were written by a man who apparently had never read a socialist book but had thought it all out for himself. (I could guess that I might be the only person who had ever taken those tomes from the library shelf.)

Gillette, of course, was pleased to hear that I knew his books. He was a large gentleman with white hair and mustache and rosy cheeks; extremely kind, and touchingly absorbed in the hobby of abolishing poverty and war. But I discovered that he had a horror of the very word *socialism*. To him that meant class struggle and hatred, whereas he insisted that his solution could all be brought about by gentle persuasion and calm economic reasoning. He would take the time to explain this to anyone on the slightest occasion. I discovered that the joy of his life was to get someone to listen while in his gentle pleading voice he told about his two-tome utopia.

He had come to me for a definite purpose. He knew that I had an audience, and he wanted me to convert that audience to his program. He had a manuscript, and he wanted me to take it and revise it—of course, not changing any of his ideas. For this service he was prepared to pay me five hundred dollars a month; and a little later when he met my wife he raised his offer. He said, "Mrs. Sinclair, if you will get him to do this for me you will never have to think about money again as long as you live." That had a good sound to Craig, and she said I would do it.

She told me so, and of course I had to do what she said. Little by little I discovered what it meant: Mr. Gillette was coming for two mornings every week to tell me his ideas—the same ideas over and over again. He was a bit childish about it. He didn't remember what he had said a week or two previously and said it again, most seriously, impressively, and kindly. It became an endurance test. How often could I listen to the same ideas and pretend that they were new and wonderful? The time came when I could stand no more, not if he had turned over to me all the royalties from Gillette razors and blades. I had to tell him that I had done everything I could do for him.

I had helped him to get his manuscript into shape, but, alas, he had scribbled all over it and interlined it. I had it recopied, and with his permission submitted it to Horace Liveright, my publisher at that time. Horace couldn't very well refuse it because Gillette offered to put up twenty-five thousand dollars for advertising. The book was published, and in spite of all the effort it fell flat.

But the dear old gentleman never gave up. He would come to see us now and then and invite us to his home. He had one down at Balboa Beach, and another far up in the San Fernando Valley. When Sergei Eisenstein came, we took him and a party up to meet Gillette, but the family were away. We had a picnic under one of the shade trees on the estate and carefully gathered up all the debris.

X

Writing books involves hard labor of both brain and typewriter. I have mentioned more than once the subject of tennis—the device by which I was able to get the blood out of my brain and into my digestive apparatus. All through those years I used to say that I was never more than twenty-four hours ahead of a headache. I had read somewhere in history that it was the law in the armies of King Cyrus that every soldier had to sweat every day. I found that I could get along with sweating three times a week. (Out of curiosity I once weighed before and after a hard tennis match in Pasadena's summer weather, and discovered that I had parted with four and a half pounds of water.)

Tennis is a leisure-class recreation, and on the courts I met some of the prominent young men of my City of Millionaires. I was amused to note that their attitude toward me on the court was cordial and sometimes even gay, but we did not meet elsewhere. Sometimes their wives would drive them to the court and call for them when the game was over; but never once was I invited to meet one of those wives. I quietly mounted my bicycle and pedaled a couple of miles, slightly uphill, to my home. On Sunday morning I had a regular date with three men: one of the town's leading bankers, one of the town's leading real-estate men, and another whose high occupation I have forgotten. We played at the ultrafashionable Valley Hunt Club, but never once was I invited to enter the doors of that club. When the game was over, I mounted my bicycle and pedaled away.

One of these cases is especially amusing, and I tell it even though it leads me ahead of my story. I had a weekly tennis date with a young man of a family that owned a great business in Los Angeles. The young man, who lived in Pasadena, called me "the human rabbit," because I scurried across the court and got shots that he thought he had put away. Every time we played, his wife would be waiting in her car, and I dutifully kept my distance.

After several years I learned from the newspapers that he had divorced his wife. Then Craig read an advertisement that all the furniture of an elegant home was being offered for sale. She wanted a large rug for the living room, so I drove her to the place and waited outside while she went in. It proved to be a long wait, but I always carry something to read so I didn't mind. Craig bought a rug, and told me that the lady who was doing the selling was the ex-wife of my tennis friend! She was a chatty lady and had told her varied social adventures, including this:

"I almost caught Neil Vanderbilt. He drove up to a boulevard stop right alongside me, and I caught his eye. If that red light had lasted fifteen seconds longer, I'd have nailed him!"

(I myself with Craig's help had already "nailed" Neil, and I shall have a bit to tell about him later on. He is the possessor of an enchanted name, which has brought him much trouble. I know only one man equally unfortunate—Prince Hopkins. When he traveled in Europe, the bellboys hit their foreheads on the ground; he changed his name to Pryns to avoid the sight.)

XI

In some trading deal Craig had come into possession of two lots on Signal Hill, near Long Beach; and now in the papers she read the electrifying news that oil had been discovered under that wide hill. I drove her down there to find out about it, and she learned that lot owners in the different blocks were organizing, since obviously there could be no drilling on a tiny bit of land. I must have taken Craig a dozen times—a distance of twenty miles or so—and I sat for that many evenings listening to the arguments. I hadn't a word to say of course; the lots belonged to Craig, and she was the business end of the family.

It was human nature in the raw, and this was the first time I had seen it completely naked. There were big lots, and there were little lots; there were corner lots—these had higher value for residences, but did they have more oil under them? Cliques were formed, and tempers blazed—they never quite came to blows, but almost. And there sat a novelist, watching, listening, and storing away material for what he knew was going to be a great long novel. He listened to the lawyers and to the oilmen who came to make offers; they told their troubles. They wanted the lease as cheaply as possible, and they had no idea they were going to be in a novel with the title *Oil!*—including the exclamation point. The book was going to be taken by a book club, translated into twenty-seven languages, and read all over the world —but all they wanted was to get that lease more cheaply.

One of them offered in exchange a goat ranch somewhere down to the south, and so we drove there; I looked at the hills, and the goats, and the people who raised them. A crude country fellow, he too was going to be translated into twenty-seven languages, of which he had never even heard the names.

I told Craig what I was doing, of course; and it pleased her because it would keep me out of mischief for a year. She got tired of the oil game herself and sold her lots for ten thousand dollars each.

Into the novel I put not merely the oil business but Hollywood, where the wealthy playboys go; also the labor struggle, which is all over America. It made a long novel, 527 closely printed pages; when it was published, a kind Providence inspired the chief of police of Boston to say that it was indecent, and to bar it from the city. After that, of course, the publishers couldn't get the books printed fast enough; and they besieged me to go to Boston and make a fight. "Would you trade on the indecency of your book?" demanded Craig; and I answered that I wished to trade on its decency. So she let me go.

In Grand Central Station when I took the train for Boston, I learned that the bookstand there couldn't keep a supply of the books; everyone bound for Boston took copies for his friends. When I reached the city, I interviewed the chief of police, an elderly Catholic gentleman who told me which passages he objected to. I had those passages blacked out in some copies and sold them on the street—the fig-leaf edition, a rare collector's item now. What shocked the Catholic gentleman most was the passage in which an older sister mentions the subject of birth control to a younger brother. I recall the soft voice of the old chief, pleading: "Now surely, Mr. Sinclair, nobody should write a thing like that." I told him I earnestly wished that someone had done me that favor when I was young. I believed in birth control, and practiced it, and I am sure that the salvation of the human race will depend on it—and soon.

XII

During my stay in Boston I paid a visit to Bartolomeo Vanzetti, who had been in prison at that time for about six years, and whom I had visited not long after his arrest. He was one of the wisest and kindest persons I ever knew, and I thought him as incapable of murder as I was. After he and Nicola Sacco had been executed, I returned to Boston and gathered material for a two-volume novel dealing with their case.

I had developed what the doctor called a plantar wart under one heel, so it was hard for me to walk; but I got myself into a Pullman car, and when I reached Boston I hobbled around the streets with a crutch, talking with everyone who had been close to the case.

I had a story half formed in my mind. Among Mrs. Gartz's rich friends I had met an elderly lady, socially prominent in Boston; Mrs. Burton was her name, and she enjoyed telling me odd stories about the tight little group of self-determined aristocrats who ruled the social life of the proud old city. Judge Alvan T. Fuller and President A. Lawrence Lowell of Harvard belonged to that group—and Bartolomeo Vanzetti didn't. Mrs. Burton had come to California, seeking a new life, and I delighted her by saying that she would be my heroine—"the runaway grandmother," I would call her.

For my story I needed to know not merely the Italian laborers, who were easy to meet, but the aristocrats, who were difficult. Soon after my arrival, still on a crutch, I read that the proprietor of a great Boston industry had died and was to be buried from his home. It was a perfect setup: a great mill in a valley, the cottages of the workers all about it, and the mansion of the owner on the height above. I went to that mansion and followed the little river of guests into the double parlor for the funeral service. When one of the sons of the family came up to me, I told him I had great respect for his father, and he said I was welcome. So I watched the scene of what I knew would be my opening chapter.

On my way back on a streetcar I was recognized by a reporter from the *Evening Transcript,* the paper then read by everybody who was anybody in and about Boston. He had come to write up the funeral, and he included me. I shall never forget the horror on the face of a proper Boston couple when I told them of my attendance at that funeral. Maybe it will shock the readers of this book. I can only say that if you are a novelist you think about "copy" and not about anybody's feelings, even your own. If I were talking to you about that scene, I wouldn't say, "Was it a proper thing to do?" I would say, "Did I get that scene correct?" When I went back to the little beach cottage, I wrote a two-volume novel in which all the scenes were correct; and the novel will outlive me.

On the way home I stopped at Denver for a conference with Fred Moore, who had been the original attorney for Sacco and Vanzetti, and had been turned away when one of the Boston aristocracy, W. G. Thompson, consented to take over the appeals. Fred was bitter about it, of course, and it might be that this had influenced his opinion. He told me he thought there was a possibility that Sacco was involved in the payroll holdup. He thought there was less chance in the case of Vanzetti. There were anarchists who called themselves "direct actionists," and Fred knew of things they had done. I pointed out to him that if Sacco had been guilty and Vanzetti innocent it meant that Vanzetti had given his life to save the life of some comrade.

Of course, I did not know and could only guess. I wrote the novel that way, portraying Vanzetti as I had known him and as his friends had known him. Some of the things I told displeased the fanatical believers; but having portrayed the aristocrats as they were, I had to do the same thing for the anarchists. The novel, *Boston,* ran serially in *The Bookman* and was published in two handsome volumes that went all over the world.

Just recently I had the honor of a visit from Michael Musmanno, who as a young lawyer came late into the Sacco-Vanzetti case and gave his heart as well as his time and labor to an effort to save the lives of those two men. Being Italian himself, he felt that he knew them, and he became firmly assured of their innocence. Now he has become a much-respected justice of the Supreme Court of Pennsylvania; but he still feels as he did, and poured out his soul as if he were addressing the jury of a generation ago. The bitter old Boston judge and the grim governor and the coldhearted president of Harvard all came to life, and I found myself sitting again in the warden's reception room at Charlestown prison, in converse with the wise and gentle working-class philosopher named Bartolomeo Vanzetti. I had sent him several of my books, and he had been permitted to have them; I wish that I could have had a phonograph to take down his groping but sensitive words.

12

More Causes—and Effects

We had made too many friends and incurred too many obligations in Pasadena; so we found a cottage down on the ocean front at Alamitos Bay, Long Beach, and moved there. During both of my trips to Boston, Craig stayed alone in the little beach cottage and never minded it. Somehow she felt safe, and the waves on the other side of the boardwalk lulled her to sleep. She had become fascinated with the problem of her own mind, and studied it with the help of scores of books that I had got for her. I still have more than a hundred volumes on psychology and philosophy and psychic research that she read and marked—Bergson, William James, William McDougall, Charcot, Janet—a long list of the best. She had had psychic experiences herself in her girlhood and was tormented with the desire to understand these hidden forces of the mind. All the time that I was writing *Oil!* and *Boston*, I was also helping her to find out what her gift actually was—and to guess what it meant. The result was the book called *Mental Radio*.

The procedure we adopted was the simplest possible: I would make half a dozen drawings on slips of paper and put each inside an envelope. Then I would bring them to Craig, who was lying on her couch. She would lay one of them over her solar plexus—having read somewhere that this might be the center of the unknown forces. We didn't know whether that was so or not; but the solar plexus was as good as any other place. I would sit quietly and keep watch so as to be able to say that she did not cheat—although, of course, I knew that she had never cheated in her life. She had only one obsession—she wanted to know for certain if these forces were *real*.

She would decide that something that had come into her mind was *the* reality, and she would take pencil and pad and make a drawing. Then we would open the envelope and compare the two. The results were amazing to us both.

I had been reading about telepathy and clairvoyance since my youth. At Columbia I had studied with James Hyslop, who had been a patient psychic researcher; then there was the Unitarian minister who had performed my first marriage—Minot J. Savage —who told me he had seen and talked with a ghost who said that he had just been drowned off the coast of Britain. The results in Craig's case settled the matter for us, and settles it for anyone who is unwilling to believe that we are a pair of imbeciles as well as cheats. There is no other alternative, for we took every possible precaution against any blunder, and there is no way to account for what happened except to say that a drawing completely invisible to the eyes can make an impression on the mind by some other means.

It was not merely from my drawings that Craig got these impressions. She got them from the mind of a professional medium, whom she employed to experiment with her. I have given the details in *Mental Radio*. I printed several thousand copies of the book, and the experiments it describes have stayed unexplained now for thirty years. It is worth noting also that *Mental Radio* has just been reissued—this time by a publisher of scientific books exclusively. This is significant.

Professor William McDougall, who had been head of the department of psychology first at Oxford and then at Harvard, wrote a preface to the book. When he came to see us at the little beach cottage, he told us that he had just accepted a position as head of the department of psychology at Duke University; he had a fund at his disposal and proposed to establish a department of parapsychology to investigate these problems. He said he had taken the liberty of bringing several cards in his pocket, and he would like to be able to say that Craig had demonstrated her power to him.

Craig, always a high-strung person, hated to be submitted to tests because they made her nervous; but her respect for McDougall was great, and she said she would do her best. She sat quietly and concentrated. Then she said that she had an impression of a building with stone walls and narrow windows, and the walls were covered with something that looked like green leaves. McDougall took from an inside pocket a postcard of a building at Oxford University covered with ivy. There were two or three other successes that I have forgotten. The outcome was that McDougall said he was satisfied, and would go to Duke and set up the new department. He did so, with results that all the world knows.

I was interested to observe the conventional thinker's attitude toward a set of ideas that he does not wish to accept. *Mental Radio* contained 210 examples of successes in telepathy—partial successes and complete successes. To the average orthodox scientist, the idea was inconceivable, and it just wasn't possible to tell him anything that he knew in advance couldn't have happened. On the other hand, the lovely personality of Mary Craig is shown all through the book, and I cannot recall that any scientist ever accused her of cheating. He would go out of his way to think of something that *might* have happened, and then he would assume that it *had* happened; it *must* have happened, and that settled the matter. He would entirely overlook the fact that I had mentioned that same possibility and had stated explicitly that it *hadn't* happened; that we had made it absolutely impossible for it *to have* happened.

I won't be unkind enough to name any scientist. One suggested solemnly that it might have been possible for Mary Craig to have gotten an idea of the drawing by seeing the movements of my hand at a distance. But in the book I plainly stated that I never made the drawing without going into another room and closing the door. That kind of oversight has been committed again and again by the critics.

While I am on this subject I will venture to slip ahead for several years and tell of one more experiment. Arthur Ford, the medium, was paying a visit to Los Angeles, and I asked him to come out to our home and see if his powers had waned. (He had never refused an invitation from us—and he had never let us pay him a dollar.) He said he would come, and Craig was so determined to make a real test that she wouldn't even let me invite our friends by telephone. Our line might be tapped! She wrote a letter to Theodore Dreiser, and one to Rob Wagner, editor of *Script*, who was a skeptic but wanted to be shown.

When evening came, my orders were to wait outside for Arthur and take him around behind the house so that he might not see who came in. This I faithfully did; so there were Dreiser and his wife, and Rob Wagner and his wife, and Craig's sister, Dolly, and her husband. They were seated in a semidark room; and when I brought Arthur in, he went straight to the armchair provided, leaned back in it with his eyes toward the ceiling, and covered his eyes with a silk handkerchief, which is his practice.

Presently came the voice that Ford calls Fletcher. "Fletcher" speaks quietly and without a trace of emotion. He said there was a spirit present who had been killed in a strange accident. He had been crossing a street when a team of runaway horses came galloping, and the center pole had struck him in the chest. And then there was a spirit victim of another strange accident. This man had been in a warship when one of the guns had somehow backfired and killed him. And then there was a newspaperman and quite a long conversation about various matters that I have forgotten. I told the full details in an article for the *Psychic Observer* but do not have a copy at hand.

At that point in the séance there came a tap on the door, and Mrs. Gartz came in with one of her nephews. She had known nothing about the séance; being highly antagonistic, she had not been invited. Fletcher said, "There is a strong Catholic influence here, but there will be a divorce."

That ended the affair, possibly because of Mrs. Gartz's hostile attitude. The lights were turned up, and the various guests spoke in turn. Bob Irwin, Craig's brother-in-law, said that his young brother had been killed by exactly such a runaway team; Rob Wagner said that his brother had been killed in the Navy in a gun accident. Theodore Dreiser had been a journalist, but he denied that he had ever known such a man or heard of any such events as had come out in the séance. Mrs. Gartz's nephew said that he was a Catholic, but there would surely not be any divorce.

So ended the evening; but the day after the next there came to Craig a letter from Helen Dreiser saying that she was embarrassed to tell us that Theodore had been drinking and had slept through the séance and not heard a word. When she had repeated to him the various statements, he admitted that he knew such a man and that the events mentioned had occurred.

The predicted divorce did not occur until a month or two later, when the wife of the Gartz nephew divorced him.

And now all the skeptics can put their wits to work and find out how Arthur Ford got all those facts about people he had never met, and about whom we had made such efforts at secrecy. I don't like to be fooled any more than the next man, but I agree with Professor McDougall and Professor Rhine that it is the duty of science to investigate such events and find out what are the forces by which they are brought about.

Just by way of fun, I will add that Professor McDougall established his department of parapsychology, and Professor Rhine has carried it on; one of the things they have proved is that when Negroes shooting craps snap their fingers and cry "Come seven! Come eleven!" they really are influencing the dice. Rhine's investigators have caused millions of dice to be thrown mechanically, and observers have willed certain numbers to come, and the numbers have come. The chances for the successes having happened accidentally are up in the billions. Most embarrassing—but it happens!

II

Much of the story of my life is a story of the books I wrote. I read a great many, too, and among those I found interesting was a history of ancient Rome—because of the resemblance between the political and economic circumstances of two thousand years ago and those I knew so well in my native land. So I wrote *Roman Holiday*, the story of a rich young American who amuses himself driving a racing automobile. He meets with an accident and wakes up in the days when he had been driving horses in a chariot race in the arena of ancient Rome. Everything is familiar to him, and he goes back and forth between the two ages of history, equally at home in both. This novel was a foreshadowing of my tragic drama, *Cicero*—although, rather oddly, this realization did not come to me until just recently, when *Cicero* was produced.

III

My next book handled the problem of prohibition, of special interest to me ever since I had seen my father and two of my uncles die as alcoholics. The whole country was boiling with excitement over the struggle between the "wets" and the "drys," so I put my youthful self into a long novel, with all the characters I had known and the battles I had fought against the saloon-keepers and the crooked politicians. *The Wet Parade* I called it. It was made into a very good motion picture, with an illustrious cast that included Robert Young, Walter Huston, Myrna Loy, Lewis Stone, and Jimmie Durante as the comic prohibition agent.

Of course, the "wet paraders" I knew, headed by H. L. Mencken, had all kinds of fun with me. But many of my oldest and best friends have been caught in that parade, and I have had to watch them go down to early graves. Jack London was one of them. I have told of his appearance and his rousing speech at a mass meeting in New York City back in the days when we were launching the Intercollegiate Socialist Society. The next day I had lunch with him. The occasion was completely spoiled for me because Jack was drinking and I wasn't, and he amused himself by teasing me with his exploits—the stories he afterward put into his book, *John Barleycorn*. Later, when I went to live in Pasadena, Jack urged me now and again to come up to Glen Ellen, his wonderful estate. I did not go because George Sterling told me that Jack's drinking had become tragic. Jack took his own life at the age of forty.

And, alas, George Sterling followed his example. Shortly before George's death, Mencken, who was in California, told me that he had seen George at the Bohemian Club in San Francisco and that he was in a terrible state after another of his drinking bouts. A day or two later George took poison—but Mencken learned nothing from that dreadful episode.

On one of my trips to New York I was asked to make a funeral speech over the body of a kind and generous publisher, Horace Liveright. I remember his weeping, black-clad mother and, sitting apart from her, the lovely young actress who had been living in his home in Hollywood when my wife and I went there to dinner, and who had taken drink for drink with him. I remember walking downtown with Theodore Dreiser after the funeral. We discussed the tragedy of drinking, and I knew the anguish that Theodore's wife was suffering. But he learned nothing from the funeral or from my arguments.

IV

As I write there comes the news of the death of Ernest Hemingway. He received an almost fatal wound in World War I, and this apparently centered all his mind upon the idea of death. It became an obsession with him—something not merely to write about but to inflict upon living creatures. His idea of recreation was to kill large wild animals in Africa, and half-tame bulls in Mexico, and small game in America, and great fish in the sea. He wrote about all these experiences with extraordinary vividness and became the most popular writer in America, and perhaps in the world. When he died, the *Saturday Review* gave thirty pages to his personality and his writings, almost two thirds of the reading matter in that issue. I read a good part of it, and found myself in agreement with just one paragraph, by a contributor:

To the present critic, who is amazed by and genuinely admires the lean virtuosity of Mr. Hemingway, the second most astonishing thing about him is the narrowness of his selective range. The people he observes with fascinated fixation and then makes live before us are real, but they are all very much alike: bullfighters, bruisers, touts, gunmen, professional soldiers, prostitutes, hard drinkers, dope fiends.

Nowhere in the thirty pages did I find any mention of the fact that all this extraordinary writing was done under the stimulus of alcohol. A decade or so ago there was published in *Life* an article by a staff man who had been permitted to accompany Hemingway and a well-known motion picture actress about the city of New York for a couple of typical days. The writer described Hemingway as unable to go for an hour without a drink of liquor. As a result of this practice his health broke, and after a long siege in hospitals he put himself out of his misery by putting both barrels of his beautiful shotgun into his mouth and blowing off the top of his head.

V

And then the mail brings a volume containing 867 pages and weighing several pounds. It is *Sinclair Lewis: An American Life,* by Mark Schorer. I have known about the preparation of this "monumental study" for several years. It is a Book-of-the-Month-Club selection, and so will be widely read; the story of a man whom I knew for almost half a century, whom I admired and helped when I could, whose books I praised when I could, and whose tragic ending I mourned because I had tried to prevent it and failed.

I have told how Hal Lewis showed up as a runaway student from Yale, expecting to find our Helicon Home Colony more interesting. He met there, not in an academic way but socially, such people as William James and John Dewey; Jo Davidson, the sculptor, who was later to do his bust; and Sadakichi Hartmann, art authority, whom Lewis had to help put out because he (not Lewis) was drunk. Also I remember that Professor W. P. Montague of Columbia University taught Lewis how to play billiards, and Professor William Noyes of Teachers College taught him how to tend the furnace. Edwin Björkman, translator of Strindberg, told him about that strange playwright, and Edwin's wife, a suffragette and editor, later became Lewis' boss. As I have already noted, Edith Summers, my secretary, became Lewis' sweetheart at Helicon Hall.

It was all quite different from what he would have gotten at Yale, and he learned a lot about the modern world and modern ideas. He left us after several months and wrote us up in the New York *Sun.* That was going to be the way of his life for the rest of his sixty-six years. He would wander over America and Europe, then settle down somewhere and write stories, long stories or short ones, about the people he had met and what he imagined about them.

Everywhere he went, both at home and in Europe, he ran into what is called "social drinking," and his temperament was such that whatever he did he did to extremes. He became one of those drinking geniuses whose talents blossom and fade.

I have known two kinds of drink victims. There are the melancholy drinkers who weep on your shoulder and ask you to help them. You try to, but you can't. Such a man was my kind father, whom I watched from earliest childhood and whom I remember introducing to Hal Lewis at Helicon Hall—shortly before my father's pitiful ending. The other kind is the fighting drunk, and Hal became one of those; you may read the painful details in Professor Schorer's book. Hal would throw his liquor into the face of the man who had offended him. He would use vile language and rush away—and rarely apologize later.

I never saw him in that condition; I was careful never to be around. That is why my friendship with him was carried on mostly by mail. I called on him once in New York, and found that he had to revise the manuscript of a play for rehearsal that afternoon; having been through that kind of thing myself, I excused myself quickly. He brought his first wife to my home in Pasadena, and he had not been drinking, so Craig and I spent a pleasant evening with them.

I have included ten of his letters in *My Lifetime in Letters*. Professor Schorer has quoted a long one in which Hal scolds me for what I had written about one or two of his least worthy novels. I am sorry to report that his biographer has left out what I did to help my old friend at the time when he was publishing his greatest novel—one that I could praise without reservation. Hal had told me about *Babbitt* during his visit in Pasadena, and he wrote me from New York, "I have asked Harcourt, Brace and Company to shoot you out a copy of *Babbitt* just as soon as possible." I read the book at once, and sent them an opinion to which they gave display in their first advertisement:

I am now ready to get out in the street and shout hurrah, for America's most popular novelist has sent me a copy of his new book, *Babbitt*. I am here to enter my prediction that it will be the most talked-about and the most-read novel published in this country in my life-time.

The book became probably the best-selling novel of the decade.

Later, when Lewis received the Nobel Prize and made his speech before the king and the notables in Stockholm, he named me as one of the American writers who might as well have been chosen for the prize. That was as handsome as anything a man could do for a colleague, and it was enough to keep me grateful to him up to the end. But I have to tell the tragic story of his "decline" and his "fall"—these two words are Schorer's labels for large sections of the biography. "Decline" occupies 103 of the book's pages, and "Fall" occupies the last 163 pages. "Decline" and "Fall" together comprise one third of the volume; and, oddly enough, when I figured up the years covered by those two sections, they cover one third of Lewis' life (22 out of 66 years).

In Professor Schorer's huge tome you may read the whole pitiful story of American "social drinking" as it affected the life of one man of genius. You may read about the parties and the rages, the various objects that were thrown into other men's faces, and so on. The Berkeley professor has produced the most powerful argument against "social drinking" that I have encountered in my eighty-four years. My own books about the problem—*The Wet Parade* and *The Cup of Fury*, which I wrote in 1956—are small ones; Schorer's contains more than half a million words—all of them interesting, many of them charming and gay, and the last of them a nightmare.

I will give only the names of the gifted people known to me who fell into the grip of John Barleycorn: Jack London, George Sterling, Eugene O'Neill, Scott Fitzgerald, O. Henry, Stephen Crane, Finley Peter Dunne, Isadora Duncan, William Seabrook, Edna St. Vincent Millay, George Cram Cook, Dylan Thomas, Sherwood Anderson, Horace Liveright, Douglas Fairbanks, Klaus Mann. Most of these persons I knew well; the others I knew through friends. At least four took their own lives. Not one reached the age of eighty, and only three got to seventy—one of these, Seabrook, because he reformed.

And I will add one more name, which will be a surprise to many people: Eugene Debs, six times candidate of the Socialist Party for president of the United States. Gene was one of the noblest and kindest men I have had the good fortune to meet. He was a tireless fighter for social justice. He was one friend of the poor and lowly who stood by his principles and never wavered. In his campaigns he went from one end of the country to the other addressing great audiences. I was one of his pupils.

I heard him first at a huge mass meeting at Madison Square Garden. I was a young writer then, and he greeted me as though I were a long-lost brother. Many years later when he came out to Los Angeles, I had the pleasure of driving him from an afternoon meeting in the Zoological Gardens to an evening meeting in the Hollywood Bowl. Theodore Dreiser was there in a front seat, I remember, and he shouted his approval.

Gene fought against the fiend all his life, and his friends helped him. I personally never saw him touch a drop of liquor, but I got the story from George H. Goebel, who had been appointed by the party leaders as the candidate's official guardian. It was Goebel's duty to accompany him on every lecture trip and stay with him every hour, morning, noon, and night. That was an old story to me of course. Many times, as a lad, I had been appointed to perform that duty for my father. But, alas, I was not as big and strong as George Goebel.

13

Some Eminent Visitors

I

ALBERT EINSTEIN came to America in 1931 to become a professor in the California Institute of Technology in Pasadena. He had been world-famous for a dozen years or so, had been awarded the Nobel Prize, and was a doctor *honoris causa* in fourteen of the world's great universities. His coming was a prestige matter to Cal Tech and had been announced weeks in advance; reporters swarmed around him, the newspapers made front-page stories of his arrival, the institute gave a banquet in his honor, and one of the town's many millionairesses contributed ten thousand dollars for the privilege of tasting that food.

I had been corresponding with Einstein for some years. He had read some of my books and had written me: "To the most beautiful joys of my life belongs your wicked tongue." He had promised to come to see me; and soon after his arrival in Pasadena, Craig's sister Dolly came in and reported, "There's an old man walking up and down on the street, and he keeps looking at the house."

Craig said, "Go out and ask what he wants." Dolly went and came back to report, "He says he's Dr. Einstein." Craig said, "Go bring him in," and called to me.

Such was the beginning of as lovely a friendship as anyone could have in this world. I report him as the kindest, gentlest, sweetest of men. He had a keen wit, a delightful sense of humor, and his tongue could be sharp—but only for the evils of this world. I don't like the word "radical"; but it is the word that the world chose to employ about me, and Albert Einstein was as radical as I was. From first to last, during his two winters in Pasadena, he never disagreed with an idea of mine or declined a request I made of him.

Of course, it was shocking to the authorities at Cal Tech that Einstein chose to identify himself with the city's sharpest social critic. I could forgive Dr. Robert Millikan, president of the great institution, because I knew he had to raise funds among the city's millionaires and so had to watch his step; but Einstein was less tolerant. He knew snobbery when he saw it, and he expressed his opinions freely. He also recognized anti-Semitism and knew when his loyal and devoted wife was slighted. Said one young instructor at Cal Tech to Craig, "The Jews have got Harvard, they are getting Princeton, and they are on the way to getting Cal Tech."

Of course, when our friends knew that we knew Einstein, they all begged to meet him; and when I told Einstein about it, he said, of course he and his wife would come to a dinner and meet our friends. We engaged a private dining room in the "swanky" Town House of Los Angeles. Craig and I went a little early to make sure that everything was in order, and we were in the dining room when Einstein and his wife arrived. He always wore a black overcoat—I think a bit rusty—and a little soft black hat. He came into the large room where a table was set for twelve and looked around as if at a loss. Then he took off his overcoat, folded it carefully, and laid it on the floor in an unoccupied corner. He then took off the black hat and laid that on top of the coat. He was ready for dinner. I was too tactful to mention that there is a hat-check room in fashionable hotels.

Another episode: Some labor leader was arrested in a strike. I felt it my duty to make a protest, but I doubted if the press services would pay heed to me. I thought they would pay heed to Einstein, and I asked him if he would care to make a protest. He told me to write out the message and he would sign it. He did so, and I turned it over to the United Press. It was not sent out. Whereupon I telegraphed a protest to Carl Bickel, head of the agency in New York. Bickel sent me a copy of the rebuke he had telegraphed to the head of the Los Angeles office, informing

him that he had made the United Press ridiculous and that here-
after anything that Einstein had to say on any subject was news.

Once I mentioned to Einstein that someone had called my social protest "undignified." The next time he came to our home
he brought a large and very fine photograph of himself, eighteen by twenty-four inches, and on it he had inscribed six lines
of verse, in colloquial German that calls for a Berliner. Needless
to say, that trophy was framed and hung on the wall, and German visitors always call for a flashlight and a footstool to stand
on.

People ask for the text of the verses, so I give it here, first in
German, then in translation:

> *Wen ficht der schmutzigste Topf nicht an?*
> *Wer klopft die Welt auf den hohlen Zahn?*
> *Wer verachtet das Jetzt und schwört auf das Morgen?*
> *Wem macht kein "undignified" je Sorgen?*
> *Der Sinclair ist der tapfre Mann*
> *Wenn einer, dann ich es bezeugen kann.*
> *In herzlichkeit*
>   Albert Einstein

> Whom does the dirtiest pot not attack?
> Who hits the world on the hollow tooth?
> Who spurns the now and swears by the morrow?
> Who takes no care about being "undignified"?
> The Sinclair is the valiant man
> If anyone, then I can attest it.
> In heartiness
>   Albert Einstein

There is an amusing story connected with those verses. *Life*
published six pages of photographs of American rocking chairs;
and I wrote them a playful note, rebuking them for having left
out the most characteristic of all American chairs, the cradle
rocker. I enclosed a photo of myself in our cradle rocker and
pointed out the photograph of Einstein just behind the chair—
which the great man had often sat in. I mentioned the poem,
and there came a phone call from *Life's* Hollywood office. The

editor, an agreeable lady, asked for the text of the poem. I said it was in German, and she didn't know German. Would I translate it for her? I said I would, but I also said it would be useless, as *Life* wouldn't publish it. She asked why, and I answered, "Because it praises *me*."

The lady laughed merrily; she thought that was a witticism, asked again for the translation, and wrote it out line by line. *Life* published the letter and the photograph, April 28, 1961. It did not mention the poem. So I knew *Life* better than one of its own editors! I had a bit of fun telling her so when next I had her on the phone.

Einstein was surprised to learn that I had never been invited to speak at Cal Tech and had never had the honor of meeting Dr. Millikan. I told him that Bertrand Russell, when he had come to speak at Cal Tech, had made an engagement to have lunch with us at the home of Mrs. Gartz. The lecture took place in the morning, and we had arranged to meet him afterward, but Dr. Millikan carried him off to lunch at the Valley Hunt Club and made no apology to us.

On one of Einstein's last days in Pasadena, I went to his home to say good-by to him. You entered his house into a hallway, and on one side was a door opening into the dining room and on the other a door leading into the living room. I was saying my farewell to Einstein in the living room; just as I was ready to leave, Mrs. Einstein came in and said in a half whisper, "Dr. Millikan is here. I took him into the dining room."

I, of course, started to get out of the way; but Einstein took me firmly by one elbow and led me out of the living room and across the hall and opened the dining-room door. "Dr. Millikan," he said, "I want you to meet my friend Upton Sinclair." So, of course, we shook hands. I said a few polite words and took myself off.

I never saw Dr. Millikan again, but I will include one more story having to do with him. At the time of our entrance into World War II, Phil La Follette was opposing our entrance and came on a lecture tour to Pasadena. Dr. Millikan's son was casting about to find someone to oppose Phil in debate, and he came to me. I was in favor of our entrance, as I had been in the case of World War I; in both cases most of my socialist friends opposed me, some of them very bitterly.

When young Millikan asked if I would be willing to enter the lists, I consented. My wife attended the debate and found herself seated just in front of a group of young socialists who were jeering at my speech; when she turned around and looked at them, they recognized her, and got up and moved to another part of the hall. When some of the ardent patriots jeered at La Follette, I got up from my seat on the platform and asked them please to hear him. Some photographer took a snapshot of that moment, and it made an amusing picture.

My friendship with Einstein continued by mail for almost twenty years. And in the course of time I received another jingle from him—he had a propensity for writing them. A pacifist lady, Rosika Schwimmer, worked up a little fuss with me over a story I had told in my book *Upton Sinclair Presents William Fox*, to the effect that she had gone to Fox with a proposal to finance a "peace ship" to Europe, and he had declined. Rosika claimed that the story was false and employed a lawyer to demand that I state in the next edition of the book that it was false. I was perfectly willing to say that she denied it, but how could I say it was false when it was a square issue of veracity between two persons, and I had no other evidence?

Rosika sued me for libel—the only time that has ever happened to me. Obviously it was no libel, for she had made the same appeal to Henry Ford, and with success as all the world knew. She carried the case to the Supreme Court of New York State and lost all the way. She also carried it to Albert Einstein, and he, friend to all pacifists, wrote me some verses, mildly suggesting I take on more weighty foes. I replied with another set of verses, pointing out that I had taken on the Francos and the Hitlers.

Postscript: When I published an article about Einstein for the *Saturday Review* of April 14, 1962, Dr. Lee DuBridge, present head of Cal Tech, wrote me a long letter protesting my statements about that institution. In reply I wrote him some of my evidence that I had been too polite to include in my article; for instance, that Mrs. Einstein had complained to my wife that she had never been able to get the use of the bus that was maintained for the convenience of faculty wives. Dr. DuBridge had sent his letter to me to the *Saturday Review*, requesting publication; but the *Saturday Review* presently informed me that he had withdrawn his request. I was left to guess that he had read my letter.

II

You may be interested to hear of another man who sat in our cradle rocker more recently. Craig's brother Allan, a Mississippi planter who has succeeded in his life purpose of buying back most of his father's lands, wrote Craig that his close friend, Judge Tom Brady, was lecturing in southern California and would like to meet us. Allan had been Craig's darling from babyhood and could have anything he asked from her. An appointment was made, and Hunter brought the Judge to our home one evening.

He was a grave and courteous Southern gentleman who was spokesman for the citizens' councils and had helped to spread them all over the Deep South. We welcomed him, and he sat motionless in the chair and in a quiet, persuasive voice repeated what was obviously the speech he had been delivering to southern California audiences. It took an hour or more, and we listened without interruption.

Then I said, very gently, that I happened to have personal knowledge of some of the events to which my guest had referred, and that several of the institutions he had named as communist were nothing of the sort. For example, the League for Industrial Democracy. I had founded it more than half a century before. I had run it from my farmhouse attic in the hills above Princeton, New Jersey, for the first year or two, and I had known about its affairs ever since. It was just what it called itself: an organization for democracy, and never anywhere in its publications was there any suggestion for the achieving of socialist aims except by the democratic process.

Then some of the persons whom the judge had called "communist-influenced" were my friends. For example, Oswald Garrison Villard, for many years publisher and editor of the *Nation*.

I had known Villard well and had read his magazine from my youth. He was a libertarian of conviction so determined that it might be called religious. It would have been impossible to name an American less apt to fall under communist influence. And so on for other names that I have now forgotten.

Our guest listened without interruption; when I finished, he said that he was surprised by what I had told him and would give careful study to the matter and not repeat the mistakes. So we parted as Southern gentlemen, and on the way back to the motel he told Hunter that he was humiliated by what had happened. When he got home he sent me his book and later one or two pamphlets; but I have not heard that the policies of the citizens' councils have been modified in this respect.

III

Early in 1933 William Fox, most mighty of the movie moguls —excuse the movie language—came into my life. He wrote that he wished to visit my home. My wife, who knew the smell of money when it came near, got a good fire burning in our fireplace and saw that a pitcher of lemonade was prepared, with no alcohol in it. The country boy from Oregon who was our servant at that time was literally trembling with excitement at the prospect of seeing the great William Fox. When the boy came in to report the arrival, Craig said, "What did you tell him?" The answer was, "I told him to rest his hat and set."

William Fox had brought his lawyer with him and was "set" for action. He had been robbed of a good part of his fortune during the recent panic; he wanted that story told—and I was the man to do it. I explained somewhat sadly that I was in the midst of another writing job and never liked to break off my work once started. Usually Craig let me make my own decisions, but not that one. She told Mr. Fox that I would accept his offer of twenty-five thousand dollars—and what could I do about *that?*

Every day Fox came with his suitcase full of documents and his little round pudgy lawyer to elucidate them. Every day he rested his hat and set, and every day he had his pitcher of prohibition lemonade. I hired two secretaries to listen on alternate days, and so in a very short time I had a book. The great mogul himself suggested the title, *Upton Sinclair Presents William Fox*; and when the mighty labor was done and the bulky manuscript complete, Fox put the check into my wife's hands—not mine! He went off to New York in the midst of loud cheers from the Sinclair establishment.

And what happened then? Well, to be precise—nothing. I waited patiently for two or three days, and then I waited impatiently for two or three weeks, and I heard not a word. Then I received a letter from my friend Floyd Dell, who happened to be in New York. How Floyd got the information I have forgotten, but the substance of it was that Fox was using the threat of publishing my manuscript in an effort to get back some of the properties of which he had been deprived. I asked a lawyer friend in New York to verify this information for me, and when it was verified I knew exactly what to do. I sent my carbon copy to my dependable printers in Hammond, Indiana, and instructed them to put the book into type, send me the proofs, and order paper for twenty-five thousand copies. Before long it occurred to me that it might be a wise precaution to tell them to order paper for another twenty-five thousand copies.

When those beautiful yellow-covered books hit Hollywood, it was with a bang that might have been heard at the moon if there was anybody there to listen. It wasn't but a few hours before I received a frantic telegram from William Fox, threatening me with all kinds of punishments; but the twenty-five-thousand-dollar check had been cashed, and the books had gone to reviewers all over the United States—and I guess William Fox decided that he might just as well be the hero I had made him. Anyhow, I heard no more protests, and I sold some fifty thousand copies of the book at three dollars a copy. (It would cost twice that today.) I was told that immediately after the book appeared, there was posted on the bulletin board of all entrances to the immense Fox lot a warning that anyone found on the lot with a copy of the book would be immediately discharged. So, of course, all the hundreds of Fox employees had to do their reading at home.

It is interesting to note that now, as I read the proofs of this book, the great Fox establishment is shut down and the company is issuing statements that it is not going into bankruptcy.

IV

It was also in 1933 that we got involved with Sergei Eisenstein, the Russian film director. He had come to Hollywood two years before to make a picture. Because he would not do what our screen masters wanted, his plans had miscarried, and now he was about to return to Russia. Then, only a few hours before he was supposed to leave, he sent a friend to us with a wonderful idea: if only someone would raise the money, he would go to Mexico and make an independent picture of the primitive Indians about whom Diego Rivera had told him.

We hated to see a great artist humiliated by the forces that had assailed Eisenstein in California; so we very foolishly undertook to raise the money. Mrs. Gartz put up the first five thousand dollars—on condition that Craig's brother Hunter Kimbrough should be the manager of the expedition.

Now, the way in which "independent" pictures are made is as follows: the director gets a certain sum of money and shoots a certain number of miles of film; then he telegraphs back to the investors that the picture is, unfortunately, not completed and that he must have more money, and more miles of film, or else, unfortunately, the investors will have no picture. Thereupon, the investors put up more money, and the director shoots more miles of film, and then telegraphs that the picture is, unfortunately, not completed and that he must have more money, and more miles of film, or else, unfortunately, the investors will have no picture. There may have been some case in the history of movie expeditions where this did not happen, but I have not been able to come upon any recollection of it in Hollywood.

Eisenstein and his staff went to the tropical land of Tehuantepec, and made pictures of Tehuana maidens with great starched ruffles over their heads, and bare feet that gripped the rough hillsides like hands, and baskets made of gourds painted with roses. He went to Oaxaca and made pictures of masonry tumbling into ruins during an earthquake. He went to Chichén Itzá and made pictures of Mayan temples with plumed serpents and stone-faced men and their living descendants, unchanged in three thousand years. He climbed Popocatepetl and made pictures of Indian villages lost in forgotten valleys. Miles and miles of film were exposed, and packing cases full of negatives in tin cans came back to Hollywood.

Meanwhile, my wife and I found ourselves turned into company promoters, addressing persuasive letters, many pages long, to friends of Soviet Russia, devotees of Mexican art, and playboys of the film colony—anyone who might be tempted by a masterpiece of camerawork and montage. We interviewed lawyers and bankers, and signed trust agreements and certificates of participating interest. We visited Mexican consuls and United States customs inspectors, and arranged for censorship exhibitions. We mailed bank drafts, took out insurance policies, telephoned brokers, and performed a host of other duties far out of our line.

And Eisenstein went to the Hacienda Tetlapayac and made endless miles of film of a maguey plantation, with peons wearing gorgeous striped serapes, singing work hymns at dawn by old monastery walls, driven to revolt by cruel taskmasters, and hunted to their death by wild-riding vaqueros. He went to Mérida and "shot" senoritas with high-piled headdresses and embroidered mantillas. He made the life story of a bullfighter— his training and technique, his footwork and capework, his intrigue with ladies of fashion, and his escape from vengeful husbands, fiercer than any bull from Piedras Negras. The most marvelous material: pictures of golden sunlight and black shadows; dream scenes of primitive splendor; gorgeous pageants, like old tapestries come to life; compositions in which the very clouds in the sky were trained to perform.

But, oh, the tens of miles of film and the tens of thousands of dollars! The months and months—until at last Craig began to cry out in protest and to demand an end. Mexico is a land of difficulties and dangers, and Hunter Kimbrough was managing the expedition; her affection for him multiplied the troubles in her mind. "Bring them home!" became her cry, day and night.

And, meanwhile, Eisenstein was in Chapala, shooting white pelicans, gray pumas, and Nayaritan damsels paddling dugouts in mangrove swamps. He was in Cholula, shooting Catholic churches with carven skulls, and images of Jesus with real hair and teeth. He was in Guadalupe, photographing miraculous healings, and penitents carrying crosses made of spiny cactus, crawling by hundreds up rocky hillsides on bare knees.

"Bring them home!" demanded Craig; and she and her husband came to a deadlock over the issue. The husband was infatuated, she declared; he was as complete a madman as a Soviet director. They argued for days and nights; meanwhile, Eisenstein tore off the roof of a Tehuantepec mansion to photograph a dance inside, gave a bullfight to keep an actor from going to Spain, and made arrangements to hire the whole Mexican Army. Again Craig clamored, "Bring them home!" And again husband and wife took up the issue; this time the husband was seized by a deadly chill and had to be taken to the hospital in an ambulance, and he lay on his back for two weeks.

The raising of money went on, and freight trains groaned under the loads of raw film going into Mexico, and exposed film coming out. Eisenstein shot the standing mummies of Michoacàn, the flower festivals of Xochimilco, and the "dead peoples' day" celebrations of Amecameca, and ordered the Mexican Army to march out into the desert to fight a battle with a background of organ cactuses thirty feet high. It was the beginning of the fifteenth month of this Sisyphean labor when Craig assembled the cohorts of her relatives and lawyers, and closed in for the final grapple with her infatuated spouse. "Bring them home!" she commanded; and for eight days and nights the debate continued. To avoid going to the hospital, the husband went to the beach for three days; then he came back, and there were more days and nights of conferences with the assembled cohorts. At times such as this, husbands and wives discover whether they really love each other!

Craig was with me in the dream of a picture—until she decided that Eisenstein meant to grind her husband up in a pulp machine and spin him out into celluloid film. She thought that thirty-five miles of film was enough for any picture. And then she stood and looked at her husband, and her hands trembled and her lips quivered; she had licked him in that last desperate duel, and she wondered if in his heart he could ever forgive her. He did.

V

The real reason for Eisenstein's delaying tactics was that he did not want to go back to his beloved Soviet Union. He had been trying to get a contract to make a picture in India, one in Japan, one in the Argentine. His relations with Craig's brother had reached a point where he cursed Hunter; and Hunter, a Mississippian, got a gun and told him the next time he cursed he would be shot. So, I sent a cablegram to Stalin, asking him to order Eisenstein to return home; in reply I received a cablegram signed by Stalin informing me that they no longer had any use for Eisenstein and considered him a renegade.

The history of that cablegram is amusing. Craig regarded it as she would a rattlesnake in her home. Anyone who saw it, including the F.B.I., would assume that I was a cryptocommunist. The evil document must be locked up in a secret treasure box that contained such things as the letters from Jefferson Davis and his daughter, Winnie. I was not even allowed to know where that box was hidden.

But I had told one or two friends about the cablegram. Way back in the early Greenwich Village days I had known Robert Minor, art editor of *The Masses*. I had played tennis with him at Croton; and much later, in the days when I was writing the Lanny Budd books, he provided me with a story of what it was like to be arrested by the French police—a story that makes a delightful ending for the first Lanny Budd book, *World's End*. Now, a friend in New York mentioned the cablegram to Bob, and reported Bob's comment, "Tell Upton if he has a cablegram from Stalin he is the only man in America who can say it."

In the end, we made a contract with Amtorg, the Russian trade agency in New York, which handled the whole Eisenstein matter. We agreed to ship the film to them with precise specifications that the boxes should not be opened in New York but should be forwarded immediately to Moscow where Eisenstein would cut the film, and the cut film would be shipped to us. So Eisenstein received orders that he could not fail to obey, and Hunter did not have to shoot him.

The director and his two associates left Mexico City in our

Buick car and drove to New York; but instead of going at once to Moscow, as the agreement specified, Eisenstein stayed in New York, and about a week later we received letters from persons in New York to whom he had been showing the film.

That settled the matter for us. We put it into the hands of our lawyer, with instructions to repossess the film, repack it, and ship it to Hollywood—which was done. We made an agreement with Sol Lesser to cut it, and that was done. And in the spring of 1934 *Thunder Over Mexico* was scheduled to open at the Rialto Theater in New York.

In the eyes of the communists, of course, we had committed a major crime. We had deprived the great Russian master of his greatest art work, and we had done it out of blind greed. All over the world the communist propagandists took up that theme, and we could not answer without damaging the property of our investors.

The situation was still more odd because my friends, the socialists, were also involved. I was just on the point of announcing my EPIC campaign for the governorship of California. I had sent a copy of my program to Norman Thomas, and he lit into it in the New York *Call*, denouncing EPIC as a "tin-can economy," and me as "a renegade to the socialist movement." The Socialist Party, which had placed a large order for seats for the opening night of Eisenstein's film, canceled the order. So, we were getting it from all sides. On opening night there was a minor riot; communists yelled protests, and some of them shook their fists in my face in the lobby of the theater.

I had one comfort, however. Among the investors in the picture was Otto H. Kahn, New York banker and art patron; he had put in ten thousand dollars at my request, without ever having met me. I invited him to dinner with my wife and me at the Algonquin Hotel on the evening of the opening. He came up to me in the lobby and took both my hands in his and said, "I am telling all my friends that if they want to invest money and want to be sure of having it carefully handled and promptly accounted for, they should entrust it to the socialist, Mr. Upton Sinclair."

Of course, *Thunder Over Mexico* wasn't a very good picture. It couldn't be because it was only a travelogue and had no form.

Sol Lesser, an experienced producer, did his best and dealt with us fairly. The investors got about half their money back, and Sol's friendship was the best thing that we got out of the whole experience.

When the film had run its course, we turned it over to the Museum of Modern Art in New York, and occasionally I see mention of its being shown here and there. As for Eisenstein, he went back to Russia; I have no report on his meeting with Stalin. But all the world knows that for many years he was put to teaching his art instead of practicing it, and that when he made another picture it was a glorification of the most cruel of all the tsars.

14

EPIC

I

I COME now to one of the great adventures of my life: the EPIC campaign. There had come one of those periods in American history known as a "slump," or, more elegantly, a "depression." The cause of this calamity is obvious—the mass of the people do not get sufficient money to purchase what modern machinery is able to produce. You cannot find this statement in any capitalist newspaper, but it is plain to the mind of any wide-awake child. The warehouses are packed with goods, and nobody is buying them; this goes on until those who still have money have bought and used up the goods; so then we have another boom and then another bust. This has gone on all through our history and will go on as long as the necessities of our lives are produced on speculation and held for private profit.

Now we had a bad slump, and Franklin Roosevelt was casting about for ways to end it. In the state of California, which had a population of seven million at the time, there were a million out of work, public-relief funds were exhausted, and people were starving. The proprietor of a small hotel down at the beach asked me to come and meet some of his friends, and I went. His proposal was that I should resign from the Socialist Party and join the Democratic Party, and let them put me up as a candidate for governor at the coming November election. They had no doubt that if I would offer a practical program I would capture the Democratic nomination at the primaries, which came in the spring. I told them that I had retired from politics and promised my wife to be a writer. But they argued and pleaded, pointing out the terrible conditions all around them; I promised to think 't over and at least suggest a program for them.

To me the remedy was obvious. The factories were idle, and the workers had no money. Let them be put to work on the state's credit and produce goods for their own use, and set up a system of exchange by which the goods could be distributed. "Production for Use" was the slogan, and I told my new friends about it. They agreed to every one of my suggestions but one—that they should get somebody else to put forward the program and run for governor.

I talked it over with my dear wife, who as usual was horrified; but the more I thought about it, the more interested I became, and finally I thought that at least I could change my registration and become a Democrat—quietly. It was a foolish idea, but I went ahead; and, of course, some reporter spotted my name and published the news. Then, of course, Craig found out and I got a mighty dressing down.

A great many people got after me, and the result was I agreed to run for the nomination at the primaries. I didn't think I could possibly win, and I was astonished by the tidal wave that came roaring in and gathered me up. I had no peace from then on; I carried the Democratic primary with 436,000 votes, a majority over the total cast for the half dozen other candidates.

So I had to go through with it, and Craig, according to her nature, had to back me. She would hate it for every minute of the whole campaign and afterward; but once I had committed myself, I was honor-bound, and quitting would be cowardice. There are no cowards in Mississippi.

II

Some months earlier I had made the acquaintance of a young man of some wealth who had established a Bellamy Society and had printed an edition of Bellamy's charming *Parable of the Water Tank*. Now I went to him and served notice that he had to be my campaign manager. I don't know what *his* wife thought of that, but I know that he dropped everything and gave his heart, his mind, and a lot of his money to that tremendous political fight. Richard S. Otto was his name, and the name of the movement was EPIC—End Poverty in California. It was a wonderful title, and went all over the world.

We had moved from our Long Beach cottage back to Pasadena, and now we had to move from Pasadena because so many people had got our address and gave us no peace. We bought on mortgage a home in Beverly Hills, where we fondly thought we could hide. I had an elderly woman secretary, and was using her little front room as an office. Now Dick Otto moved the EPIC movement into that little front room, and presently the elderly secretary had to find a new home and leave the whole cottage to EPIC.

It wasn't long before Dick had to hunt up a bigger place; he moved three or four times and at the end leased a whole office building. People came from all over the state, and brought funds when they had any; if they had none, they offered their time, often when they had nothing to eat. The movement spread like wildfire—quite literally that. The old-men politicians were astonished, and the newspapers, which had kept silent as long as they dared, had to come out and fight it in the open.

As for me, it meant dropping everything else, and turning myself into a phonograph to be set up on a platform to repeat the same speech in every city and town of California. At first I traveled by myself and had many adventures, some of them amusing, others less so. I had an old car, which had a habit of breaking down, and I would telephone to the speech place to come and get me. Once I was late and was driving fast, and I heard a siren behind me; of course, I stopped and told my troubles to the police officer. He looked at my driver's license before he said anything; then, "Okay, Governor, I'll take you." So I rode with a police escort blazing a mighty blast and clearing traffic off one of the main highways of central California. The phonograph arrived, and the speech was made!

I am joking about its being the same speech, because as a matter of fact something kept turning up and had to be dealt with. Our enemies continually thought up new charges, and I had to answer them. I would try to get them to come and debate with me, but I cannot recall one that ever accepted. That doesn't mean that I was a great orator, it simply means that I had the facts on my side, and the facts kept on growing more and more terrifying. The Republican opposition had no program—it never does, because there is no way to defend idle factories and workers locked out to starve. We have the same situation now, as I write, in 1962; but we don't quite let them starve, we give them a stingy "relief"—and they can thank EPIC for that, though they do not know it.

III

Self-help co-operatives had sprung up all over the state, and of course that was "production for use," and those people automatically became EPIC's.

Our opponents would not debate; however, there were challenges from the audience, and now and then I would invite the man up to the platform and let him ask his question and present his case. That was fair play, and pleased the audience. There were always communists, and several times they showered down leaflets from the gallery. They called EPIC "one more rotten egg from the blue buzzard's nest." (The "blue buzzard" was the communists' name for the New Deal's "blue eagle.") When the shower fell, I would ask someone in the audience to bring me a leaflet, and I would read the text and give my answer. It was a simple one: We wanted to achieve our purpose by the American method of majority consent. We might not win, but if we cast a big vote we would force the Roosevelt administration to take relief measures, and we would have made all America familiar with the idea of production for use; both these things we most certainly did.

That campaign went on from May to November, and the news of it went all over the United States and even further. We had troubles, of course—arguments and almost rows at headquarters. I would be called in to settle them, but all I told anybody was to do what Dick Otto said. That brave fellow stood everything that came, including threats to kill him. There was only one thing he needed, he said, and that was my support.

More important yet, he had Craig's. She never went near the
headquarters, but when I was on the road, she spoke for me—
over the telephone.

Sometimes she went to meetings that were not too far away.
She always sat back toward the rear and was seldom recognized.
At the outset of the campaign, at a meeting in a church, she observed that everybody sat still, and it occurred to her to applaud
something I had said; instantly the audience woke up, and the
applause became continuous. That was a trick she did not forget.

We had an eight-page weekly paper called the *EPIC News,*
and I had to write an editorial for it every week, and answer our
enemies and keep our organizers and workers all over the state
alive to the situation. Sometimes Craig wrote for that.

A big advertising concern had been hired to defeat EPIC.
They made a careful study of everything I had written, and they
took passages out of context and even cut sentences off in the
middle to make them mean the opposite of what I had written.
They had had an especially happy time with *The Profits of Religion.* I received many letters from agitated old ladies and gentlemen on the subject of my blasphemy. "Do you believe in
God?" asked one; and then the next question, "Define God." I
have always answered my letters, and the answer to question
one was "Yes," and the answer to question two was "The Infinite
cannot be defined." There wasn't the least trouble in finding quotations from both the Old and New Testaments that sounded
like EPIC, and it wasn't necessary to garble them.

IV

When we carried the primaries, we were the Democratic Party
of California, and under the law we had a convention in Sacra-
mento—the state capital. I remember that Mrs. Gartz came with
us to that convention. Craig had been too busy to manage her
now, and another lady as large and stout as Mrs. Gartz had gotten hold of her. This lady had herself nominated as EPIC candidate from her assembly district; also she had a son and was
frantically beseeching me to make him state commissioner of
education. She owned a half-dozen houses in California and

rented them, and had the wonderful idea that all homes should be exempt from taxation. Poor Mrs. Gartz never knew what was being done to her, and at the convention I had to tell those two large ladies to go back to their seats and let me alone. The upshot was that Mrs. Gartz's daughter took her for a trip around the world until the EPIC nightmare was over.

Halfway through the campaign I wrote a little dramatic skit called *Depression Island.* I imagined three men cast away on a small island, with nothing to eat but coconuts. One was a businessman, and in the process of trading he got all the coconuts and trees into his possession. Then he became the capitalist and compelled the other two to work for him on a scanty diet of coconuts. When the capitalist had accumulated enough coconuts for all his possible needs, he told the other two that there were "hard times." He was sorry about it, but there was nothing he could do; coconuts were overproduced, and the other two fellows were out of jobs.

But the other two didn't starve gracefully. They organized themselves into a union and also a government, and passed laws providing for public ownership of the coconut trees. The little drama carefully covered every point in the national situation, and nobody in that EPIC audience could fail to get the idea.

A group of our EPIC supporters in Hollywood undertook to put on the show in the largest auditorium available. I went to see Charlie Chaplin, who said he would come and speak at the affair—something he had never been known to do previously. I remember trying to persuade several rich people to put up rent for the auditorium. I forget who did, but there was a huge crowd, and nobody failed to learn the geography lesson—location of Depression Island on the map.

V

In the month of October, not long before election day, I made a trip to New York and Washington. I stopped off at Detroit and visited Father Coughlin, a political priest who had tremendous influence at that time. I told him our program, and he said he endorsed every bit of it. I asked him to say so publicly, and he said he would; but he didn't. He publicly condemned some of

the very things he had approved, and he denied that he had
given his approval.

In New York, of course, there were swarms of reporters. EPIC
had gone all over the country by that time. I had an appointment with President Roosevelt at Hyde Park. It was five o'clock
one afternoon, and some friends drove me up there. The two
hours I spent in the big study of that home were among the
great moments of my life. That wonderfully keen man sat and
listened while I set forth every step of the program, and he
checked them off one after the other and called them right.
Then he gave me the pleasure of hearing his opinion of some of
his enemies. At the end he told me that he was coming out in
favor of production for use. I said, "If you do, Mr. President, it
will elect me."

"Well," he said, "I am going to do it"; and that was that. But
he did not do it.

I went to Washington to interview some of Roosevelt's cabinet members and get their support if I could. Harry Hopkins
promised us everything in his power if we got elected. Harold
Ickes did the same—the whole United States Treasury, no less.
Also, I spent an evening with Justice Louis Brandeis—but he
couldn't promise me the whole Supreme Court.

I addressed a luncheon of the National Press Club, and that
was an interesting adventure. There were, I should guess, a
couple hundred correspondents of newspapers all over the country, and indeed all over the world. I talked to them for half an
hour or so, and then they plied me with questions for an hour or
two more. I was told afterwards that they were astonished by
my mastery of the subject and my readiness in facing every
problem. They failed to realize the half year of training I had received in California. I can say there wasn't a single question
they asked me that I hadn't answered a score of times at home.
I not only knew the answers, but I knew what the audience response would be.

I had all the facts on my side—and, likewise, all the fun. I can
say that EPIC changed the political color of California; it scared
the reactionaries out of their wits, and never in twenty-eight
years have they dared go back to their old practices. The same
thing can also be said of civil liberties; they have never dared to

break a strike as they did at San Pedro Harbor before our civil-liberties campaign in the early twenties.

> Say not the struggle nought availeth,
> The labor and the pains are vain!

In the last few days of the campaign, Aline Barnsdall, a multi-millionairess, came to Craig and told her she had decided to put ten thousand dollars into the fight. Craig told her to take it to Dick Otto, and needless to say she was welcomed at headquarters. Among other things we did with that money was to put on a huge mass meeting in the prize-fight arena in Los Angeles. I had never been in such a place before and have not since. Speaking from the "ring," I could face only one fourth of the audience at any one time, so I distributed my time and spoke to each fourth in turn. There were four loudspeakers, so everybody could hear, and the audience enjoyed the novelty. The speech was relayed and heard by an audience in the huge auditorium in San Francisco; so I dealt with the problems of southern California for a while and then with those of the north.

I remember on the afternoon before the election a marvelous noon meeting that packed the opera house in Los Angeles. Our enemies had made much of the fact that the unemployed, otherwise known as "bums," were coming to the city on freight trains looking for free handouts. This had been featured in motion pictures all over the state and had front-page prominence in the Los Angeles *Times*. I told the audience that Harry Chandler, owner of the *Times*, had himself come into Los Angeles on a freight train in his youth. I shouted, "Harry, give the other bums a chance!" I think the roar from the audience must have been audible as far as the *Times* building.

No words could describe the fury of that campaign in its last days. I was told of incidents after it was over. A high-school girl of Beverly Hills told me of being invited to the home of a classmate for dinner. The master of that home poured out his hatred of the EPIC candidate, and the schoolgirl remarked, "Well, I heard him speak, and he sounded to me quite reasonable." The host replied, "Get up and get out of this house. Nobody can talk like that in my home." He drove her out without her dinner.

Another woman in Hollywood, a poet rather well known, told

me of a businessman she knew who had made his will and got himself a revolver, and was going to the studio where I was scheduled to speak on election night; if I won he was going to shoot me. I did not win, and in my Beverly Hills home that night a group of our friends, including Lewis Browne, sat and awaited the returns. Very soon it became evident that I had been defeated, and Craig, usually a most reserved person in company, sank down on the floor, weeping and exclaiming, "Thank God, thank God!" Our dear Lewis, whom she knew and trusted, came to her and said, "It's all right, Craig. We all understand. None of us wanted him to win."

Many people rejoiced that night, and many others wept; I was told that the scenes at the EPIC headquarters were tragic indeed. I won't describe them, but will take you back to that old home in Greenwood, Mississippi, where an elderly judge sat listening to his radio set. It was Craig's Papa, the one who had "overspoke himself" a little more than twenty years earlier. He had owned a great plantation, much land, and two beautiful homes. He was the president of two banks, vice president of others—one of which he had founded; and in all of them he was a heavy stockholder. The panic had come, the banks had failed, and under the law he was liable to the depositors up to twice the amount of his own holdings. It had wiped him out.

I had warned him of what was coming. I had warned his son, Orman, who also was a lawyer and ran the law business that had been his father's. Orman had replied, "To show you how much I think of your judgment I will tell you that I am buying a thirty-thousand-dollar property." That may sound ungracious, but it wouldn't if you knew Orman, who was a great "kidder." He bought the property on credit, and he was in trouble too.

Interesting evidence of the respect in which Leflore County held "the Judge": the people who took over his homes did not let him know it; they let him use both houses for his remaining years. I suppose they did it by a secret arrangement with Orman; anyhow, he was there in his Greenwood house, with his large gardens. All his Negroes were dependent upon him; they worked the gardens and lived on the food—corn and beans, tomatoes, and milk from the cows.

Such was the situation when the Judge sat at his radio set, listening to the news of the California election. It should not surprise you to learn that he was hoping for his son-in-law's victory, and disappointed at his son-in-law's defeat.

He was a proud old gentleman. With Craig's approval, I had sent him a check for two hundred dollars—and that check was in his pocket, uncashed, when he died. But one other gift he did accept. One of his daughters wrote that his greatest trouble was that he had nothing to read. I was taking some fifty magazines, and still do. Every week, after I had read them, my secretary would bundle them up and mail them to the Judge, and it touched our hearts to hear of his pleasure.

15

Grist for My Mill

I

It was a relief to me to have coughed up that EPIC alligator, and to Craig it was the coughing up of a whole aquarium. It was days before she could be sure that we were really out—and by then she discovered that we couldn't be, because there were still the headquarters and the *EPIC News*, and all those poor people who had put everything they had into the campaign. It was unthinkable to quit, but—we had no money. I sat myself down and wrote the story of the campaign as I have told it here, and offered it for serial purposes to California newspapers. Some thirty accepted. I had based the price upon the circulation of the newspaper, and some of them actually paid. Those that failed to pay I suppose had been calling EPIC dishonest. I put the whole story into book form: "I, Candidate for Governor—and How I Got Licked." What I have written here is a summary for a new generation.

I had made plans for a lecture trip, to travel over the country and tell about the campaign and answer questions about production for use. A friend had presented us with a lovely German shepherd, and we had the protection of that affectionate creature all over the United States. No one could ever come close to our car.

We crossed the continent twice, and I could make quite a story out of our adventures. In Seattle the governor of the state called out the troops, and I didn't know whether his idea was to protect me or to arrest me. Anyhow, I made the speech. In Portland I spoke in a baseball park, and there I had the company of a young newspaperman, Dick Neuberger, who later became United States Senator. In Butte we found ourselves in a hotel amid a convention of rifleshooters, and discovered that some shooter had either bored or shot a hole through the door of our hotel room so that he could peek in at us. It was the wild and woolly West.

Once we got lost in lonely mountains, and because we were desperately tired we asked shelter in one of two shacks by the roadside, where some rough-looking men were living. One shack was given to us in all kindness. Craig was a little scared of our hosts; but in the morning we were politely asked how we had slept, and when Craig asked the price, she was told, "It's hard times, lady, would twenty-five cents be too much?" She gave him a couple of dollars.

Also, I never get tired of telling my experience in St. Louis, where there was a large auditorium and a distinguished gentleman to introduce me—the head of the astronomical observatory, I was told. The gentleman made a most gracious speech and concluded, "And now ladies and gentleman, I have great pleasure in introducing Mr. Sinclair Lewis." The audience began to laugh, the astronomer looked worried, and his son jumped up and ran to him. I comforted him by saying that I had had much experience with that mistake.

In Chautauqua I debated before a huge audience with Congressman Hamilton Fish, Republican aristocrat from Franklin Roosevelt's district up the Hudson. Fish had come to know me well, as we had had the same debate in Hollywood and in Chicago. Craig never went in to my talks but sat in the car under the protection of "Duchess." When the debate was over the audience strolled by, and Craig listened. Presently came "Ham," and Craig heard him say, "I really think he got the better of me." But you may be sure he didn't say that from the platform!

At Princeton I lectured in the university auditorium. Albert Einstein was teaching there, and I spent the afternoon with him. He had consented to introduce me at the debate, which was to be with a chosen representative of the senior class. To our pained surprise there were not more than twenty or thirty persons in that auditorium. I was interested to hear Albert Einstein tell the students and faculty of Princeton University what he thought of their interest in public affairs.

My opponent in the debate was a well-bred young gentleman, and I didn't want to be hard on him. I told the audience how I had lived in a tent north of Princeton just thirty years previously. I had come to know some of the students then and had walked in the hills with a senior who had specialized in economics. I was interested now to discover that instruction at Princeton had not changed a particle in thirty years; what my opponent had said in 1935 was exactly the same as my student friend had said in 1904. America had changed, but Princeton stood like a rock in the middle of a powerful stream.

We made two trips from coast to coast, lecturing about EPIC —including the detours, a distance of sixteen thousand miles, and I drove every mile of it. It took more than that long for the EPIC political movement to fade away; the self-help co-operatives hung on for years. I had visited many of them, and talked with hundreds of their members.

They included the inhabitants of what was known as Pipe City near Oakland, California. A most unusual name, but it was literally exact. The city of Oakland had been in the process of putting down a main sewer line with pipe six feet in diameter. The money had run out, and sections of pipe were lined up along the highway. They provided shelter from the rain if not from the cold, and hundreds of unemployed men wandering the roads ducked in and made Oakland their begging center.

Three of them happened to be men with education and business experience, and they had conceived the idea of a self-help co-operative. Instead of begging for food, let them beg for the means of production—the tools and goods that people possessed and could no longer either use or sell. Let the co-operators offer to do useful work in exchange for such goods. In the city where so many thousands were idle there was no kind of work, and no kind of material that could not be found and bartered for services. An idle building was found, and the people piled into it and before long were actually working. In the course of the depression the co-op became a successful business, and the lesson was learned. Before the New Deal had brought Amer-

ican industry back to life there were two or three hundred of
these self-help co-operatives scattered all over the state.

I had conceived a form in which these events could be woven
into a story. Each chapter would tell of some individual or family of a different character and a different occupation, either
hearing about the co-op in a different way or stumbling upon it
by accident, and so coming into the story. I saw it as a river,
flowing continuously, and growing bigger with new streams
added. So came the novel *Co-op*.

II

Craig didn't like communists. I am sad to have to report that
there were also some socialists with whom she failed to get
along. Indeed, they almost disillusioned her with the socialist
movement—for she was a personal person and thought that
idealists ought to live up to their programs.

During the EPIC campaign, old Stitt Wilson, California socialist leader and several times candidate for governor, had seen
that the EPIC movement was a tide and had decided to swim
with it. He spoke at our huge Fourth of July celebration in the
Arroyo Seco. He was one of those orators who take off their
coats and wave their arms and shout, even in a Fourth of July
midday sun. After it was over, he was driven to our home and
ordered Craig to draw him a bath. She wouldn't have minded
helping an old man, but she did mind taking an order; so, while
he got his bath he lost her regard.

Then came Lena Morrow Lewis, tireless lecturer and strictly
orthodox Marxian. She was a guest in my absence and followed
Craig around the house, insisting on reading passages from Marx
to her. Then she asked to be allowed to stay in the house for a
week or two while Craig was away, and she left everything in a
state of disarray—including the soiled dishes. If Craig had been
a guest in anybody's house, there would not have been a pin out
of place, and every dish would have been polished. So, the socialist movement went still lower in my lady's esteem.

Oddly enough, those who won her favor were the IWW. They
had a most terrible reputation in the capitalist newspapers.
They were said to drive copper nails into fruit trees. I made in-

quiries among arboriculturists, but could not find a single one who could see what harm copper nails could do in a fruit tree. Anyway, the "wobblies" were freely sent to jail in California, and when they got out of jail, they would frequently come to me because I had written a play about them—*Singing Jailbirds*. They wanted to tell me their stories and have me write more. Without exception they were decent and honest men, and they won Craig's heart. They would not even let her give them money—only, in one case, fifty cents to get back to Los Angeles.

As the years passed, the communists succeeded more and more in their effort to take possession of the word "socialism." Craig saw no possibility of countering this—especially when the effort had to be made by her husband. More and more she wanted me to give up the word, which I had worn as a badge all my life. Craig's effort was supported by her brother Hunter, who was with the government in Washington prior to World War II and knew many labor men. It was amusing when now and then a newspaper reporter would come for an interview, and Craig and Hunter would conspire together to make me into an ex-socialist.

I have mentioned the Intercollegiate Socialist Society, which I founded in 1905 and which later changed its name to the League for Industrial Democracy. "Now surely," Craig pleaded, "that is a good-enough name. Why not be an Industrial Democrat?" It is a rather long name to say, but I do my best to remember, and Hunter Kimbrough helps by reminding me it was he, after all, who persuaded Harry Flannery, head of the educational department of the AFL-CIO, to make use of books such as *The Jungle, King Coal,* and *Flivver King;* they did, and a great deal about them has gone out in print and over the radio. That, of course, is what I have lived for.

III

All through the EPIC campaign I had been asked questions regarding my ideas about God; so I decided that I would arm myself for the future, and I wrote and published a book, *What God Means to Me*. The largest of all subjects, of course; but I made the book small and tried to make it practical—that is, I told the ideas by which I had guided my life. I content myself here by quoting the concluding sentences, and you can have more for the asking.

Somehow love has come to be in the world; somehow the dream of justice haunts mankind. These things claim my heart; they speak to me with a voice of authority. I know full well how badly the idealists fare in our society. I know that Jesus was crucified, and Joan burned, and Socrates poisoned; I know that Don Quixote was made ridiculous, and Hamlet driven mad. But still the dream persists, and in every part of the world are men determined "to make right reason and the will of God prevail."

This God whom I preach is in the hearts of human beings, fighting for justice; inside the churches and out—even in the rebel groups, many of which reject His name. A world in which men exploit the labor of their fellows, and pile up fortunes which serve no use but the display of material power—such a world presents itself to truly religious people as a world which must be changed. Those who serve God truly in this age serve the ideal of brotherhood; of helping our fellow-beings, instead of exploiting their labor, and beating them down and degrading them in order to exploit them more easily.

The religion I am talking about is not yet "established." It rarely dwells in temples built with hands, nor is it financed with bond issues underwritten by holders of front pews. It does not have an ordained priesthood, nor enjoy the benefit of apostolic succession. It is not dressed in gold and purple robes, nor are its altar cloths embroidered with jewels. It does not honor the rich and powerful, nor sanctify interest and dividends, nor lend support to political machines, nor sprinkle holy water upon flags and cannon, nor send young men out to slaughter and be slaughtered in the name of the Prince of Peace.

My God is a still, small voice in my heart. My God is something that is with me when I sit alone, and wonder, and question the mystery. My God says: "I am here, and I am now."

My God says: "Speak to Me, and I will answer; not in sounds, but in stirrings of your soul; in courage, hope, energy, the stuff of your life." My God says: "Ask, and it shall be given you. Seek, and you shall find. Knock, and it shall be opened unto you."

My God is the process of my being; nothing strange, but that which goes on all the time. I ask, "Can I pray?" and He answers: "You are praying." He says: "The prayer and the answer are one."

To pray is to resolve. To pray is to take heart. The motto of the Benedictine order tells us that "To work is to pray." Mrs. Eddy tells us that "Desire is prayer."

The old-time prophets knew this God of mine. Jesus said: "Believe me that I am in the Father, and the Father in me." That was not egotism, nor was it theology; it was elementary psychology.

The philosophers have known this God; Emerson wrote: "The simplest person who in his integrity worships God, becomes God."

The poets have known this God; Tennyson wrote:

Speak to Him thou, for he hears, and spirit with spirit can meet;
Closer is He than breathing, and nearer than hands and feet.

My God is a personal God; for how else can I be a person? If He does not know me, how can I know myself?

My God is a God of freedom. He says: "Anyone may come to Me."

My God is a God of mercy. He says: "Come unto Me all ye that travail and are heavy laden, and I will refresh you."

My God is a God of justice. Of Him it was said: "He hath put down the mighty from their seats, and exalted them of low degree."

My God is a God of love, in a world of raging madness. He has put into the hearts of His people the idea of subduing the hate-makers.

My God is an experimental God. He says: "I have made a world, and am still making it." He says to men: "I am still making you, and you are still making Me."

IV

Much of this book, as you will have noted, is the story of other books, their origins and their fates. This is something I could not help if I tried, because my whole life has been a series of books.

On our first motor trip up the Pacific Coast we had gone through one of the redwood forests, and I was fascinated by those marvelous trees. One of them was so big that the one-lane road had been cut through its trunk. I got out and wandered about in the fern-covered forest, and when I drove on, there popped into my mind a delightful story for children. Two little gnomes, a young one and his grandfather, were the last of their race to survive. A human child, wandering about in the ferns, was greeted timidly by the grandfather and begged to help in finding a wife for the younger gnome.

The little girl promised to help, and the two gnomes were taken into the automobile, which of course immediately became a "gnomobile"—the title of the book. There followed a string of adventures extending all the way from California to the forests of the East. The two gnomes were kept in a large basket, and the playful young man of fashion who did the driving told everybody that the basket contained Abyssinian geese. Thereafter he was hounded by newspapermen who wanted to see those rare and precious creatures. When the gnomes were stolen and put on exhibition in a circus, the story indeed became exciting.

This book for children was published with a lot of gay pictures; it was also published in France, and is about to be republished here. Walt Disney read it and told me that he had never done anything with live characters, but if ever he did he would do *The Gnomobile*. Now, almost thirty years later, he is setting out to keep the promise. I have a contract.

V

Next story: I thought it most amusing when my cousin, Wallis Warfield of Baltimore, came near to wrecking the British Empire by running away with its king; so I wrote a one-act play showing exactly how a Baltimore belle went about fascinating any male animal, whether he had a crown or a dunce's cap on his head—or both at the same time. I called it *Wally for Queen*. I thought it was hilariously funny; but when I sent it to my friend, Arch Selwyn, movie producer, he wrote back, "Upton, are you crazy, or do you think that I am?" So the crazy little play remains unproduced. But I can wait, and maybe I'll outlast my cousin and her ex-king, and my story will be history and can be made into a musical comedy, as happened to Bernard Shaw's *Pygmalion*.

VI

Sometime in the twenties Henry Ford had come for a winter's vacation and lived on an estate in Altadena not far from our home. Henry fancied himself a sociologist, an economist, and an authority on what should be done for his country. I wrote a note offering to call, and received an invitation. I duly presented my card to the guard at the gates and was admitted. I found the unpretentious great man in the garage with his son, Edsel, busy looking over some junk they had found in this rented place.

They had in their hands a discarded carburetor and were twisting it this way and that, trying to figure out what purpose the various openings could have served. I don't think I quite knew what a carburetor was, so I was not able to help.

Presently we went into the house; Henry's wife was there, a quiet little woman—I can't recall anything that she said. Henry had a great deal to say, and his wife listened. Henry thought he knew what was wrong with America and told me. I saw that he liked to talk, and I let him, only putting in a mild suggestion now and then. That suited him, and when I left he suggested that I should come again and we would take a walk in the hills.

So we took a walk. Henry was a spare man and a fast walker even on hills. I expressed the opinion that the American people needed educating on economic questions, and Henry agreed with me. I asked him why he didn't do some of the educating himself, and the idea pleased him. I suggested that he start a magazine, and he said he thought that when he got back to Dearborn he would buy one. I suggested some of the topics for the magazine—"Production for Use" and "Self-Help Co-operatives"—and Henry said those things sounded good to him. He did start a magazine. It was the *Dearborn Independent*; and from the outset it was the most reactionary magazine in America.

I had told Henry about King C. Gillette and his books. Gillette was another multimillionaire, not quite so multi as Henry, but plenty. Henry was interested. He consented to come and exchange ideas with Gillette, and the appointment was made. A houseboy and two schoolboys whom my wife employed for work on the place just couldn't be persuaded to do any work that morning. They lined up beside the drive to see the Flivver King and the Razor King come in. (Razor King is a pun, but it was made by fate, not by me.)

The Flivver King was lean and spry, and the Razor King was large and ponderous. They sat in easy chairs in front of our fireplace and exchanged ideas. As I wrote shortly afterward, it was like watching two billiard balls—they hit and then flew apart, and neither made the slightest impression upon the other. America remained and still remains what it always was—a land of vast riches and cruel poverty. Gillette's book fell flat, and Henry's magazine died unmourned.

As fate willed it, I was to have more to do with Ford, indirectly. And though I never heard from him again, I feel quite sure that he knew what I did—and didn't like it. In the thirties, the CIO set out to organize industrial workers, including those who worked in the big automobile plants. Henry Ford was blindly and stubbornly opposed to unionization and declared that he would close his plants rather than have them organized. There was a strike, and he fought ruthlessly. Frank Murphy, mayor of Detroit, said to me at the dinner table of Rob Wagner in Beverly Hills: "Henry Ford employs some of the worst gangsters in Detroit, and I can name them."

Because I had known Ford, I was much interested in what was going on; as usual, I decided to make a novel of it. I called the book *Flivver King,* and when it was done I sent a copy of the manuscript to one of the strike leaders in Detroit. I expected a prompt response and was not disappointed. They wanted that story, and they wanted it quickly. I offered them 200,000 pamphlet copies to be retailed at fifty cents a copy. However, I insisted on having the book done by my own printer, a union shop, because I wanted the plates and the control. After some dickering they accepted the offer, and the result was that in Ford plants all over the world Ford workers could be seen with a little green paperbound book, folded once lengthwise and stuck in their back pants pocket. I was told that they put it there on purpose, where it could be seen. It was a sort of badge of defiance.

The story of the humble mechanic who had built the first self-moving vehicle in his own garage and had revolutionized the traffic of mankind all over the world—look at it now!—was a wonderful story, and I would have been a bungler if I had not made it interesting.

Ford's battle with the union had a surprising ending. He suddenly gave way and permitted his plants to be organized. It wasn't until some years later that I learned the reason—his wife told him that if he did close the plants she would leave him. I can't reveal the source of this information, but I know that it is true. As I have already related, I had met Mrs. Ford during my acquaintance with her husband. She had scarcely said a word and had never expressed an opinion during my arguments with Henry. But she had listened. She couldn't have heard such arguments as mine very often in her life—and perhaps they played a part in persuading her that Ford's workers should be allowed to have a union. It pleases me to believe that.

VII

My next book was a novelette called *Our Lady*, and I think it is my favorite among all my too-many books.

I had been brought up as a very religious little boy; I had been confirmed in the Episcopal Church of the Holy Communion in New York at the age of about fourteen. I remember that I attended service every day during Lent. Later on in life I had found the New Testament an excellent way of learning foreign languages. I knew the text so well that I could save myself the trouble of looking up words in the dictionary; so I read the New Testament first in Latin, then in Greek, then in German, then in French, and then in Italian.

I had conceived a real love, a personal affection, for the historical Jesus; it seemed to me that he had been a social rebel who had been taken up and made into an object of superstition instead of human love. I had been particularly repelled by the deification of his mother; I found myself thinking what she must have been in reality and what she would have made of the worship of the Catholics. And so came my story:

A humble peasant woman of Judea, named Marya, sees her beloved son go off on a mission that terrifies her. In her neighborhood is a Nabatean woman, a "dark-meated one," a sorceress, much dreaded. Marya goes to her and asks to see the future of her son. The sorceress weaves a spell, and Marya in fright falls unconscious. She wakes up to find herself in the modern world, walking on an avenue in Los Angeles, in the midst of a great crowd on its way to a football stadium at which the Notre Dame team is to be pitted against some local team. Since not all my readers are scholarly persons, I point out that Notre Dame means "Our Lady"—in other words, Marya, the mother of Jesus.

Arriving at the gates, the woman in a humble peasant costume is assumed to have been lost from one of the many floats; so she is seated in another, goes in, and sees the game with all its uproar, having no idea that it is being held in her name. She finds herself seated next to a young Catholic priest from Notre Dame University; he is a student of ancient languages and is astounded to hear her speak to him in ancient Aramaic. He decides that this is a problem for the authorities of the Church, and he takes her to a convent. He calls the bishop, and ceremonies of exorcism are performed that send Marya back where she belongs. She is disturbed by the strange experience and sternly rebukes the Nabatean sorceress: "All this has nothing to do with me!"

As I said, I think it is my favorite story, and I think that last line has a special "punch." I must add that I could never have written the story if it had not been for the gracious and loving help of my friend Lewis Browne, a scholar who knew those languages and cultures and gave me all the rich details. That is why I think it is a good story, and will be read as long as anything of mine. But perhaps not by my Catholic friends.

VIII

I would guess that I have earned a million dollars in the course of my life; ninety-nine per cent of it came from writing and one per cent from lecturing. First it was the half-dime novels; then it became serious books, and my troubles and the readers' began. Always I had been advocating unpopular opinions, swimming against the current. I can hear the voice of my dear mother, long since departed from this earth, pleading with me not to make things so hard for myself but to write things to please other people—and incidentally help my dear mother so that she would not have to wear the discarded clothes of her well-to-do sisters.

But there was something in me that drove me to write what I believed and what other people ought to believe: always something unpopular, something difficult; a play about Marie Antoinette, for example—what could be more unlikely from Upton Sinclair, or less likely to please his readers? "Upton Sinclair just *loves* Marie Antoinette," said the *New Republic*, jovially.

No, I didn't exactly love her, but I pitied poor human creatures in their dreadful predicaments. A girl child had been raised and trained to believe that she was destined by Almighty God to rule over millions of people—or at least to sit on the throne beside the ruler and bring a future ruler into the world; and she was destined instead to be dragged from her throne and hauled through avenues packed with screaming, cursing people crowding in to see her head chopped off upon a high public platform. Who was she really, and what did she make of it—she and the God whom she worshiped.

She had a lover, the Swedish Count Fersen, quite proper according to the customs of her time. I found that pitiful love story touching, and I think I wrote a good play; but it would have been expensive to produce, and no one here or in Paris has come forward.

I did my homework on it, as I always do, and the book was highly praised. There sticks in my mind a letter from an old gentleman who took exception to my interpretation of the revolutionary slogan, "*Les aristocrats à la lanterne!*" There was a French song at the time that I translated, "The aristocrats, they shall hang from lanterns"; the old gentleman found that an amusing blunder. But in the music room of the Pasadena Library I had dug up a book of those historic revolutionary chants, and had found a footnote explaining that in those days at street and highway intersections high posts had been set up and chains strung across, so that a lantern could be hung above the center of the roads. It was literally true that the aristocrats had been hung from lanterns.

16

Lanny Budd

I

I come now to what I suppose is the most important part of my literary performance. The Second World War was on the way. I had been predicting it and crying out against it for many years —indeed, ever since the First World War had been settled with so little good sense. At the end of that awful peace settlement I had published my protests in the little magazine, *Upton Sinclair's*; but few had heeded. Now, at the age of sixty, I decided to try once more, going back and picturing the half-dozen years of the war and peace that had so tormented my soul. I was going to write a real novel this time, not propaganda, but history—a detailed picture of the most tragic five years in the story of the tragic human race.

I had enough money to last me for a year, and my dear wife had provided me with a quiet and pleasant home. At one end of our place was a garden fenced in and hidden by rose vines. And there was a lovely German shepherd who was trained to lie still and never bark at the birds while I was pecking on the typewriter. Nothing more could be asked for. The greatest of all historic subjects, perfect peace to write in, a faithful secretary to transcribe the manuscript, attend to the book business and keep all visitors away; a garden path to walk up and down on while I planned the next paragraph, and a good public library from which I could get what history books I needed for the job.

The year I was writing in was 1939, and the years I was writ-

ing about were 1913 to 1919. For the opening scene I used our
experience, already described, in the German village of Hellerau
or "bright meadow." That meadow had been bright, not merely
with sunshine but with hope and joy and art and beauty—and
also with the golden beard of George Bernard Shaw, when we
attended the festival at the Dalcroze temple of art and saw a
performance of Gluck's *Orpheus*. What setting could be more appropriate for the beginning of a novel about everything that was
gracious and kind in the civilization of old Europe?

I knew I had something extra this time and was shivering
with delight over it. The lovely American lady, "Beauty" Budd,
and her charming and eager son, Lanny, were at that festival.
Our old friend Albert Rhys Williams read my opening chapter
and said to my wife, "You had better watch out; Upton is in love
with Beauty Budd." So I was, all through that enormous task;
eleven volumes, 7,364 pages, over four million words. When I
began, I planned one novel to cover five years of Europe's history. I wonder if I would have had the nerve to go on with it if I
had known that it was going to cover more than forty years and
take a dozen years of work.

I have read patronizing remarks about the Lanny Budd
books from high-brow critics. But some very distinguished indi-
viduals and journals have done them honor. I quote a few of
these opinions; they gave me courage to go on writing the
books, and they may give the reader courage to read them.

George Bernard Shaw: "When people ask me what happened
in my long lifetime I do not refer them to the newspaper files
and to authorities but to your novels."

Albert Einstein: "I am convinced that you are doing very
important and valuable work in giving to the American public
a vivid insight into the psychological and economical background of the tragedy evolving in our generation. Only a real
artist can accomplish this."

Thomas Mann: "Someday the whole cycle will certainly be
recognized as the best founded and best informed description
of the political life of our epoch."

New York *Times Book Review*: "Something of a miracle . . .
one of the nation's most valued literary properties."

New York *Herald-Tribune Books*: "This greatly daring, ambitious history in story form of our times."

New York *Post*: "This planetary saga . . . We see a whole civilization on these pages."

Times Literary Supplement, London: "The inventive power, intellectual resource and technical craft of these volumes, indeed, are easily underrated. . . . How full, varied and decisive a job he makes of it! For the fascination of *la haute politique* in our time of destiny he adds the wonders of the worlds of art, finance, Marxism, travel, spiritualism and a good deal more. At the same time how irrepressible and all but disinterested is the storyteller in Mr. Sinclair, who switches from a burst of left-wing elucidation to a chapter of thrills without turning a hair. The first impression he leaves here is of the sweep and diversity of his knowledge."

Manchester *Guardian*: "Lanny Budd is the romantic rider of a documentary whirlwind. . . . Criticism kneels."

II

Beginning in 1939, the Lanny Budd books occupied practically all of my working time and a good part of my playtime over a ten-year period; then, after an interval, for another year. I thought about little else when I was writing them, and Craig was delighted to have me at home and out of mischief.

I knew some people who had been through the war, and I found others. I had been in Britain, France, Germany, and Holland, and had friends who lived there and would answer my questions. I had my own writings, including my little magazine, which had covered the time. I had met all kinds of people who had lived and struggled through that war—businessmen, politicians, soldiers, radicals of every shade. In spite of my wife's anxieties about communists I had known Jack Reed and Bob Minor and Anna Louise Strong—I could compile quite a list of persons whom I oughtn't to have known.

Near the end of my story I found that the men who had been on Wilson's staff of advisors in Paris were willing to write long letters, answering questions and giving me local color. Also there was Lincoln Steffens, who had been in Paris at the time of the peace conference; he had been close to Woodrow Wilson, and had known everything that was going on in those dread days of the peace making—or the next war preparing. He told me the details; and I had already learned a lot from George D. Herron, who had been Woodrow Wilson's secret agent, operating in Switzerland. I have told about Herron earlier in this book.

So I wrote the story of a little American boy, illegitimate son of a munitions-making father, living on the French Riviera with an adoring mother called Beauty.

Those lively scenes unfolded before my mind, and I was in a state of delight for pretty nearly a whole year. I began sending bits of the manuscript here and there for checking, and I found that other people were also pleased. How Lanny grew up and went out into the world of politics and fashion—there were a thousand details I had to have checked; and there may have been someone who ignored me, but I cannot recall him. Whatever department of European life Lanny entered, there was always someone who knew about it and would answer questions. That went for munitions and politics and the intermingling of the two. It went for elegance and fashion, manners and morals, art and war.

I have to pay tribute to several of these friends, new or old. There was S. K. Ratcliffe, journalist and man of all knowledge. I had met him in England, and once every year he came on a lecture trip to California; we became close friends. I asked if he would read a bit of manuscript, and he said he would read every page. Little did the good soul realize what that promise meant! I sent him chapter by chapter straight through that whole series, and I found him a living encyclopedia. The details that he knew, the little errors he caught—it was wonderful, and every time I tried to pay him, he would say no. He would be proud, he said, to have helped with the Lanny Budd books.

There was my old classmate, Martin Birnbaum. He had been in my class in grammar school and for five years in City College —I figure that meant six thousand hours. Then he became my violin teacher, and always he remained my friend. He made himself an art expert, and what he did and what he knew you can

read in his book, *The Last Romantic,* for which I wrote a preface. It may have been his suggestion that being an art expert
would give Lanny Budd a pretext to visit all the rich and powerful persons in both Europe and America. I knew, and still know,
very little about art, but Martin would tell me anything I
wanted to know—always exactly what my story required.

I put Martin himself into the story; he is of Hungarian origin,
and gave me the Hungarian name Kerteszi, which means Birnbaum, which means "pear tree." Armed with Martin's vast
knowledge, Lanny could become a pal of Hermann Goering and
sell him wonderful paintings, or sell some of the wonderful
paintings that Goering had stolen. Armed with that art alibi,
Lanny could travel to every country in Europe, and come back
to America when he became a "presidential agent."

III

Incidentally, I actually knew a presidential agent, and he
helped me with Lanny Budd. This was Cornelius Vanderbilt,
Jr.—"Neil" to the thousands who know him. We met him early
in California when he was trying to start a liberal newspaper
and came to persuade the Gartz family to invest. I liked him, and
what was more important, Craig liked him; we saw a great deal
of him, and watched his gallant fight to finance a liberal newspaper in a reactionary community.

In 1943 when I had gotten volume four to the printers and
was thinking about volume five, Neil happened along. I remember that two of Craig's nieces were visiting us, and Neil had recently obtained one of his divorces. Maybe Craig had a certain
notion in her head—I do not know, and would not tell if I did—
but anyhow the two young ladies prepared a lunch of cold
chicken and sundries, while I sat out by the little homemade
swimming pool and listened to Neil's stories about his dealings
with Franklin Roosevelt during the Second World War.

Neil really was a Presidential agent. He traveled to Europe
on various pretexts and came back and reported secretly to the
boss. He had been able to go into Germany and into Italy. He
had been taken for a long drive by Mussolini. The dictator did
his own ferocious driving, and when they ran over a child and

killed it, Il Duce did not stop. (When Neil published this story, Mussolini denied it, but that of course meant nothing.)

Neil told me of the secret door by which he had entered the White House, and what Franklin wore and how he behaved. Presently, I said with some excitement and hesitancy, "That would make a wonderful story for Lanny Budd." Neil said, "That's why I'm telling it to you." It was a magnificent gift, and I here express my gratitude. *Presidential Agent* became the title of volume five of the series.

Thereafter whenever I met Neil—I was about to say that I pumped him dry, but I realize that that metaphor is wrong; he is a bubbling spring, the most entertaining talker I ever listened to. Other people can be interesting for half an hour, perhaps, but Neil—well, I will give the statistics on our last meeting. He arrived at our home about three o'clock in the afternoon and talked steadily until seven o'clock, when I thought he ought to have some dinner; we got into his Cadillac—the only time I ever rode in a Cadillac—and he talked all the way to dinner and during dinner and on the way back to the house. Then he talked until eleven o'clock in the evening. We listened to every word.

Such stories! He has been married five times, and each marriage was a set of mishaps. One dissatisfied wife forced her way into the great Fifth Avenue mansion and refused to leave. When the servants shut off the light and heat to get rid of her, she dumped armfuls of papers on the tile floor and burned them, while she looked on. They included all the letters Neil had had from Roosevelt. Such is life, if you happen to be born an American millionaire!

Craig was especially amused, because in her girlhood she had been for two years a pupil at Mrs. Gardner's fashionable school, directly across Fifth Avenue from the Vanderbilt mansion. Curtains were drawn over all the front windows of the school, and it was strictly against the rules to open them. But don't think the young ladies didn't peek! Craig had watched the family come out to their carriages and had seen a tiny boy, two or three years old, toddling out with one or two attendants. She could not know that this child would grow up to tell her muckraking stories.

Neil gave me not merely the title, *Presidential Agent*, he provided me with many incidents and much local color, all accurate—for be sure that millions of people read those stories in some twenty of the world's great languages, and few were the errors pointed out to me. Now Lanny Budd is being prepared for TV, and Neil is somehow connected with it. Maybe he is going to furnish local color. I hope for the best.

One other person to whom I owe a heavy debt of thanks: Ben Huebsch, old friend from the first days of the Civil Liberties Union in New York. He was then an independent publisher, and later became editorial head of Viking Press. It was to him that I sent the completed manuscript of *World's End*—one thousand or more pages. He afterward stated that he had known in the first twenty-four hours that they would publish the book.

They published it beautifully; the Literary Guild took it, which meant something over a hundred thousand copies at the start. Ben had pointed out errors, and thereafter I sent him every chapter of the succeeding ten volumes. He found many errors and gave much advice; he is one more to whom the reader is indebted for the assurance that the books can be read as history, as politics, art, and science, and a little bit of everything— business, fashion, war and peace and human hope.

I wrote the first three of the Lanny Budd books in Pasadena, and then we moved to Monrovia. I remember because one day the telephone rang, and the editor of the local newspaper asked me if I had heard that volume three, *Dragon's Teeth*, had just been awarded the Pulitzer Prize. I hadn't heard it and, of course, was thankful for the call. Bernard Shaw and a large group of others had tried to get me the Nobel Prize but had failed. Another try is now being prepared.

I interrupted the writing of the Lanny Budd series only once —to do a play about the atomic bomb, which everybody was speculating about at the end of the 1940's. They have been speculating ever since, and are continuing as I write. Is our world going to be ended with a bang—or will it take several? I put my speculations into a play called *A Giant's Strength*. "Oh, it is excellent to have a giant's strength," says Shakespeare, "but it is tyrannous to use it as a giant." It seems to me not excellent to have a giant's strength entrusted to persons with the mentality of pigmies. My play pictured a Princeton professor of physics fleeing with his family to hide in a cave somewhere in the Rocky Mountains; and not even the caves were safe.

Then I wrote the tenth volume of the Lanny Budd books, *O Shepherd, Speak!* The shepherd who was asked to speak from the grave was Franklin Roosevelt, and I thought that was to be the end of my series. I was entitled to a little fun, so I wrote *Another Pamela*—in which I took Samuel Richardson's old-time serving maid and exposed her to temptations in a family that, I must admit, bore many resemblances to that of our friend Kate Crane-Gartz. It pleased her wonderfully. She never objected to publicity. The story is now being prepared as a musical comedy.

Also I wrote *A Personal Jesus*, in which I speculated about what that good man must have been in actuality. Having been brought up on the Bible, in later years I was tempted to go back to those old stories and old formulas and see them through a modern pair of spectacles. Needless to say, they turned out to be somewhat different. I tried to imagine Jesus as a human being.

And then another light novel: What would happen if a modern man suddenly found himself with the power to work miracles—miracles like those in the Testaments both New and Old? How would he be received, and what would he accomplish? So came *What Didymus Did*. My "Thomas called Didymus" was a humble and rather ignorant American youth, and what he did got him into a lot of trouble—and made a lot of fun. Oddly enough, the book was translated and made an impression in the far-off native land of the original Didymus. Just recently they had a communist overturn in Kerala, and I earnestly hope that my little story was not to blame. You see, in my story the communists got hold of Didymus in Los Angeles and brought to smash the new religion he was trying to found. I would hate to think that I had put evil ideas into any heads on the southwest coast of modern India!

After an interval of four years, I wrote *The Return of Lanny Budd*, dealing with the postwar struggles against the communists. Some of my friends objected to the episode in which Lanny encouraged an anti-Nazi German youth to betray the secrets of his Nazi father. All I can say is that it was a civil war as well as a social war, and that Lanny was saving American lives. I happened to know of one such case, and have no doubt there were hundreds. War is hell, and books should not prettify it.

After I had finished with Lanny Budd, I turned my attention to a subject that I had not touched upon since *The Wet Parade* a couple of decades earlier. I called the book *The Cup of Fury*. My maternal grandfather was a deacon in the Methodist Church, and on a lower shelf of his bookcase was a row of bound volumes of the *Christian Herald*. They were full of pictures, and as a little fellow I used to pull out a volume and lie on the floor and learn to spell out words and read the titles and the stories underneath. Now, seventy years later, I submitted the manuscript of *The Cup of Fury* to Daniel A. Poling, now editor of the *Christian Herald*. He was enthusiastic about it and turned it over to his publishers; it is still one of my best-selling books.

IV

I have already told a great deal about Kate Crane-Gartz who played such an important part in our lives. My wife loved her as a sister, and my wife was the most loyal of friends. She had done a great deal of work for Kitty; she had been well paid for it, and was sure that she had earned the pay. In addition there was friendship, which cannot be bought for money and can be repaid only with more friendship. But Craig had a higher loyalty, which was to truth and to the human society in which we have to live.

Little by little, Mrs. Gartz's mind had been laid siege to by the communists. They had high-sounding phrases, they were trained in subtlety, and they had no loyalty except to their cause of social revolution. Directly or indirectly, they were subsidized by Moscow. Mrs. Gartz was an easy mark because she was kindhearted; she believed what she was told, and they knew exactly what to tell her. They told her that we socialists were dreamers, out of touch with the real cruelties of militarism and the corruptions of our political life. They told her that she alone had the insight and courage to be a real pacifist and to support the only real steps that could prevent another world war. They pointed out that when the showdowns had come, Upton Sinclair and his wife had supported two cruel world wars and that she, Kate Crane-Gartz, was the only true and dedicated pacifist. She was the one who had been right all along!

I can't say that Mrs. Gartz accepted all this, because I was not present to investigage her mind, and she changed it frequently. All that she asked of us was that we would come up to her home and answer the communists; and that was what Mary Craig had made up her mind to do no more. We had seen enough of their trickery and their success in flattering our old friend. After we had been confronted by communists several times without warning, Craig decided that we would stay away —and that she would cash no more of Mrs. Gartz's checks. (Years later, she discovered half a dozen that she had put away; but the estate had been closed.)

All this had its humorous aspect if you could forget the pain on both sides. Craig could not shut our door to Mrs. Gartz, so her decision was that we would go into hiding. I don't know how many cottages Craig bought and moved me into in order to keep Mrs. Gartz from finding us. I can tell you those that come to my mind and of which I remember the names.

In 1946 we found a little cottage in the hills up above Arlington. A lovely location, a great high plateau with no smog in the air, and hills all around with flocks of sheep tended by shepherds who were Basques. There was a highway in the distance, and at night when the cars passed over it, the long row of lights made a beautiful effect. Wandering over those ridges I came upon a level spot with a half-dozen boulders laid around in a circle, and it was easy for my imagination to turn it into an Indian assembly place. I pictured there a gathering of departed spirits, including Lincoln Steffens and Mrs. Gartz's eldest son, who had taken his own life. I imagined them discussing the state of the world, each according to his own point of view; I wrote down the discussion and called the little pamphlet *Limbo on the Loose*.

And then there was a place in the hills above Corona, the most comfortable cottage we ever had. We lived there a year or two and came back to it after Craig's first heart attack, as I shall narrate. There were always troubles, of course. Boys played baseball on the place when we were away and damaged the tile roof. Also, some of the neighbors thought we were unsociable, which was too bad. The main trouble was that our highway went wandering through the hills, and the traffic was fast and heavy; so every time I went to town Craig was worried.

In 1948 we found a lovely concrete house on the slope just above Lake Elsinore. It had an extra building that had been a billiard room and made a fine office for me. But, alas, we had no sooner fallen in love with that beautiful lake than it proceeded to disappear. I don't know whether it went down through the mud or up into the air; anyhow, there was no more lake, but only a great level plain of dust. I can't remember why we moved from there, and, alas, Craig is no longer here to tell me. If she were here she probably wouldn't let me be telling this story anyway.

I am giving a playful account of our game of hide-and-seek with Mrs. Gartz; that is my way—especially if the troubles are past and I can no longer undo them. It really seems absurd to say that we spent several years of our lives keeping out of reach of one woman to whom my wife felt in debt and whose feelings she could not bear to hurt. It wasn't the devil who was after us, it was a dear friend who wanted nothing except to make us meet communists.

Whenever we took a trip to some other region of California, Craig would buy a picture post card of that place, sign it "With love," and mail it to Mrs. Gartz. Later on, Albert Rhys Williams, who had written a book about Russia and didn't mind knowing communists, told Craig that Mrs. Gartz had received one of these cards and had sent him on a hunt. He went to San Jacinto and asked at the post office and the hotels and wherever there might be a possibility of finding out where the Upton Sinclairs lived. All the Upton Sinclairs had done in San Jacinto was to eat one lunch and write one post card.

V

The time came when ill-health put an end to that strange game of hide-and-seek. Craig had to go back to our comfortable Monrovia house and lock the big wooden gates and keep them locked no matter who came. One man climbed over the gates and told her that he had just been released from the psycho-pathic ward at the Veterans' Home in Sawtelle; that time, Craig called the police.

Her anxieties were the result of many experiences, extend-ing over many years. I will tell one more story, going back to the Pasadena days. A Swedish giant, who must have been seven feet high, entered my study and told me in a deep sepulchral voice, "I have a message direct from God." I, only five feet seven and cringing at a desk, said politely, "Indeed—how inter-esting; and in what form is it?" Of course, I knew what the form was because I saw a package under his arm. "It is a manuscript," he said.

It was up to me to say, "You wish me to read it?" The sepul-chral voice replied, "No human eye has ever beheld it. No hu-man eye ever *will* behold it."

I asked timidly, "What do you wish me to do?"

Then I heard Craig's voice in the doorway, "Upton, the plumber is waiting for you."

When it comes to hints I am very dumb. "What plumber?" I asked. Craig, used to my dumbness, continued, "There's a leak in the basement, and you have to go and let the plumber in." I got it that time and followed her, and we fled down to the other house and locked ourselves in.

As to Mrs. Gartz, Craig had finally made up her mind to face it out. When the celebrated "Red Dean" of Canterbury Cathe-dral visited Pasadena and Mrs. Gartz wrote demanding that we meet him, Craig locked our gates and let them stay that way. Mrs. Gartz came, with the communist prelate by her side. Her chauffeur got out and pounded on the gate, while Craig peered through a tiny crack in an upstairs window curtain. Afterward she wept, because of what she had done to an old and beloved friend.

Years later, another friend was driving Craig on one of the business streets of Pasadena, and they passed a mortuary. "Just think," said the friend, pointing. "In there is all that is left of Kate Gartz—in an urn, on a shelf."

17

Harvest

I

WOMAN, the conservator. She is traditionally that, and from the first moment we united our destinies, Craig had set herself to saving all the papers that were lying about our house. She put them into boxes and stacked the boxes in a storeroom. When she built the five old houses into one house on Sunset Avenue, she had a mason come and build a concrete room. She didn't know about concrete so she did not supervise the job, and very soon she had a leaky roof to torment her. She got old Judd, the carpenter, and really laid down the law to him. She was going to build four storerooms, each a separate airtight and watertight little house; she was going to supervise that job herself.

Old Judd had one set comment for all of Craig's jobs: "Nobody ever did anything like that before." But he gave up and did what he was told; soon on the long front porch and on the several back porches of that extraordinary home were four tiny houses, three of them eight by ten and one of them eight by sixteen, built as solidly as if they were really houses, each with its double tar-paper roof—and all that under the roofs of the regular porches.

So at last the Sinclair papers were safe and dry. When we moved to the new house in Monrovia each of those little houses was picked up with its contents undisturbed, put on a truck, and transported a dozen miles or so to the new place. Craig did all these things without telling me; I was writing a new book while she was taking care of the old ones.

303

The big double garage at the Monrovia place didn't suit her because one had to circle around the main house to get into it, and she didn't trust her husband's ability to back out around a curve; so the big double garage, which was of concrete, became my office, and the four little houses were emptied and set therein. Later, a long concrete warehouse was built, as well as an aluminum warehouse, and all the precious boxes of papers were at last sheltered safely.

I lived and worked in that Monrovia office over a period of some fifteen years, and I managed to fill all the storerooms with boxes of papers. The ceilings were high, and shelves went up to where you could only reach them by ladder. I had over eight hundred foreign translations of my books, not counting duplicates. I had what was estimated to be over a quarter of a million letters, all packed away in files. I had practically all the original manuscripts of my eighty books, and also of the pamphlets and circulars.

We decided that the time had come to find a permanent resting place for our papers. I called the head librarian of the Huntington Library, and he came with two assistants. They spent a couple of weeks going through everything and exclaiming with delight. Leslie E. Bliss, an elderly man, said it was the best and the best-preserved collection he had ever seen. He asked what we wanted for it, and at a wild guess I said fifty thousand dollars. He said that was reasonable, and he would take pleasure in advising his trustees to make the deal.

Alas, I had forgotten to ask about those trustees. I quailed when I learned that the chairman of the board was Mr. Herbert Hoover; and the other members were all eminent and plutocratic. I was not favored by the Pasadena gentlemen who control the Huntington Library; my collection was declined.

Dear, good Mr. Bliss was sad. He was kind enough to tell me of a wonderful new library, both fireproof and bombproof, that was being built at Indiana University with a million dollars put up by the pharmaceutical firm of Lilly. He advised me to approach them; and in April 1957 Cecil Byrd, the head of all that university's libraries, and also David Randall, head of the Lilly Library, came to see me. They said just what Bliss had said, that ours was the most extensive and the best-preserved collection they had ever seen.

You remember the story I told about the Stalin telegram. I said to Byrd and Randall, "If someone were to come upon a genuine document signed by Tamerlane, or Genghis Khan, or any other of the wholesale slaughterers of history, what do you think it would be worth?" One of them said, "Oh, about a million dollars." I laughed and said, "What we are asking for the collection is ten thousand a year for five years." They said, "It's a deal."

One of the great sights of my life was the arrival of a huge van from a storage company, and the packing of those treasures. The three packers were experts. They had sheets of heavy cardboard, already cut and creased, so that with a few motions of the hand each sheet became a box. Into those boxes went all the priceless foreign editions, the original manuscripts, the manila folders with the two hundred and fifty thousand letters. The whole job was done in three or four hours, and off went our lifetime's treasure. Off went the bust by the Swedish sculptor, Carl Eldh, and the large photograph of Albert Einstein with the poem to me, written in German; off went all the books, pamphlets and manuscripts.

I could fill a chapter with a listing of those treasures. There were thirty-two letters from Einstein and a hundred and eighty-six from Mencken, and a long one from Bernard Shaw about the Nobel Prize that he had asked for me—in vain; also his letter that I quoted earlier, praising the Lanny Budd books. Any scholar who really wants to know about the pains I took with those eleven volumes will find the thousands of letters I wrote to informed persons, checking details of history and biography. Anyone can see the pains I took with a book like *The Brass Check*, which contained, as Samuel Untermyer told me, fifty criminal libels and a thousand civil suits, but brought no suit whatever. (I ought to add that Untermyer's statement was hyperbolical, and my memory of it may be the same. It was something like that.)

The collection rolled away, and the place seemed kind of empty—all those storerooms and nothing in them! Only the outdoors was full—of the grocery cartons the truckmen had discarded. They were piled to the very top of the office, and I remember it cost us thirty-five dollars to have them carted away. But we could afford it!

II

So far I have said little about my efforts at playwriting. I have always had aspirations to the stage, and no interest in "closet dramas"; I wanted to write for producers, actors, and audiences. But, alas, I had to write on subjects that appealed to few in those groups. Stage plays are supposed to portray things as they are, and I wanted to portray things as they ought to be—or to portray people trying to change them. I spent a lifetime learning the lesson that no matter how real such characters may be, no matter how lively their struggles may be, no producer thinks that the public wants to see or hear them.

One day I estimated that I had written thirty plays; half a dozen of them one-acters, and the others full length. On the same day, oddly enough, I received a letter from a graduate student who has been doing research on my collection at Indiana University. He told me that in half a year of research and reading he had found a total of twenty-eight plays—thirteen published and fifteen unpublished. (I had two others in my home.) The list may interest other students.

Revolutionary or reform themes: *Co-op; Depression Island; Singing Jailbirds; The Second-Story Man; After the War Is Over; Oil!; Prince Hagen.*

Indirect demands for reform: *The Machine; The Millennium; Doctor Fist; The Great American Play; John D; Love in Arms; Bill Porter; The Grand Duke Lectures; The Pamela Play; The Saleslady; The Convict; The Naturewoman; Hell.*

Those on topical subjects: *A Giant's Strength; The Enemy Had It Too.*

Nonreform subjects: *The Pot Boiler; Marie and Her Lover; The Emancipated Husband; The Most Haunted House; Wally for Queen; Cicero.*

Lost and forgotten: *The Jungle* dramatization.

III

The latest of my plays, *Cicero: A Tragic Drama in Three Acts*, was written in the winter of 1959–60. I had been reading a history of ancient Rome and was impressed by the resemblances between the time of Cicero and the time of Eisenhower: the extremes of contrast between the rich and the poor; the rich exhibiting their glory by fantastic extravagances; the unemployed poor crowding into the cities, existing in slums on doles; the farmers deserting their land and rioting—they were doing it in Oklahoma; the domination of public affairs by big money; and the total blindness of the public to all these manifest evils.

I did not intend to preach a sermon; on the contrary, I determined to leave the resemblances to the discernment of the audience. I was going to show what Cicero faced and what happened to him. He was a rich man himself, a consul, a senator; he had all the honors. A lawyer, he tried criminal cases and made fortunes; a statesman, he was driven into exile, and when his party came into power he came back. In the end his enemies triumphed, and he fled and was captured; his head and hands were cut off and exhibited in the forum. That hasn't happened as yet to anybody in America—but who knows?

Most terrifying in ancient Rome was—and in our own land is—the sexual corruption. When I was young I wrote a book about love and marriage, *Love's Pilgrimage*. It contained a bridal scene and a birth scene that were detailed and without precedent; but every line was clean and true, and every doctor and every married person knew it. I was told there would be trouble, but there wasn't. I was told there would be trouble in England, and I asked the English publisher to send a copy of the book to every bishop of the Church of England. He did so, and I got some kind letters from these gentlemen; you will find examples in the volume, *My Lifetime in Letters*. There was no trouble.

But the vileness that is being published today is revolting to every decent-thinking person. It is deliberately advertised and sold as vileness, and one after another the books enter the best-seller list. I have chosen to stay out of that competition; all I say here is that it is exactly what Cicero saw in ancient Rome. He blistered it in his courtroom speeches; he named names— and that was a contributing cause to his murder.

I had the three-act *Cicero* mimeographed, and one of the persons who I hoped would honor it was Albert Camus. He wrote me cordially, and I quote the first three sentences of his opinion —first in French and then in translation:

J'ai été bien touché par la confiance que vous m'avez faite en m'envoyant votre *Ciceron*. C'est une tragédie pleine de sens et plus actuelle q'il n'y paraît. On y comprend mieux un certain classicisme qui finissait dans les rains coupées et l'horreur.

I have been indeed touched by the confidence you have shown me in sending me your *Cicero*. It is a tragedy full of sense and more real than it would seem. One there understands better a certain classicism which would finish with the kidneys cut and the horror.

I, and others, were puzzled by the *rains coupées*—"the kidneys cut." It was explained to me that the phrase approximates "a rabbit punch" in American parlance.

Camus went on to say that he had been "promised a theater" and would be able to deal with the play "with more precision." Soon thereafter I read in the news that he had been assigned the directorship of the Théâtre Française, perhaps the most famous in the world. My hopes rose high. Then, alas, I read that he had been killed in a motorcar accident.

III

Taking my cue from Camus, I decided that the play might be "classical" in more than one sense, and might appeal to university audiences. I submitted the script to John Ben Tarver, then in the department of dramatic arts at New York University. With his permission I quote from his reply, dated April 3, 1960:

I have gone through *Cicero* several times. It is a splendid play, and I want to thank you again for sending it to us. Here are some of my reactions:

1. It has color, contrast, variety. Too many modern dramas labor one theme to death and never try to vary the thread of the story.

2. It is told in dramatic terms. The finest writing in the world will not play in the theatre unless it is suited to a stage.

3. It makes a statement which has general meaning, a statement which has meaning for today's audience.

4. The characters are sharp. All parts are good for actors. Every role is clearly defined. Cicero, in particular is superbly written.

5. It calls for all the elements of the theatre to be brought into play.

Tarver undertook to give the play a commercial production Off Broadway in New York. He set out to raise the money, and I gave him the names of friends who might be interested. That, alas, made my dear Craig unhappy, because I had caused friends to lose money in the past, and I had been forbidden ever to do it again.

One of the names was that of Dick Otto, campaign manager of EPIC a quarter of a century back. Craig considered him one of the finest men she had ever known; she had stood by him all through those horrible two or three years (for EPIC had gone on after my defeat in the election). Then Dick had gone off on a small yacht to recuperate, and had come back to his business and had extraordinary success. Craig forbade him to put any money into the play, but he disobeyed her to the extent of ten thousand dollars, and that was sad and mad and bad indeed.

After elaborate preparation and numerous rehearsals, the play went on in a small theater on Second Avenue. Whatever power controls the weather in New York must have disapproved of my political and social opinions, for there fell such masses of snow that it was impossible for most people to get about. A few did get to the theater, and sent me enthusiastic telegrams, which gave me hope for a day or two. But, alas, the critics were luke-warm—most of them didn't like the subject of the play. When I read accounts of the stuff they have to witness and praise, I am not surprised.

Cicero ran for about six weeks, and Dick Otto lost his ten thousand dollars. I lost the advance paid to me, which I had put back as an investment. Dick was sorry about the play but un-troubled about the money—in the meantime he had developed a deposit of quicksilver on his property, and will now be richer than ever. The trouble is, it takes more of his time, and he de-lays writing the autobiography that he has been promising me —including, of course, the story of our EPIC campaign as he saw it.

18

A Tragic Ordeal

I

I COME now to the tragic, the almost unbearable part of my story. Craig had been overworking and overworrying, for many years. Nobody could stop her; when there was something to be done she did it, because she was the one who knew *how* to do it. She had got so that she no longer wanted a servant. We had moved about so much.

Also, there was the smog. The growth of industry in Los Angeles, especially of the oil industry, had become tremendous; the fumes were brought our way by the sea breeze, and they settled around the mountain that went up directly back of our home. Everybody talked about smog, and even the newspapers had to discuss it, bad as it was for business.

So, in the spring of 1954, we moved again; this time to the Arizona desert, as far away from industry as possible. Phoenix was where Hunter lived, and he could come to help us. We found a cottage, and Hunter had a seven-foot concrete wall put around the lot. Those four boxes that had been built for storerooms, and which had been transported from Pasadena to Monrovia, were now transported from Monrovia to Buckeye, and set down in a row with an extra roof over them for coolness. One was to be my workroom, and the others were to hold my stock of books. I still could not get away from book orders.

Craig worked as she had always done, unsparing of her strength. In the middle of the night she called to me, terrified—

she could not breathe. Lying down asleep, she had almost choked, and to get her breath she had to sit up. There were two doctors in the town, and I called one. He told us she had an enlarged heart, and it was due to overexertion: what she had now was a "congestive" heart attack. The heart was no longer equal to pumping the blood out of the lungs, and she had to sit up in order that part of her lungs could be clear.

So there we were, in a strange place, both of us possessed by dread. A specialist was brought from Phoenix, and he confirmed the diagnosis. "The patient should be taken to a hospital." She was taken to Phoenix and treated for a couple of weeks, and she got a little better; but the specialist gave us no hope.

She was brought back to our Buckeye home, and I had her sole care. I had her care for the next seven years, and there were few days when we did not confront the thought of her doom.

II

I came upon an article about a treatment for such heart conditions advocated by Dr. Walter Kempner of Duke University, in Durham, North Carolina. I wired asking for literature, and there came a copy of a magazine published in Los Angeles called *G.P.*, meaning "General Practice." It gave an account of Kempner's treatment, and included x-ray photographs of hearts before and after treatment. The difference was striking, and I made up my mind that Craig was going to have Dr. Kempner's rice-and-fruit diet. (His belief is that the cause of the heart enlargement is excess of salt in the blood, and rice is the all-nourishing food that has the lowest quantity of salt).

It was out of the question to move Craig to North Carolina. I phoned to a physician we knew in Riverside and asked if he would give the rice diet according to Kempner's specifications. He said, "I will do it if you will take the responsibility." Then he gave a little laugh and added, "If you will take half." I said, "I will take all." I arranged for a hospital plane to take us to Riverside next morning.

She didn't want to go, but for once she was too weak to resist, and I was in a position to have my way. We had to make an early start because we had mountains to fly over, and when the sun was up the rising air would make turbulence. At five o'clock in the morning Hunter was there, and we carried Craig to our car and drove her to the little airfield of the town, not much more than a cow pasture.

It was a four-hundred-mile trip, my first by air. We flew over the road I had driven many times, and it was fascinating to see it from above. I told Craig about the sights; but, alas, she hadn't much interest. At the airport there was an ambulance waiting, and soon she was in a hospital bed.

I doubt if anybody in the hospital had ever heard of the rice diet, and it was hard to get a large plate of well-cooked rice without gravy or butter on it. In fact, it was hard to get anything that Craig wanted, including quiet; but even so, the miracle began right away. She got well and was able to breathe lying down. After a couple of weeks she was able to walk a little.

My mind turned to that little cottage up in the Corona hills only seven miles away. In that cottage there would be no nurses gossiping outside her door at midnight. I would be the one to take care of her, and I would move on tiptoe whenever she slept. I persuaded her to let me take her there; the doctor consented, on condition that I bring her down twice a week for the blood tests that were necessary—to make sure that the supply of salt in her blood wasn't below the minimum required. I promised so to do.

So for half a year more we lived in that cottage. I was nurse, cook, housemaid, chauffeur, and guardian angel. I cooked a pot and a half of rice for Craig every day, and she was so well that it was a miracle. Even the cautious doctor had to use extravagant language when he set the newest x-ray photograph beside the earliest one. I said to him, "Don't you think that is remarkable?" His answer was, "I should say it is spectacular."

The results of the rice-and-fruit diet were so spectacular that I decided to try it myself. I didn't want to bother with blood tests, so I added celery to the diet—it is a vegetable of which I happen to be fond, and it gave me what I thought was the necessary bulk for safety. I added a spoonful of dried-milk powder for a little more salt. We were both having large quantities of fruit juice, mine being pineapple because it is the sweetest. Both of us took vitamins.

Throughout most of my writing life, certainly for a half century of it, I had been accustomed to say that I was never more than twenty-four hours ahead of a headache. But from the time I adopted the diet of rice and fruit, which I still follow, I ceased to have headaches, and I have even forgotten, now, what a headache feels like. Nor have I had any other ailment, not even a cold.

But to return to my story. With the good doctor's permission I took Craig back to our Monrovia home, and we got some apparatus that was supposed to take the smog out of our bedrooms. We lived there in peace and happiness for a while; but then Craig discovered that she could no longer bear to eat any more rice. She began trying all other kinds of health foods, in particular bread stuffs that were supposed to be low in salt. Also, she could no longer stand the blood tests, because the nurses couldn't find the vein in one wrist, and the other wrist had become sore from too much puncturing.

So all the heart troubles came back; and there was something worse, called fibrillation—an endless quivering of the heart that was most distressing and kept her awake at night. I had gotten an oxygen tank; she would call me, and I would get up and put the little cap over her nose and turn on the valve and wait until she had had enough, and then turn off the valve and go back to bed and sleep, if I could, until she called again. Neither of us wanted a stranger in the house, so I had her sole care. I cooked her food, served it, and cleaned up afterward.

Every day I took her outdoors. I took care of her flower beds, and she would gaze at them with rapture—her poppies, her big red rosebush, her camellia bush that bloomed every April, and a wonderful golden oleander that bloomed all summer.

Every night I put her to sleep with prayers. "Dear God, make her well," was what I wanted to say over and over again, but Craig insisted it must be, "Dear God, make *us* well." I didn't need any help so far as I could see, but I said it her way; when the fibrillations got bad, I would say it over a hundred times, or maybe two hundred, until at last she went to sleep. I could never tell when she was asleep; so I would let my voice die away softly, and wait and see if she spoke.

That was our life for several years. Every now and then I would try to persuade her to have some rice, just a little at a time; and that little, alas, was not enough. She was tired of it and forbade me to mention it. Month after month her condition got worse, her pain harder to endure. The kind doctor would try pills with some new outlandish name, and I would get the prescription filled and do my best to learn which was which.

III

It was during this period of long-drawn-out pain and struggle that Craig wrote the beautiful book, *Southern Belle*. She wrote about herself and her lovely childhood and girlhood, all because I pleaded with her to do it. She wrote about her life with me, because she wanted to set me straight with the world. Sometimes I would sit by the bed, and write to her dictation; but most of the time she would write lying in bed with her head propped forward, holding a pad with one hand and a pencil with the other.

It was a tiring position, and after she had been doing it for months, she developed a pain near the base of the spine. I knew from the beginning that it was a question of posture and tried to persuade her of that, but in vain. I would take her to specialists, and they would examine her and give their verdicts—and no two verdicts were the same. I am quite sure that none of these doctors had ever had a patient who had treated her spine in that fashion. Craig wouldn't let me tell them; I wasn't a specialist— only a husband—and I must not influence their judgment.

How many of these dreadful details shall I put into a book? Of course, anyone may skip them; but I had no way to skip them. Craig had stood by me through my ordeals, and she was all I had in this world—apart from the books I had written and the one I was writing. The only other person who could help us was Hunter, and he would arrive from Phoenix eight hours after I telephoned. He was there when Craig became delirious from pain or from the injections that the doctors had given her. He would comfort me when I, too, was on the verge of becoming delirious at the sight of her suffering. She would say that she was suffering from cold and would have me pile every blanket in the house on top of her; then she would say that she was suffocating and would throw them all off. I remember a night of that, and then I could not sleep in the day. We had to have her taken to a hospital; and she hated hospitals, each one had been worse than the last.

IV

I cannot bring myself to tell much about the end. I do not think that many could bear to read it. At times she became delirious, and wasn't herself any more; I had to make up my mind to that. Then suddenly she *would* be herself—her beautiful self, her dear, kind, loving self, her darling self, agonizing about me and what I was going to do, and how I could manage to survive in a dreadful world where everybody would be trying to rob me, to trap me, to take away the money that she had worked so desperately to keep me from spending.

Three times during that long ordeal I found her lying on the hard plastone floor of the upstairs kitchen that we had made for her. The first two times we were alone in the house, and since I could not lift her, I had to call the ambulance to get her back in bed. The second time she was unconscious, and I called the doctor again. He thought these were "light strokes," and later on the autopsy confirmed the opinion; but she had not been told.

The third time was less than a month before the end. Her nephew, Leftwich Kimbrough, was with us, so we two carried her to bed. I sat by, keeping watch, and presently I heard her murmuring; I listened, and soon went and got a writing pad and pen. They were fragments of a poem she was composing while half-conscious, and I wrote what I heard:

> Stay in their hearts, dear Jesus,
> Stay and make them kind.

And then, after an interval:

> Oh, the poor lonely nigger,
> Bring love to his soul.

Later, I wrote underneath, for the record: "Craig's murmured singing after bad fall. I mentioned to her, it was Good Friday Eve, 1961."

You will recall my account of the visit of Judge Tom Brady, founder of the citizens' councils all through the Deep South. From earliest childhood little Mary Craig Kimbrough had wrestled with that race problem of her homeland. She heard and saw both sides; the fears of the whites, for which they had reason, and the pitiful helplessness of the ignorant blacks. Now, in her last hours, she was pleading, in the first couplet for the whites whom she loved and in the second for the blacks, whom she also loved.

One day she would eat nothing but soft-boiled eggs, and the next day she would eat nothing but gelatine. So the icebox was full of eggs and then of gelatine. One elderly doctor told her that the best remedy for fibrillation was whisky; so here was I, a life-long teetotaler who had made hatred of whisky a part of his religion, going out to buy it by the quart. Craig insisted that I should never buy it in Monrovia where I was known; I must drive out on one of the boulevards and stop in some strange place and pay for a bottle with some imbecile name that I forgot. That went on for quite a while, and the time came when Craig was so weak that I couldn't manage to hold her up while she tried to walk the length of the room.

V

She wouldn't let us call the doctor because he would order her to the hospital. But the time came when we had to call the doctor, and he called the ambulance, and poor Craig was carried away on her last ride. She was in the hospital for three weeks, and it cost us close to four thousand dollars. This seems an ungracious thing to mention, but I am thinking about what happens to the poor—how do *they* die? Perhaps they do it more quickly, and don't have day and night nurses by their bedside. This sounds like irony, but I let it stand.

In addition to the nurses and the husband, there were Hunter and Sally, his wife, two nieces, and a sister who had come on from Alabama. What they saw was a hideously tormented human being. I pleaded with the doctor—surely there must be some ethical code that would give him the right to end such torment! But he said that stage had not yet been reached.

I won't tell much about my own part in it. I would sit and gaze at the features of my beloved who no longer knew me; or if she did know me she was angry because I had let her be brought to the hospital. I would sit there blinded with my own tears, and then I would get up and try to get out of the hospital without making a spectacle of myself.

Why do I tell such a story? Well, it happened. It was life. It is our human fate. It happened to me, and it could happen to you. This universe is a mystery to me. How beauty, kindness, goodness, could have such an end visited upon it will keep me in agony of spirit for the rest of my days on this planet. I do not know what to make of it, and I can draw only this one moral from it: that nature has been, and can be, so cruel to us that surely we should busy ourselves not to commit cruelties against one another. I know that I had for half a century the love of one of the kindest, wisest, and dearest souls that ever lived upon this earth; why she should have died in such untellable horror is a question I ask of God in vain.

She died in St. Luke Hospital, Pasadena, on April 26, 1961. Her ashes were shipped to a brother in Greenwood, Mississippi, and were interred in a family plot in the cemetery in that town.

19

End and Beginning

THE death of Craig left me with a sense of desolation beyond my power to describe. Hunter and his wife Sally went back to Arizona. The sister and nieces scattered to their homes, and I was in that lovely old house in which every single thing spoke of the woman who had bought it, arranged it, used it—and would never see it again. I had lived in a town for twenty years and never entered a single home; I had no one to speak to but the clerks in the post office, the market, the bank. In my early days I would not have minded that; I had camped alone all summer, in a tent on an island in the St. Lawrence, and again in an "open camp" on an Adirondack lake, and had been perfectly happy. But I no longer had the firm conviction that the future of mankind depended upon the words I was putting on paper; on the contrary, I was obsessed by memories of horror, inescapable, inexcusable. The house was haunted—but I had no other place to go.

For more than seven years, ever since her first heart attack, Craig had been insisting that I could not live alone. It had become a sort of theme song: "Oh, what will you do? What will become of you? You *must* find some woman to take care of you." Then she would add, "Oh, don't let some floozie get hold of you!" My answer was always the same: "I am going to take care of you and keep you alive." But now she was gone, and I could say it no more.

We had friends, but they were mostly far away; elderly married couples who came to see us once or twice in a year: Sol Lesser, who had produced *Thunder Over Mexico* for us; Richard Otto, who had run the EPIC campaign for us; Harry Oppenheimer, New York businessman who had promised to come and run the state of California for me if I had had the misfortune to get elected. Now I spent several weeks wondering which of these good friends I should ask to help me find a wife.

For decades I had been a friend and supporter of the *New Leader*; and every week had read the gay verses of Richard Armour. He had sent me his books, beginning with *It All Started with Columbus,* and continuing with *It All Started with Eve* and *It All Started with Marx.* I was so pleased that I wrote him some lines in his own style; I recall the last two lines:

> And if you find that I'm a charmer
> You'll know that I've been reading Armour.

He is dean of Scripps College, some twenty miles east of my home; but for many years we did not meet. It happened that Hunter Kimbrough was a classmate of Frederick Hard, president of the college, and Hunter was in the habit of stopping by on his way to and from Arizona. He and Dick Armour became friends, and several months after Craig's death, Hunter invited Dick and his wife to my home for a picnic lunch. So it was that I met Kathleen Armour, gracious, kind of heart and with a laugh as merry as her husband's verses.

After days and nights of thinking about it, I composed a letter to Kathleen, putting my plight before her. The unmarried women I knew could be counted on the fingers of one hand, and not one of the four was suitable. In a woman's college Kathleen must know many; I didn't mean a pupil, but a teacher, or member of such a family.

I received a cordial reply, and soon I was invited to Kathleen's home. There I met the sister of Hunter's friend, Fred Hard, president of the college. She was a widow, and her years were seventy-nine, appropriate to my eighty-three. She was twice a mother, once a grandmother, and three times a great-grandmother. She was of a kind disposition, with a laugh as happy as Kathleen's and an abundance of good sense. She was born in South Carolina and had lived in several parts of the United

States. She was well read and was part of a cultured environment. She was staying in the lovely home of the college president, keeping it during summer while he and his wife were in Europe. Her name was May, and Dick Armour had written her some verses:

> For her, two cities vie and jockey:
> First Claremont claims her, then Milwockey.
> The West and Middle West both crave her,
> To both she brings her special savor,
> For in the one or in the other'n,
> She's still herself, completely Southern.
> But here alone we can rejoice
> With lifted hearts and lifted voice
> And happily and smugly say:
> When it is August, we have May.

I invited her to my home. The large downstairs rooms were dark, she said; and I pointed out to her that the long velvet curtains could be thrown back. In the living room are four double windows, from floor almost to ceiling, and in the dining room are five more of the same; the rooms are practically one, because the wide double doors roll back into the walls. But she said she would be lonely in that half acre of gardens surrounded by a high hedge of two hundred eugenia trees. She said she might marry me if I would come to live in Claremont; but I saw myself living in a town full of college boys and girls who would come to ask for interviews, and who would consider me snobbish if I put a fence around my house. I do my work outdoors, weather permitting—as it does most of the time in southern California.

So, back I went to my lonely existence. Hunter was disturbed, for to him the Hard family represented the best of culture, that of the South. Maybe the Armours had something to do with it— I did not ask—but I met May at their house again, and she was cordial. More time passed, and there came a birthday letter, telling me of her interest in my work and wishing me happiness. So I went to see her again; this time I did not stand on ceremony, but put my arms around her, and it was all settled in a few minutes.

II

We were to be married in the Episcopal Church, and the rector was called in to hear my story. I had obtained a divorce half a century before, I being the innocent party in the suit. I had been remarried by an Episcopal clergyman, on the banks of the Rappahannock River—with jonquils blooming on the riverbank and behind me the heights on which twenty thousand Union soldiers had given their lives. The rector in Claremont said that if the church had given its sanction once, it would not refuse it again; so all was well.

We wanted the wedding as quiet as possible. All my life I have sought publicity—but for books and causes, not for myself, and if we could have had our way, no one but the family would have known. But the law in California requires that both parties appear at the county office building and sign an application for a license—and this two days before the marriage can take place. The license is valid anywhere in the state; so I had an idea: "Let's go into another county, where there's less chance of our being known." We motored to San Bernardino, where two kind ladies gave us the blanks and instructions, and gave no sign that there was anything unusual about us. But soon after we got back to Claremont, the telephone calls began, and we knew that all the cats were out of the bag. Later we learned that courthouse reporters make it a practice to inspect the lists daily before closing time.

The clergyman had agreed that only members of the family and half a dozen invited friends were to be admitted: the Armours, of course, and the Sol Lessers, and the Richard Ottos of the far-off EPIC campaign. Dr. Hard gave his sister away, and the bride's granddaughter, Barbara Sabin, was matron of honor. Hunter acted as my "best man." The doors were guarded, and the morning ceremony was performed with the customary age-old dignity. But when the bride and groom emerged from a side door, there was what appeared to be a mob. A flood of questions was poured out, and cameras before our eyes were making little clicking noises. There was a crony of the far-off EPIC days, Hans Rutzebeck, a sailor who had written a grand book about his life,

The Mad Sea. He had had plenty of time to talk to the reporters, and when I greeted him his claims of friendship were confirmed.

So the story was lively, and it appeared in all the evening papers. More detailed stories with photographs were in the morning papers all over the world. I do not exaggerate; friends, and strangers too, cut them out and sent them to us from half a dozen capitals of Europe, and from Brazil, Tokyo, India, Australia. College president's sister, aged 79, marries muckrake man, aged 83—you can see how it was, and May was amused. She even got an album in which to keep the clippings for her great-grandchildren.

So this story has a happy ending. We both enjoy good health, and age does not bother us. We live with our books and papers in a wonderful fireproof house that a rich banker built, got tired of, and sold cheaply some twenty years ago. There is a half acre of land, completely surrounded by the hedge of eugenia trees. There are twenty-one kinds of fruit trees, and instead of lawns there are lantana and sweet alyssum, which do not have to be mowed. There is a camellia bush, and a golden oleander as big as a cottage; there are rosebushes, an iris bed, poppy beds that are a dream—and when I get tired of hammering on a typewriter, I go out and pull weeds from the poppies.

Now the house is fixed up May's way; the velvet curtains are drawn back, and there are bright curtains and new paint in spots and everything is gay. Her friends come and carry her off to luncheons and musicales and exhibitions of paintings; in the evenings we read some of the fifty magazines that I take, or play the word game called Scrabble, which she has taught me. She is ahead one day, and I the next.

III

Ordinarily I do not attend luncheons or dinners—my diet of rice and fruit cuts down my social life. But as I write, my wife and I have just returned from a trip to the East that was one long round of luncheons and dinners. (I kept to my diet—and probably left a trail of puzzled waiters behind me.)

Some months ago the New York chapter of the American Newspaper Guild wrote to inform me that a Page One Award in

Letters was to be presented to me and invited me to attend the ceremony late in April. Then, shortly afterward, came a letter from Walter Reuther, president of the United Automobile Workers, telling me that the UAW was also giving me an award —at its annual convention in Atlantic City early in May—and would like to present it to me in person. I could scarcely resist two such invitations.

The trip by air was a miracle to me. I had made only two short flights before. Now I saw the whole of the United States spread under me like a map, and I marveled at the nearness of the mountaintops and the vast spread of the plains. On the bare, brown deserts I observed great black spots, and I puzzled my head as to what could be growing on a desert floor; until I realized suddenly that these were the shadows of clouds, also beneath me. It was fascinating to observe how the shape of every spot corresponded exactly to the shape of its cloud. In the Middle West the farms were all laid out in perfect rectangles with the quarter sections clearly distinguishable; but as we got farther east, the irregularities increased until everything was chaos, including the roads.

All kinds of enterprises like to make use of celebrities, and the airport was no exception. The management, learning of my age, had taken the precaution to send a wheelchair to the plane. When May saw it she said to the porter, "You get in and let him wheel you."

My son, David, was on hand with his wife and his car. An engineer, he publishes pamphlets about his technical discoveries of which his father is unable to understand a sentence. One of the problems he has solved is that of spinning a plastic thread so fine that one spool of it would reach all the way around the world. Both May and I are fortunate, in that we can love and admire our "in-laws."

The American Newspaper Guild presented me with a handsome gold figure, which now stands on our mantel. The citation runs as follows:

Page One Award in Letters to Upton Sinclair, author of hundreds of books and papers, including *The Jungle* and *The Brass Check,* over a span of 60 years, all of which contributed immeasurably to the advancement of democracy and public enlightenment. 1962.

Some sixteen hundred people were present, and I made a short speech.

IV

A few days later David and his wife drove us down to Atlantic City, where the sixty-five hundred delegates of the United Automobile Workers throughout the world were having a week's assembly. I had never met either Walter Reuther or his younger brother, Victor, and this was a pleasant occasion for both me and my family. Present also was Michael Angelo Musmanno, who as a young lawyer had plunged into a last-hour effort to save the lives of Sacco and Vanzetti. A wonderfully kindhearted and exuberant person, now close to the seventies, he has become a judge of the Supreme Court of Pennsylvania. When I asked him how this miracle had come about, he answered with a smile: "It is an elective office."

On a Sunday evening we found ourselves confronting the sixty-five hundred cheering delegates, many of whom no doubt had read *Flivver King*. It was a dinner affair, and I found myself seated between my wife and Mrs. Eleanor Roosevelt, whom I had not seen since a visit to the White House in 1935, just after the EPIC campaign. There was plenty of time for conversation, especially since I had had my rice-and-fruit meal an hour or so earlier.

Walter Reuther presented to me the Social Justice Award of the United Automobile Workers—an ebony plaque that carries this citation:

With admiration and affection and in thankful appreciation for the great moral courage and social conscience that motivated your writings as you exposed the inhuman exploitation of labor in American industrial jungles. Your life and your work have contributed immeasurably to the extension of the frontiers of *Social Justice*. May 1962.

In my speech of acceptance I told how I had made a socialist, or a near-socialist, out of Henry Ford's wife; and how, when he saw that he could not win the strike, he made all his plans to close up his plants—and was only deterred from it at the last moment by his wife's announcement that if he carried out this evil purpose she would leave him. The story was new to those delegates, and I will not attempt to describe the enthusiasm with which they received it.

Mrs. Roosevelt also gave one of her warmhearted talks, and so it was a worthy occasion to those labor men and their wives. I imagined that newspaper readers might also be interested in it, but I examined the New York morning and afternoon papers and discovered that they had nothing whatever to say about the affair. I am used to newspaper silence about my doings, but I had really thought they would have something to say about the eloquence of Eleanor Roosevelt, and of the welcome she had received from that vast throng. But not one word in the Monday morning and afternoon papers! I paid a call on the labor editor of the New York *Times,* and he was cordial—he took me about and introduced me to several other editors—but he had nothing to say about the paper's failure to say anything about the UAW assemblage.

The award from the UAW included a check for a thousand dollars. I had written Walter that I would use the money to put a copy of *Flivver King* in the libraries of all the branches of the union throughout the world. In Atlantic City Victor Reuther told me that they planned to reissue *Flivver King* themselves and make it available to all their members. So I shall use the money to put in the union libraries copies of this present book and of the memorial edition of *Southern Belle.*

V

Meanwhile, in New York, I met many old friends. Also, I was asked to appear on several TV programs, and my interviews with Eric Goldman, Mike Wallace, and Barry Gray were great fun. One of the most unusual occasions was a luncheon given by my faithful agent, Bertha Klausner, who invited only those people who are working, in one way or another, with my various books —publishing or reissuing or dramatizing them for stage or screen. And there was a roomful of them!

Happily, there seems to be a revival of interest in my books. *The Jungle* is now in paperback, and students are reading it and teachers are talking about it in their classes. *World's End* and

Dragon's Teeth, two of the Lanny Budd volumes, are also in paperback. So is *Manassas,* under the title of *Theirs Be the Guilt.* *Mental Radio,* my precise and careful study of Craig's demonstrations of her telepathic power, has just been reissued by a publisher of scientific books, with the original preface by William McDougall and, in addition, the preface that Albert Einstein wrote for the German edition. *The Cry for Justice: An Anthology of Social Protest* is to be republished with modern additions. And *A Personal Jesus,* an attempt at a modern insight, is also being reissued.

Our Lady is being dramatized. *Another Pamela* is being converted into a musical comedy. Walt Disney is now setting out to make a movie of *The Gnomobile,* my story for children, which is also going to be reissued with gay illustrations from the French edition. And there is to be a TV series drawn from the Lanny Budd books. I cannot attempt to control this last and can only hope for the best.

20

Summing Up

I

A READER of this manuscript asked the question: "Just what do you think you have accomplished in your long lifetime?" I give a few specific answers.

I begin with a certainty. At the age of twenty-eight I helped to clean and protect the meat that comes to your table. I followed that matter through to the end. I put the shocking facts into a book that went around the world in both directions. I set forth the details at President Theodore Roosevelt's lunch table in the White House, and later put them before his trusted investigators. I put their true report on the front page of the New York *Times*, and I followed it up with letters to Congressmen. I saw the laws passed; from friends in the Chicago stockyards, I learned that they were enforced. The stockyard workers now have strong unions; I know some of their officials, and if the old conditions had come back, I would have been told of it and would be telling it here.

Second, I know that we still have many bad and prejudiced newspapers, but many are better than they were. I think that *The Brass Check* helped to bring about the improvement. It also encouraged newspapermen to form a union. And the guild, among other things, has improved the quality of newspapers.

Third, I know that our "mourning parade" before the offices of Standard Oil in New York not merely ended slavery in the mining camps in the Rocky Mountains but also changed the life course of the Rockefeller family; and this has set an example to others of our millionaire dynasties—including the Armours and the Fords.

Fourth, I think that Mary Craig Sinclair, with my help, did much to promote an interest in the investigation of psychic phenomena. Professor William McDougall, an Englishman who became known as "the dean of American Psychology," told us that it was Craig's demonstrations that decided him to set up the department of parapsychology at Duke University. It was McDougall who appointed J. B. Rhine, and the work that has been done by these two men has made the subject respectable. *Mental Radio* is now issued by a scientific publishing house.

Fifth, I know that the American Civil Liberties Union, which I helped to organize in New York and of which I started the southern California branch in 1923, has put an end to the oppression of labor in California and made it no longer possible to crowd six hundred strikers into a jail built to hold one hundred.

Sixth, I know that the EPIC campaign of 1934 in California changed the whole reactionary tone of the state. We now have a Democratic governor and a Democratic state legislature, and the Republicans are unhappy. In the depression through which we passed in 1961, no one died of starvation.

Seventh, I know that I had something to do with the development and survival of American democratic ideas, both political and social, in Japan. From 1915 on, practically every book I wrote was translated and published in Japan, and I was informed that a decade or two in that country were known as the *Sinkuru Jidai*, which means "the Sinclair Era." Every one of the Lanny Budd books was a best seller there; and in September 1960, when the Japanese students appeared on the verge of a procommunist revolution, my faithful translator, Ryo Namikawa, cabled, begging me to send a message in favor of the democratic process of social change. I paid over four hundred dollars to send a cablegram to *Shimbun,* the biggest newspaper in Japan, and it appeared on the front page the next day. Of course, I cannot say how much that had to do with it. I only know that the students turned away from their communist leadership and chose the democratic process and friendship with America.

Eighth, my two books on the dreadful ravages of alcoholism

may have had some effect. The second, called *The Cup of Fury*, was taken up by the church people, and it has sold over a hundred thousand copies. I get many letters about it.

Ninth. Way back in the year 1905, I started the Intercollegiate Socialist Society, now the League of Industrial Democracy. I had had nine years of college and university, and I hadn't learned that the modern socialist movement existed. I held that since the educators wouldn't educate the students, it was up to the students to educate the educators—and this was what happened, partly because so many of our students of those days are educators now.

Tenth and last, there are the Lanny Budd books. They won the cordial praise of George Bernard Shaw (who made them the basis for recommending me for the Nobel Prize), H. G. Wells, Albert Einstein, and Thomas Mann. I worked at those books like a slave for a dozen years, and if they contain errors of historical fact, these have not been pointed out. The books have been translated into a score of languages. They contain the story of the years from 1911 to 1950, and I hope they have spread a little enlightenment through the world.

The English Queen Mary, who failed to hold the French port of Calais, said that when she died, the word "Calais" would be found written on her heart. I don't know whether anyone will care to examine my heart, but if they do they will find two words there—"Social Justice." For that is what I have believed in and fought for during sixty-three of my eighty-four years.

II

In politics and economics, I believe what I have believed ever since I discovered the socialist movement at the beginning of this century. I have incorporated those beliefs in a hundred books and pamphlets and numberless articles. My books have been translated into forty languages, and millions of people have read them. What those millions have found is not only a defense of social justice but an unwavering conviction that true social justice can be achieved and maintained only through the democratic process. The majority of my books have been translated and published in communist lands; of course, it may be that the texts have been altered. If they were published as I wrote them, their readers learned the ideals of democratic freedom.

Despite my fight and the struggles of many others, communist dictatorships have taken over half the world. Meanwhile, for the first time, proud man, dressed with a little brief authority, has so perfected the instruments of destruction that he is in a position to put an end to the possibility of life on our earth and condemn this planet to go its way through infinite space, lonely and forgotten. Whether this will happen depends entirely upon the decision of two men—or possibly on the decision of one of them. Both are known to the world by one initial, "K." What can a poor fellow whose name happens to begin with "S" do about it? He can only say what he thinks and hope to be heard. He can only go on fighting for social justice and the democratic ideal, hope that man does not destroy himself, by design or by accident, and trust that eventually the peoples of the world will force their rulers to follow the ways of peace, of freedom, and of social justice.

Books by Upton Sinclair

Springtime and Harvest 1901 (*Reissued as* King Midas 1901)
The Journal of Arthur Stirling 1903
Prince Hagen 1903
Manassas: A Novel of the War 1904 (*Reissued as* Theirs Be the Guilt 1959)
A Captain of Industry 1906
The Jungle 1906
The Industrial Republic 1907
The Overman 1907
The Metropolis 1908
The Moneychangers 1908
Samuel the Seeker 1910
The Fasting Cure 1911
Love's Pilgrimage 1911
Plays of Protest 1912
The Millennium: A Comedy of the Year 2000 1912
Sylvia 1913
Damaged Goods 1913
Sylvia's Marriage 1914
The Cry for Justice 1915
King Coal 1917
The Profits of Religion 1918
Jimmie Higgins 1919
The Brass Check 1919
100%: The Story of a Patriot 1920
The Book of Life 1921
They Call Me Carpenter 1922
The Goose-Step 1923
Hell: A Verse Drama and Photoplay 1923
The Goslings 1924
Singing Jailbirds: A Drama in Four Acts 1924
The Pot Boiler 1924
Mammonart 1925
Bill Porter: A Drama of O. Henry in Prison 1925
The Spokesman's Secretary 1926
Letters to Judd 1926
Oil! 1927
Money Writes! 1927
Boston 1928
Mountain City 1930
Mental Radio 1930, 1962
Roman Holiday 1931
The Wet Parade 1931
American Outpost 1932
Upton Sinclair Presents William Fox 1933

The Way Out 1933
I, Governor of California—and How I Ended Poverty 1933
The Epic Plan for California 1934
I, Candidate for Governor—and How I Got Licked 1935
We, People of America 1935
Depression Island 1935
What God Means to Me 1936
Co-op 1936
The Gnomobile 1936, 1962
Wally for Queen 1936
The Flivver King 1937
No Pasaran 1937
Little Steel 1938
Our Lady 1938
Terror in Russia 1938
Expect No Peace 1939
Letters to a Millionaire 1939
Marie Antoinette 1939
Telling the World 1939
Your Million Dollars 1939
World's End 1940
World's End Impending 1940
Between Two Worlds 1941
Peace or War in America 1941
Dragon's Teeth 1942
Wide Is the Gate 1943
Presidential Agent 1944
Dragon Harvest 1945
A World to Win 1946
Presidential Mission 1947
A Giant's Strength 1948
Limbo on the Loose 1948
One Clear Call 1948
To the Editor 1948
O Shepherd, Speak! 1949
Another Pamela 1950
The Enemy Had It Too 1950
A Personal Jesus 1952
The Return of Lanny Budd 1953
What Didymus Did 1955
The Cup of Fury 1956
It Happened to Didymus 1958
Theirs Be the Guilt 1959
My Lifetime in Letters 1960
Affectionately Eve 1961

Index

333